T0136200

Transfer Learning Through Embedding Spaces

Transfer Learning Through Embedding Spaces

Mohammad Rostami

CRC Press

Taylor & Francis Group

Boca Raton London New York

CRC Press is an imprint of the
Taylor & Francis Group, an **informa** business

First edition published 2021
by CRC Press
6000 Broken Sound Parkway NW, Suite 300, Boca Raton, FL 33487-2742

and by CRC Press
2 Park Square, Milton Park, Abingdon, Oxon, OX14 4RN

© 2021 Mohammad Rostami

CRC Press is an imprint of Taylor & Francis Group, LLC

Library of Congress Cataloging-in-Publication Data

ISBN: 9780367699055 (hbk)
ISBN: 9780367703868 (pbk)
ISBN: 9781003146032 (ebk)

Typeset in Nimbus font
by KnowledgeWorks Global Ltd.

*To my wife
and
my parents.*

Contents

List of Figures

List of Tables

Preface

The unprecedented processing demand, posed by the explosion of big data, challenges researchers to design efficient and adaptive machine learning algorithms that do not require persistent retraining and avoid learning redundant information. Inspired from learning techniques of intelligent biological agents, identifying transferable knowledge across learning problems has been a significant research focus to improve machine learning algorithms. In this book, we explore the challenges of knowledge transfer through embedding spaces that capture and store hierarchical knowledge.

In the first part of the book, we focus on the problem of cross-domain knowledge transfer. We first study the problem of zero-shot image classification, where the goal is to identify images from unseen classes using semantic descriptions of these classes. We then study feasibility of using this idea to match data distributions of two visual domains in a shared cross-domain embedding space. In the second part of the book, we investigate the problem of cross-task knowledge transfer. Here, the goal is to identify relations and similarities of multiple machine learning tasks to improve performance across the tasks. We first study the problem of zero-shot learning in a lifelong machine learning setting, where the goal is to learn tasks with no data using high-level task descriptions. The idea is to relate high-level task descriptors to the optimal task parameters through an embedding space. We then study the problem of catastrophic forgetting within continual learning setting of deep neural networks, where the idea is to enforce the tasks to share the same distribution in an embedding space. We further demonstrate that we can address the challenges of domain adaptation in the continual learning setting through matching distributions in an embedding space. Finally, we consider the problem of cross-agent knowledge transfer in the third part of thesis book. We demonstrate that multiple lifelong machine learning agents can collaborate to increase individual performances by sharing learned knowledge using an embedding space in a fully distributed learning setting.

We demonstrate that despite major differences, problems within the above learning scenarios can be tackled through learning an intermediate embedding space. Implementation of some of the algorithms presented in this book is publicly available at https://github.com/mrostami1366.

Acknowledgments

I am grateful to many people who helped me to make this work possible. This book is primarily based on my PhD dissertation [187]. I apologize in advance to those whom I have not mentioned in this part. I would like to express my appreciation to my PhD supervisors, my MASc supervisors, my dissertation committee members, and my research collaborators who helped me during all the PhD studies years. Without their help and support, this work would not be possible.

Although this book is a result of my studies at the University of Pennsylvania and later at the University of Southern California, I think prior training for many years before graduate studies significantly contributed to development of this book. In particular, I would like to thank my professors at Sharif University of Technology who helped me to gain the background knowledge I needed for graduate school. I also thank my teachers at Shahid Beheshti elementary and high schools in my hometown, Zanjan, whose teachings have influenced my abilities forever.

Finally, my family members have played a crucial role in fulfillment of this book. I would like to thank my parents for their endless love and support. My upbringing played a primary role in pursuing higher education. I also thank my brothers who performed duties that were also partially on me in my absence. I thank my in-law family, who supported me and my wife to pursue higher education. Last but certainly not the least, my deep gratitude goes to my dear wife and best friend who patiently helped me to go through years of graduate studies while we were thousands of miles away from our homeland.

CHAPTER 1

Introduction

The emergence of data-driven industries, high-performance computing technologies, the Internet of Things (IoT), and crowdsourcing platform has led to the unprecedented deployment of Machine Learning (ML) algorithms and techniques in a broad range of applications. These applications include problems within computer vision, natural language processing, robotics, complex network science, and decision-making, among many others. Despite the diversity of these applications, the common goal for practical purposes is to develop algorithms and techniques that can mimic humans and replace or augment them in tasks at which humans are slow, inefficient, or inaccurate.

Some of the current ML algorithms have reached human-level performance, readily are used in practice, and their impact on the economy can be observed. In the consumer market, we can see that commercial personal assistant robots are available to purchase, the first commercial drone delivery service kicked off recently, autonomous vehicles are being tested at the moment, and even some ML-based medical diagnosis algorithms are as good as trained specialists. Progress in ML and Artificial Intelligence (AI) is not limited to handful of examples. In the stock market, we can see that nine of the ten largest companies by market capital are companies that heavily invest in and use ML [1]. In the labor market, a study predicts that if the current trend continues for another decade, 30 percent of work activities in sixty percent of current occupations will be automated by the year 2030 [138]. It is not easy to judge how accurate this or other similar predictions are, but there are clear signs that demonstrate even the general public is concerned. For example, one key issue in presidential campaigns is addressing the potential socioeconomical consequences of the rapid changes that are going to happen to the labor force as a result of AI and ML advancement [183]. All the above demonstrates that the importance of AI and ML has gone far beyond just a research area and many unexplored aspects need to be addressed by people outside the AI academic community.

Unsurprisingly, research interest in ML has gained huge momentum in academic circles recently as well, partially as the result of commercial successes of ML algorithms. For example, the number of papers that are submitted to main AI conferences has tripled over just the past five years [2] and attendance at the major AI and ML conferences has grown to unprecedented numbers. However, despite their dramatic progress, current ML algorithms still need significant improvement to replace humans in many applications; machine learning is still a fertile ground for academic research. A major deficiency of ML is that current state-of-the-art ML algorithms depend on plentiful and high-quality datasets to train ML models. Generating such datasets has been challenging until quite recently when crowd-sourcing platforms such as Amazon Mechanical Turk (AMT) were developed. Since then, data labeling has become a business of its own. Although data labeling has been resolved for common applications, generating high-quality labeled datasets is still time-consuming and potentially infeasible for many more specific applications [192]. Even if a model can be learned using a high-quality labeled training dataset, the data distribution may change over time. Drifts in data distributions will result in distribution discrepancy for the testing data samples, leading to poor model generalization and the need to continually retrain the model. Despite considerable advancement of computing technologies, ML models such as deep neural networks are becoming consistently more complex and more challenging to train. On the other hand, continual model training is not feasible given the current computational power resources. For these reasons, it is important to develop algorithms that can learn selectively to use computational resources efficiently, reuse previously learned knowledge for efficient learning, and avoid redundant learning.

Further improvement seems possible because, in contrast to current ML methods, humans are able to learn much more efficiently. Humans can learn some tasks from only a few examples, generalize their knowledge to conditions that have not been experienced before, and continuously adapt and update their skills to perform a wide range of tasks and problems. This seems possible because humans effectively use knowledge acquired from past experiences and identify similarities across different learning problems. Humans also benefit from collective and collaborative learning by sharing their expertise. Building upon the experiences of other humans eliminates the need to learn everything from scratch. Inspired from these abilities of humans and due to the fact that performance of single-task ML techniques is reaching theoretical learning upper-bounds, research in ML has shifted from learning a single task in isolation to investigating how knowledge can be transferred across different domains, tasks, and agents that are related. A term that has been used to refer to this broad research area is transfer learning. The goal of transfer learning is to improve learning quality and speed of the current ML algorithm through overcoming labeled data scarceness, avoiding redundant learning and model retraining, and using computational power resources efficiently. In particular, since deep neural networks are becoming dominant models in machine learning, training complex models with several millions of parameters has become a standard practice which makes model retraining expensive. Transfer learning can be very useful since labeling millions of data points is not practical for many real-world problems. For these reasons, it has been predicted that "transfer learning will be the next driver of ML success" [158].

In a classic supervised learning setup, the goal is to train a model for a specific task or domain using a labeled training data. Many ML algorithms are implemented by parameter-izing a model to form a hypothesis space. The model selection process is implemented by learning parameters through solving an optimization problem over the set of the labeled training dataset. The idea behind this process is that the training dataset represents the data distribution and hence, the optimal model over this set approximates the Bayes-optimal solution. Under quite well-studied conditions, the trained model will generalize well on testing data points that are drawn from the data probability distribution. However, this framework is inapplicable when sufficient labeled data for the learning problem does not exist, i.e., training dataset does not represent the data distribution well, or when the data distribution changes after training the model. As a result, often trained models underperform on new tasks and domains that are not encountered during training. knowledge transfer techniques tackle challenges of labeled data scarceness and distributional drifts through exploiting the knowledge that is gained by learning related tasks or during past experiences.

Various learning scenarios and applications can benefit from knowledge transfer. For example, in many multi-class classification problems in vision domain, there are classes without sufficient labeled data points, potentially none. Learning to transfer knowledge from classes with sufficient labeled data points can help to recognize images that belong to classes with few labeled data points. In some problems within natural language processing, there exists sufficient labeled data in few common-spoken languages, but the labeled data is scarce in many less common-spoken languages. It is desirable to transfer knowledge from more common-spoken languages with sufficient annotated data to learn similar tasks on less common languages. In many robotics applications, e.g., rescue robots, a robot explores the external world and almost certainly encounters situations and conditions that are new and has not been explored before. Transferring knowledge from past experience can help to learn to handle such conditions fast. Even when labeled training data is accessible, knowledge transfer can help to learn more efficiently either in terms of starting from a better initial point, learning speed, or asymptotic performance. We can use many ideas to implement and use knowledge transfer. In this book, we focus on transferring knowledge through embedding spaces that relate several ML problems and capture dependencies and structures across the ML problems. We demonstrate that this common strategy can be used to address the challenges of various learning scenarios. Implementation of some of the algorithms presented in this book are publicly available at `https://github.com/mrostami1366`.

1.1 KNOWLEDGE TRANSFER THROUGH EMBEDDING SPACE

In a knowledge transfer scenario, the problem that knowledge is gained from is called the *source problem*, and the problem that knowledge is transferred to is called the *target problem*. The primary question that needs to be addressed is "how can we transfer knowledge successfully to the target problem(s) given the source problems?". Many different approaches have been proposed to answer this question. A major goal of AI and ML is to mimic and replicate the abilities of humans. Hence, an approach inspired by the nervous system can be helpful and lead to successful algorithms, e.g., algorithms for blind source separation [45, 188] or reinforcement learning [236]. More specifically, works within *Parallel Distributed Processing (PDP)* framework suggest that embedding spaces can be used to model cognitive processes as cognition is a result of representing data using synaptic connections that are changed based on experiences [143]. An embedding space can be considered as a way of representing data such that the data representations become meaningful and discriminative for a particular task. Throughout this book, we loosely are inspired from this idea to find relations and correspondences between ML problems by coupling their data representations in a shared embedding space.

PDP framework has not been the dominant framework for AI. In the early days of AI, modal logic was more a source of inspiration for AI researchers. Following modal logic,

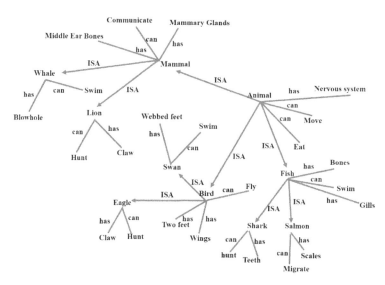

Figure 1.1 Quillian's hierarchical model for the broad concept of animals (inspired and adapted from [143]). Each straight line denotes a proposition from the predicate in its start and the subject in its tail with the relation written on it, e.g., "can" and "has". The arrows denote "IS A" relations and denote one more level of the hierarchy. In addition to direct propositions, hierarchical propositions can be deduced through the ancestor nodes, e.g., "salmon has gill" and salmon "can move".

early AI models were developed based on using categories and propositions [149]. Quillian suggested that concepts can be organized in hierarchical tree structures similar to *tree of life* (as denoted in Figure 1.1). In this structure, specific categories are denoted by leaves of more general categories, then propositions that are true about a group of concepts can be stored at the first common ancestor node that all those concepts are leaves of it. Upon forming this structure, we can use it to answer whether a proposition is true about a concept. It only suffices to start from the concept and look into its immediate ancestor node to see if the proposition is stored in that node. If not, we can search the higher level ancestor nodes until the proposition is found, or reaching the root node, which means the proposition is not true.

Despite intuitiveness of Quillian's framework, experiments on the human nervous system do not confirm its predictions. For example, this model predicts that it is easier for humans to verify more specific properties of concepts compared to boarder properties. Because these properties are stored closer to the concepts, less search is required. But psychological experiments do not confirm this prediction [156]. Additionally, this idea implies that more specific properties of a concept form a stronger bond with the concept compared to more general properties, but this does not seem to be the case either. Findings related to a special type of neurological disorder, called *semantic dementia*, provide evidence for an alternative model for cognition. Patients with this disease progressively lose the ability to associate properties with concepts [143]. However, they lose specific properties first, e.g., a zebra has stripes, and gradually lose more general properties, e.g., a zebra has four legs. When the patients lose specific properties of two similar concepts, then he/she cannot distinguish between the two concepts, e.g., a zebra versus a donkey. As a result, patients would draw those concepts similarly which demonstrate that those concepts are encoded similarly in the nervous system. These observations suggest that concepts are grouped according to their properties in the brain in a hierarchical structure. However, concepts that have the same property are grouped such that similar synaptic connections encode all those concepts. As we will see in the next chapters, this process can be modeled mathematically, by assuming that those concepts are mapped in an embedding space that is shared across those concepts. This means that if we represent the human semantic space with a vector space in which each dimension denotes a specific property, e.g., having stripes or being able to swim, then concepts that share many common properties, lie close to each other in this space. An important advantage of this approach is that it is feasible to train models that encode data according to abstract similarities in an embedding space.

Following the above discussion, our goal throughout this book is to represent the data from different ML problems in an embedding space such that the resulting representations would capture relations among several learning domains and tasks. Upon learning this embedding space, we can map data points from different domains and tasks to the shared embedding space and use the relationships in the embedding space to transfer knowledge from (a) source domain(s) to the target domain(s). The common challenge that we need to address in different learning scenarios is how to enforce the embedding space to capture hyper-relations among the ML problems.

1.2 STRUCTURE AND ORGANIZATION OF THE BOOK

Knowledge transfer problems and challenges can be manifested in a wide range of research areas and learning scenarios. In this book, our contributions are in three major areas of knowledge transfer: cross-domain knowledge transfer, cross-task knowledge transfer, and cross-agent knowledge transfer. Implementation of some of the algorithms presented in this book is publicly available at `https://github.com/mrostami1366`.

1.2.1 Cross-Domain Knowledge Transfer

Knowledge transfer across related domains is our first focus, e.g., visual and textual domains, which are the two dominant information domains. Cross-domain knowledge transfer is helpful in performing tasks for which obtaining information in a particular domain might be challenging, but easier in a related more accessible domain. Humans always benefit from this type of knowledge transfer. For example, in dark lighting conditions, people usually rely on a combination of haptic perception and imagination to improve their visual perception of an object. This is an example of transferring knowledge from the haptic domain to the visual domain. This seems possible for humans because the brain is able to relate haptic and visual sensory information. Similarly, consider image retrieval ability of Google search engine for a query. Handling the image search query directly in the visual domain is a challenging task, but the task becomes a lot easier through asking the user to provide a textual description about the query or automatically extracting a textual description of the input image and then transferring knowledge from textural domain, e.g., processing and comparing the captions that are normally provided or the surrounding texts for images in the database against the textual description for the query.

More specifically, we first focus on the problem of zero-shot learning for multi-class image classification in chapter 3. The goal in this learning scenario is to recognize images from unseen classes, i.e., without any labeled training data. Humans can easily recognize objects that they have not seen before but are given their semantic descriptions. From ML perspective, successful implementation of this strategy is highly beneficial because with the help of open-source web-based encyclopedias such as Wikipedia, and recent NLP techniques, acquiring semantic descriptions of almost any class is very cheap compared to acquiring a large number of annotated images. Data labeling is, in particular, more challenging when classification involves a large number of classes or persistent emergence of new classes. Our idea is to learn a shared embedding between these two domains that allows mapping data from one domain to the other. To this end, we assume that for a subset of classes, both visual labeled data and semantic descriptions are available, i.e., seen classes. This is a major assumption that makes cross-domain knowledge transfer between the visual and textual domains feasible. We use these seen classes to learn an embedding that couples the visual and semantic domain. In particular, we learn two coupled dictionaries [275] that coupled the visual and the semantic domain knowledge. Our contribution in chapter 3 is to train these two dictionaries jointly by enforcing the visual and the semantic features for all seen images to share the same sparse vector in the embedding space. Upon learning these dictionaries, we can map an unseen class image to the learned embedding using the visual dictionary and sparse vector recovery methods. Classification then can be performed in the embedding space by searching for the class with the closest semantic description in the embedding space. Additionally, our approach is able to address the problems of *domain shift* and *hubness* with ZSL.

We then investigate the problem of domain adaptation through learning a domain-invariant embedding space in chapters 4 and 5. In this learning setting the goal is to solve a task in a target domain, where labeled data is scarce, by transferring knowledge from a source domain, where sufficient labeled data is accessible to solve the task. We consider the multiclass classification task in two visual domains. Humans always are very good at this task. For example, upon learning numeral characters, most humans are able to classify numeral characters in a new domain, e.g., calligraphy font, very fast by observing few and potentially no samples. This means that when a class concept is formed in the human brain, this concept can be generalized and identified in new domains quite fast. This ability suggests that the concepts are encoded in higher levels of the nervous system that can be modeled as an embedding space. Inspired by this intuition, we propose to transfer knowledge by minimizing the discrepancy between the probability distributions of the two source and target visual domains in an intermediate embedding space. To this end, we consider deep encoders that map data points from two domains to a joint embedding space in its output such that the discrepancy between the probability distributions is minimized. A shared deep classifier network is trained to map the data points to the labels. Learning a shared and domain-agnostic embedding space provides an effective solution to use the deep classification network that is trained on the source domain on the target domain. Due to minimal distribution discrepancy, the network will generalize well on the target domain with unlabeled training data. Such an embedding allows for cross-domain knowledge transfer by training the classifier network via solely labeled data from the source domain.

More specifically, our contribution is that we use a shared end-to-end model across the two domains in chapter 4 and align the distributions of both domains class-conditionally in the embedding space. We select two problems with small domain-gap which allows to use a shared end-to-end model. In chapter 4, we use two domain-specific encoders that share their output and a shared classifier from this shared output to the label space. This stricture allows for more domain gap. We consider a few-shot domain adaptation setting and use the target domain labeled data to match the distributions class-conditionally. In both of these chapters, we use the Sliced Wasserstein Distance metric to minimize distribution discrepancy.

1.2.2 Cross-Task Knowledge Transfer

Our second area of focus is knowledge transfer across related tasks. We use the term *task* to refer to a common problem in classic ML, e.g., regression, classification, or reinforcement learning tasks. Humans extensively use cross-task knowledge transfer by identifying the prior learned skills that can be used to solve a new task. This means that challenging tasks are broken into subtasks that are more basic and can be used across different tasks. This suggests the existence of hierarchies in acquiring skills that relate the tasks through embedding spaces that encode similarities.

We first investigate the problem of zero-shot learning within a multi-task learning setting in chapter 6. Chapter 6 can be considered as an extension of chapter 3 to a continual learning setting. Here, the goal is to transfer knowledge from past experiences to learn future tasks using no data. We consider both sequential online lifelong learning setting and offline setting. In the offline setting, a group of tasks is learned simultaneously before switching to tasks with no data. We assume that the tasks are described using high-level descriptions. The core idea is to learn a mapping from the high-level task descriptors to the optimal task parameters through an intermediate embedding space which couples the optimal task parameters and the task descriptors. To learn this embedding, initially, some tasks with both data and descriptors are used. Similar to chapter 3, we train two dictionaries jointly such that the task descriptor and the task optimal parameter share the same sparse vector in the shared embedding space. We demonstrate that using task descriptors not only improves the learning performance, but upon learning this embedding one can learn a task with no data, through recovering the optimal parameter using high-level task descriptors. It suffices to recover the shared sparse vector using the task descriptor dictionary and then recover the task optimal parameters through multiplication with the optimal parameter distribution.

In chapter 7, we focus on addressing the problem of *catastrophic forgetting* in a sequential multi-task learning setting. When humans learn a new task, more often they do not forget what they have learned before. This is not the case with most ML algorithms that use non-linear models as usually new learned knowledge interferes with what has been before, causing performance degradation on previously learned task. To overcome this challenge, we explore the idea of mapping the tasks to an intermediate embedding space such that the distributions of the tasks are matched, i.e., the embedding space becomes invariant with respect to the input task. As a result, when a new task is learned, the newly acquired knowledge is added to the past learned knowledge consistently, which in turn prevents catastrophic forgetting. To implement this idea, we train a shared end-to-end model across the tasks. We also amend this model with a decoder to make it generative. We learn a shared multi-mode distribution in the embedding space to generate pseudo-data points that can represent the past learned tasks. These data points are replayed along with the current task data to mitigate catastrophic forgetting.

We then focus on the problem of continual concept learning in chapter 8, where the goal is to extend and generalize a concept to new domains using only a few labeled data points. This chapter can be considered as an extension of chapter 5 to a sequential online learning setting. We use the idea of chapter 7 to extend the learned distribution for a task to incorporate new instances of a number of concepts in a new domain. Our architecture is similar to chapter 7, but we can learn the shared distribution using few labeled data points in future tasks. Since the learned distribution in the embedding is enforced to remain stable, the concepts can be generalized to new domains by observing only a few labeled data points.

1.2.3 Cross-Agent Knowledge Transfer

Finally, we focus on the problem of distributed lifelong learning in chapter 9. Here, we assume that multiple agents try to learn related tasks, and the goal is to improve learning quality and speed through collaboration, i.e., cross-agent knowledge transfer. This area is less explored compared to the previous two areas in the literature. But since IoT is becoming a common characteristic of daily life, addressing ML problems in a distributed setting is becoming more important. We consider a network of agents that learn sequential tasks in an online setting. Each agent is assumed to be a lifelong learner which sequentially receives tasks and learns the current task through transferring knowledge from past learned tasks and collaboration with neighboring agents. We extend the idea of lifelong learning from a single agent to the network of multiple agents that potentially collectively learn a series of tasks. Each agent faces some (potentially unique) set of tasks; the key idea is that knowledge learned from these tasks may benefit other agents that are learning different (but related) tasks. To enable knowledge transfer, we assume that a shared embedding can be learned for task parameters. This embedding space captures structures of the tasks and allows knowledge transfer among the agents. Our algorithm provides an efficient way for a network of agents to share their learned knowledge in a distributed and decentralized manner while preserving the privacy of the locally observed data as the data is not shared. We solve the learning problem in a decentralized scheme, as a subclass of distributed algorithms, where a central server does not exist, and in addition to data, computations are also distributed among the agents.

1.2.4 Book Organization

Figure 1.2 summarizes the problem and the challenges we address for each chapter of the book as well as relations between the chapters in a nutshell. In this tree structure, we have listed the five main challenges that need to be addressed in each part and chapter of the book. We have listed five common ML topics to incorporate all challenges that need to be addressed in each chapter. These topics are common in the machine learning literature, but our goal is to address them through learning an intermediate embedding space. We have developed an ML algorithm in each of the chapters 3 to 9 using "knowledge transfer through an embedding space". The solid arrows in Figure 1.2 denote the challenges that need to be addressed for each chapter and part. The dotted blue arrows denote that in some chapters, reading the previous chapters can be helpful to understand those chapters. Readers who might be interested in reading a particular aspect of the book can use Figure 1.2 to identify the proper part and chapter.

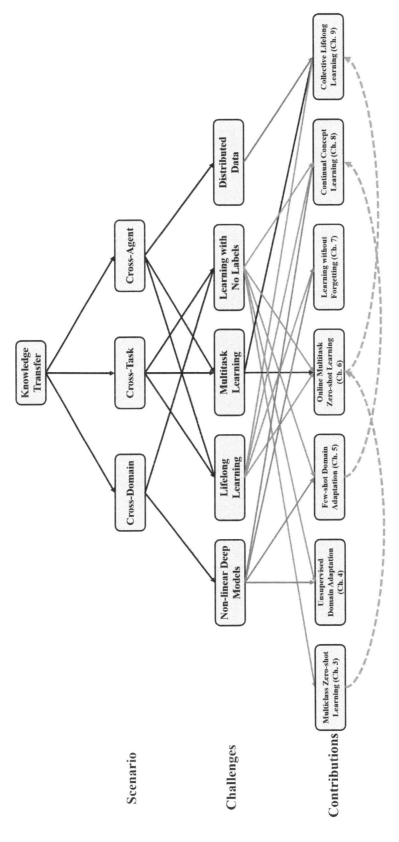

Figure 1.2 Contributions of the book and the challenges that are addressed for each contribution.

CHAPTER 2

Background and Related Work

In this chapter, we explain and survey the machine learning problems that we investigate in this book and survey recent related works that address challenges of knowledge transfer by learning an embedding space to provide a background on prior similar works and introduce the specific problem that we investigate throughout the book. We review the proposed algorithms in the literature that use this strategy to address few- and zero-shot learning, domain adaptation, online and offline multi-task learning, lifelong and continual learning, and collective and distributed learning. We mainly focus on the works that are the most related works to the theme of the book and many important less relevant works are not included in this chapter. For broad surveys on transfer learning/knowledge transfer, interested readers may refer to the papers such as the paper by Pan et al. [163] or Taylor and Stone [240].

From a numerical analysis point of view, most machine learning problems are function approximation problems. Throughout the book, we assume that the goal for solving a single ML problem is to find a predictive function given a dataset drawn from an unknown probability distribution. A single ML problem can be a regression, classification, or reinforcement learning problem, where the goal is to solve for an optimal parameter for the predictive function [221]. This function predicts the label for an input data point for classification tasks, the suitable value for independent input variable for regression tasks, and the corresponding action for an input state for reinforcement learning tasks. The prediction of the function must be optimal in some sense; usually Bayes-optimal criterion is used, and the broad challenge is to approximate such a function. Each problem is Probably Approximately Correct (PAC)-learnable. This assumption means that given enough data and time, solving for an optimal model for each problem is feasible. Due to the various types of constraints that we covered in the previous chapter, our goal is to transfer knowledge across similar and related problems that are defined over different domains, tasks, or agents to improve learning quality and speed, as compared to learning the problems in isolation. The strategy that we explore for this purpose is transferring knowledge through an embedding space that couples the underlying ML problems.

The idea of learning a latent embedding space has been extensively used for single-task learning, where the goal is to learn a mapping such that similar task data points lie

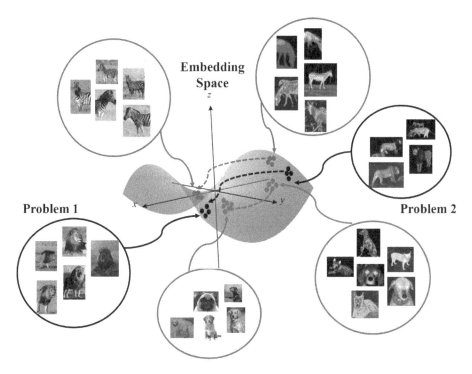

Figure 2.1 knowledge transfer through an embedding space: in this figure, the solid arrows denote functions that map the abstract notions, e.g., images, into the embedding space, the dots in the embedding space denote the data representations in the embedding space, and the dotted arrows indicate correspondences among across two problems, e.g., two classes that are shared between two classification problems. Throughout this book, we focus on learning these arrows in terms of parametric functions. The global challenge that we address in this book is how to relate two problems through the embedding space.

nearby on a space which can be models as lower-dimensional embedding space. The goal is to measure an abstract type of similarity, e.g., objects that belong to a concept class, in terms of well-defined mathematical distances. Figure 2.1 visualizes this idea using visual classification tasks. The notion of "zebra" and "lion" are abstract concepts that form human mental representations which remain consistent for a large number of input visual stimuli (for the moment, consider only problem 1 in Figure 2.1). Humans are able to identify these concepts on a wide range of variations which supersede many current computer vision algorithms. The idea that Figure 2.1 presents for solving a single classification problem is to learn how to map input visual stimuli that correspond to a concept to an embedding space such that, abstract similarities can be encoded according to geometric distance, as evident from Figure 2.1. We have represented this procedure in Figure 2.1, by showing that images that belong to the same class in problem 1 form a cluster of data points in the embedding space. Simultaneously, the class clusters have more distance from each other, which means that geometric distance in the embedding space correlates with similarities in the input space. We can see that instances of each concept form a cluster in the embedding space. The hard challenge would be to learn the mapping, i.e., feature extraction method, from the input data space to the embedding space. This process converts abstract similarities to measurable geometric distances which makes data processing and model training a lot more feasible as it is usually tractable to solve optimization problems using geometrical distance as a similarity measure in the embedding space. As it can be seen in Figure 2.1, the abstract classes are separable in the embedding space for problem 1. This has been inspired from the way that the brain encodes and represents input stimuli in large populations of neurons [220]. Note that this idea can be applied to a broader range of ML problems. We just used visual classification as an example which gives a more intuitive explanation for this idea.

Knowledge transfer across several problems is a further step to learn a problem-level similarity among multiple probability distributions and captures relations between several ML problems. In this book, our goal is to extend the idea of learning a discriminative embedding space for a single ML problem to transfer knowledge across several ML problems. We use a shared embedding space across several machine learning problems to identify cross-problem similarities in order to make learning more efficient in some problems. We have presented this idea in Figure 2.1. In this figure we see three classes of "zebra", "lion", and "dog" in two ML problems. For each concept-class, we have two types of input spaces: electro-optical and infrared (IR) images. In each input space, we can define independent classification problems. However, these problems are related as they share the same abstract concept-classes. As demonstrated in Figure 2.1, if we can learn problem-independent relations between the classes in the embedding space, then we may be able to transfer knowledge from one domain to the other domain. For example, if the geometric arrangement and relative location of classes with respect to each other are similar (as in Figure 2.1), then it is easy to use knowledge about these relations in the source problem, to solve the target problem. This is a high-level description of the strategy that we explore in this book to improve learning performance and speed in a target domain(s) by transferring knowledge from the source domain(s). There are various approaches to relate two ML problems. As we will see, many learning scenarios may benefit from this knowledge transfer strategy. In what follows, we explain about learning settings that can benefit from this idea and survey the related papers in each scenario to give the reader an insight into the prior works.

2.1 KNOWLEDGE TRANSFER THROUGH SHARED REPRESENTATION SPACES

Let $\mathcal{Z}^{(u)}$ denote an ML problem with an unknown probability $p^{(u)}(\boldsymbol{x}, \boldsymbol{y})$ which is defined over the input and output spaces $\mathcal{X}^{(u)}$ and $\mathcal{Y}^{(u)}$. The goal of learning is to find a predictive function $f^{(u)} : \mathcal{X}^{(u)} \to \mathcal{Y}^{(u)}$ such that the true risk is minimized $\mathcal{R} = \mathbb{E}_{(\boldsymbol{x}, \boldsymbol{y}) \sim p^{(u)}}(\ell(f^{(u)}(\boldsymbol{x}), \boldsymbol{y}))$, where ℓ is a point-wise loss function. For a single PAC-learnable problem, usually we are given a training dataset $\mathcal{D}^{(u)} = \langle \boldsymbol{X}^{(u)}, \boldsymbol{Y}^{(u)} \rangle$, the function $f^{(u)}(\cdot)$ is parameterized to form a hypothesis class, and the optimal parameter $\theta^{(u)}$ is computed using Empirical Risk Minimization (ERM) to approximate the Bayes-optimal predictive function. Almost all parametric ML algorithms can be fit into this framework. Moreover, for many common base hypothesis classes there are learning bound that relate the accuracy of ERM-optimal model to the accuracy of the Bayes-optimal model in terms of the size of the training dataset.

As we explained, we can benefit from knowledge transfer when the goal is to learn multiple learning problems, i.e., $u \in \mathbb{U}$ for countable set $\mathbb{U}$. To implement the idea of "using a shared embedding space for transferring knowledge", we assume that the functions $f^{(u)}(\cdot)$ can be decomposed as $f^{(u)}(\cdot) = h^{(u)}(\psi^{(u)}(\cdot))$, where $\psi^{(u)}(\cdot) : \mathcal{X}^{(u)} \to \mathcal{Z}$ map data points of the corresponding problem into the shared embedding space $\mathcal{Z}$, where similarities and structures between the distributions of problems are captured. Doing so, we can formulate the following training problem to benefit from knowledge transfer:

$$\min_{f^{(1)},\dots,\mathbf{f}^{(u)}} \underbrace{\sum_{u=1}^{U} \lambda^{(u)} \mathcal{L}^{(u)}(f^{(u)}(\boldsymbol{X}^{(u)}))}_{\text{Problem-Specific Regularization and Loss Terms}} + \underbrace{\sum_{u,v=1}^{U} \gamma^{(u,v)} \mathcal{M}^{u,v}(\psi^{(u)}(\boldsymbol{X}^{(u)}), \psi^{(v)}(\boldsymbol{X}^{(v)}))}_{\text{Problem Alignment Terms}} ,$$

(2.1)

where $\lambda^{(u)}$ and $\gamma^{(u,v)}$ are trade-off parameters, $\mathcal{L}$ is a loss function over $\mathcal{D}^{(u)}$, and $\mathcal{M}$ is a functional to measure some notion of pairwise-distance between two problems.

The terms in the first sum in Eq. 2.1 can be thought of regularization terms which are either computed using some prior knowledge about the problem distribution or most often are empirical risk terms (if $\boldsymbol{Y}^{(u)}$ is available). These terms are problem-specific and are computed for each problem, irrespective of other problems. The second sum consists of pairwise problem alignment terms that couple the problems and are computed after mapping data into the shared embedding. The goal is to use problem/class-wise relations and shared representations to enforce knowledge integration in the embedding to transfer knowledge across the problems.

Given a specific learning setting and prior knowledge, a suitable strategy should be developed to define the loss and alignment functions. Throughout this book, we investigate several important knowledge transfer scenarios (analogous to categorizations that we provided in the previous chapter):

- If the input spaces are different, we face a **cross-domain knowledge transfer scenario**. In this scenario, usually, $U = 2$ (sometimes more for) multi-view learning and the problems are mostly classification tasks. There may be data scarcity in all domains or, in one domain we may have sufficient labeled data and labeled data maybe scarce in the other domain(s). Domain adaptation, multi-view learning, and zero/few-shot learning are common settings where cross-domain knowledge transfer is helpful. This area is becoming important as nowadays sensors are becoming cheaper and usually various data modalities are recorded and processed to perform a learning task.

- If $\mathcal{X}^{(u)} = \mathcal{X}$, $\mathcal{Y}^{(u)} = \mathcal{Y}$, and $U \gg 1$, we face a **cross-task knowledge transfer scenario**. Each problem can be either a classification, regression, or reinforcement learning task. Transfer learning, multi-task learning, and lifelong learning are common settings for cross-domain knowledge transfer. Cross-task knowledge transfer is in particular important when learning is performed at extended time periods, where usually distributions change. Hence, even the same task is not going to be the same in the future.

- Finally, the datasets $\mathcal{D}^{(u)}$ might not be centrally accessible and be distributed among a number of agents. This would be a **cross-agent knowledge transfer scenario**, where the goal is to learn the problems without sharing full data by sharing individual knowledge of the agents. Distributed learning, collective learning, and collaborative learning are common settings for this scenario. Development of wearable devices and Internet of Things (IoT) has made this area an important learning scenario.

The above terminologies and categorizations are not universal, nor they are exclusive, but they help to categorize the knowledge transfer literature, which covers a broad range of ML literature. For this reason, we use this categorization to arrange the topics of the book.

2.2 CROSS-DOMAIN KNOWLEDGE TRANSFER

For cross-domain knowledge transfer, the challenge is to explore correspondences across domains $\mathcal{X}^{(u)}$ via prior information. In this book, we investigate two important sub-problems within cross-domain knowledge transfer: zero-shot learning and domain adaptation.

2.2.1 Zero-Shot Learning

In the zero-shot learning (ZSL) setting, the problem of multi-class classification is investigated, where while for some classes sufficient labeled data is accessible (seen classes), for some classes, no labeled data is accessible (unseen classes). ZSL is a common situation in modern applications where new classes constantly emerge over time, and hence, continual data labeling is not feasible. Additionally, even if data labeling is feasible, re-training a model from scratch to incorporate the new classes is inefficient and time-consuming. The goal is to learn unseen classes through knowledge transfer from the semantic textual domain. This is a helpful strategy as textual descriptions about a category is easy to obtain nowadays, e.g., using the internet. A major line of ZSL methods learn a shared embedding space to couple the visual and the semantic domains using the seen classes as information about both domains is accessible for seen classes. Let $\mathcal{X}^{(v)}$ denote the visual domain and $\mathcal{X}^{(t)}$ denote the textual domain. In a standard ZSL setting, we are given the training dataset $\mathcal{D}^{(v)} = \langle \boldsymbol{X}^{(v)}, \boldsymbol{Y}^{(v)} \rangle \in \mathbb{R}^{d \times n} \times \mathbb{R}^{k \times n}$ which denotes visual features, e.g., deep net features, and the labels of n images for k seen classes. Additionally, we have a second training dataset $\mathcal{D}^{(t)} = \langle \boldsymbol{X}^{(t)}, \boldsymbol{Y}^{(v)} \rangle \in \mathbb{R}^{d' \times n} \times \mathbb{R}^{k \times n}$ of textual feature descriptions for the same images in the semantic domain, e.g. word vectors or binary semantic attributes. Note that textual descriptions are mostly class-level and hence values in $\boldsymbol{X}^{(t)}$ can be repetitive. For unseen classes, we have access only to textual descriptions of the class in the semantic space. Since we have point-wise level cross-domain correspondence for the data points of seen classes through $\boldsymbol{Y}^{(1)}$, we can solve the following instance of Eq. 2.1 to couple the two domains:

$$\min_{\theta^{(v)}, \theta^{(t)}} \sum_i \ell(\psi_{\theta^{(t)}}^{(t)}(\boldsymbol{x}_i^{(t)}), \psi_{\theta^{(v)}}^{(v)}(\boldsymbol{x}_i^{(v)})) \; , \tag{2.2}$$

where $\theta^{(v)}$ and $\theta^{(t)}$ are learnable parameters, and ℓ is a point-wise distance functions, e.g., Euclidean distance.

For simplicity, it is assumed that only unseen classes are present during testing in the standard ZSL setting. Upon learning $\psi^{(v)}$ and $\psi^{(t)}$, zero-shot classification is feasible by mapping images from unseen classes as well as semantic descriptions of all unseen classes to the embedding space using $\psi^{(v)}$ and $\psi^{(t)}$, respectively. Classification then can be performed by assigning the image to the closest class description, using ℓ. Variations of ZSL methods result from different selections for $\psi^{(v)}$, $\psi^{(2)}$, and ℓ. An important class of ZSL methods considers the semantic space itself to be the embedding space and project the visual features to the semantic space. The pioneering work by Lampert et al. [113] use a group of binary linear SVM classifiers, identity mapping, and Euclidean distance (nearest neighbor), respectively. Socher et al. [230] use a shallow two-layer neural network, identity mapping, and Gaussian classifiers. Romera et al. [182] use a linear projection function, identity mapping, and inner product similarity. Another group of ZSL methods, consider a shared intermediate space as the embedding space. Zhang et al. [292] use the class-dependent ReLU and intersection functions, sparse reconstruction-based projection, and inner product similarity. Kodirov et al. [103] train an auto-encoder over the visual domain. In Eq. (2.1), this means $\psi^t = (\psi^v)^{-1}$ and $\psi^t \circ \psi^v(x_i^{(v)})$ is enforced to match the semantic attribute. They use Euclidean distance for classification.

ZSL algorithms that solely solve Eq. (2.2) face two major issues: domain shift and hubness problem. Domain shift occurs when the visual feature mapping $\psi^{(v)}$ is not discriminative for unseen classes. As a result, the embedding space is not semantically meaningful for unseen classes. The reason is that this mapping is learned only via seen classes during training, while the distribution of unseen classes may be very different. To tackle this challenge, the mapping $\psi^{(v)}$ that is learned using seen classes attributes, needs to be adapted towards attributes of unseen classes. Kodirov et al. [102] use identity function, linear projection, and Euclidean distance for ZSL. To tackle the domain shift problem, we can learn the linear projection such that the visual features become sparse in the embedding. The learned linear projection is then updated during testing by solving a standard dictionary learning problem for unseen classes.

The hubness problem is a version of the curse of dimensionality for ZSL. It occurs because often the shared embedding space needs to be high-dimensional to couple the semantic and the visual domains. As a result, a small number of points, i.e., hubs, can be the nearest neighbor of many points. This counterintuitive effect would make the search of the true label in the embedding space impossible because the nearest neighbor search mostly recovers the hubs regardless of the test image class [54]. The hubness problem has been mitigated by considering the visual space as the embedding space [287]. More recent, ZSL methods focus on the more realistic setting of generalized zero-shot learning, where seen classes are present during testing [265]. In this book, we consider ZSL in both chapter 3 and chapter 6. Chapter 3 considers a classic ZSL setting as we described above but chapter 6 focuses on a cross-task ZSL scenario where the goal is to learn a task without data using what has been learned from other similar past learned tasks. Despite this major difference, we use a similar strategy to tackle the challenges of ZSL in both learning setting.

2.2.2 Domain Adaptation

In domain adaptation settings, usually $\mathcal{Y}^{(t)} = \mathcal{Y}^{(s)}$ for both source and target domains. Usually, the problems are classification tasks with the same label space. This is a common situation when a task distribution is non-stationary. As a result, after training a classifier, when the task distribution changes over time, it is desirable as well as efficient to adapt the learned classifier using minimal labeled data to generalize well again. Domain adaptation is a common strategy to address problems in computer vision beyond the visible spectrum as collecting labeled data is challenging. Since similar problems likely have been addressed in the visible domain, transfer from visible spectrum domains can be helpful. Personalizing a service is another area when we want to adopt a general predictive function for each user using minimum labeled samples. A major assumption in ZSL setting is that we have point-wise correspondence in the training data as the textual and visual features of seen images are given. However, point-wise correspondences are not always accessible.

Unsupervised domain adaptation (UDA) is a more common scenario where we are given a labeled training dataset $\mathcal{D}^{(s)} = \langle \boldsymbol{X}^{(s)}, \boldsymbol{Y}^{(s)} \rangle \in \mathbb{R}^{d \times n} \times \mathbb{R}^{k \times n}$ in a source domain and a second unlabeled dataset $\mathcal{D}^{(t)} = \langle \boldsymbol{X}^{(t)} \rangle \in \mathbb{R}^{d' \times m}$ in a target domain. The goal is transferring knowledge from the source domain to train a model for the target domains. Due to lack of point-wise correspondences in UDA, solving Eq. 2.2 is not feasible. Instead, we solve:

$$\min_{\theta^{(s)}, \theta^{(t)}, \kappa^{(t)}} \mathcal{L}^{(s)}(h_{\kappa^{(s)}}^{(s)}(\psi_{\theta^{(s)}}^{(s)}(\boldsymbol{X}^{(s)})), \boldsymbol{Y}^{(s)}) + \gamma \mathcal{M}(\psi_{\theta^{(s)}}^{(s)}(\boldsymbol{X}^{(s)}), \psi_{\theta^{(t)}}^{(t)}(\boldsymbol{X}^{(t)})) \;, \qquad (2.3)$$

where the predictive functions are parameterized and, $\theta^{(s)}, \theta^{(t)}, \kappa^{(t)}$ are learnable parameters. The first term is the Empirical Risk Minimization (ERM) objective function for the labeled domain, and the second term minimizes the distance between the distributions of both domains in the embedding space. Upon learning $\psi^{(t)}, \psi^{(s)}$, and $h^{(s)}$, the learned embedding would be discriminative for classification and invariant with respect to both domains. Hence, the classifier $h^{(s)}$ would work and generalize well on the target domain even though it is learned solely using source domain samples. Since the target domain data is unlabeled, usually the distance between marginal distributions, $\psi^{(s)}(p^{(s)}(\boldsymbol{x}))$ and $\psi^{(t)}(p^{(t)}(\boldsymbol{x}))$, in the embedding is minimized, i.e., $\mathcal{M}(\psi_{\theta^{(s)}}^{(s)}(\boldsymbol{X}^{(s)}), \psi_{\theta^{(t)}}^{(t)}(\boldsymbol{X}^{(t)})) = \mathcal{A}(\psi_{\theta^{(s)}}^{(s)}(p(\boldsymbol{X}^{(s)})), \psi_{\theta^{(t)}}^{(t)}(p(\boldsymbol{X}^{(t)})))$ where $\mathcal{A}$ is probability distance measure, e.g., KL-divergence.

Different UDA methods select suitable models $\psi^{(t)}, \psi^{(s)}, h^{(s)}$, and the probability distance measure $\mathcal{A}$ and then solve Eq. (2.3). For simplicity, some UDA methods do not learn the mapping functions and use common dimensionality reduction methods to map data into a shared linear subspace that can capture similarities of distribution of both domains. Gong et al. [67] use PCA-based linear projection, PCA-based linear projection, and KL-divergence, respectively. Fernando et al. [60] use PCA-based linear projection, PCA-based linear projection, and Bregman divergence. Baktashmotlagh et al. [12] use Gaussian kernel-based projection, and maximum mean discrepancy (MMD) metric. Another group of methods, learn the mapping functions. Ganin and Lempitsky [65] use deep neural networks as mapping functions. The challenge for using deep networks is that common probability distance measures such as KL-divergence have to vanish gradients when two distributions have non-overlapping supports. As a result, they are suitable for deep net models as first-order gradient-based optimization is used for training deep models. Ganin and Lempitsky [65] use $\mathcal{H} \triangle \mathcal{H}$-distance instead, which has been introduced for theoretical analysis of domain adaptation [17]. Intuitively, $\mathcal{H} \triangle \mathcal{H}$-distance measures the most prediction difference between two classifiers that belong to the same hypothesis class on two distinct distributions. Courty et al. [48] use optimal transport distance for domain adaptation. In addition to having a non-vanishing gradient, a major benefit of using is that is can be computed using drawn samples without any need for parameterization. On the other hand, the downside of using optimal transport is that it is defined in terms of an optimization problem, and solving this problem is computationally expensive.

The above-mentioned methods minimize the distance between distributions by directly matching the distributions. Development of generative adversarial networks (GAN) has introduced another tool to mix two domains indirectly. In the UDA setting, $\mathcal{M}$ can be set to be a discriminative network which is trained to distinguish between the representations of the target and the source data points. This network is trained such that it cannot distinguish between the two domains, and as a result, the embedding space becomes invariant, i.e., the distributions are matched indirectly. Tzeng et al. [248] use this technique to match the distributions for UDA. Zhu et al. [297] introduce the novel notion of *cycle-consistency loss*. The idea is to concatenate two GANs and then train them such that the pair forms an identity mapping across the domains by minimizing the cycle-consistency loss. This is very important as no pair-wise correspondence is going to be necessary anymore.

In this book, we address domain adaptation in chapters 4 and 5. Chapter 4 focus on UDA where both domains are from the same data modality, whereas in chapter 5, we address semi-supervised DA, where the data modality between the two domains is different. More specifically, we consider knowledge transfer from electro-optical (EO) domains to Synthetic Aperture Radar (SAR) domains.

2.3 CROSS-TASK KNOWLEDGE TRANSFER

Since the input and output spaces are usually equal for cross-task knowledge transfer, the challenge for knowledge transfer is to identify task relations and similarities. If the data for all tasks are accessible simultaneously, the learning setting is called multi-task learning. In contrast, if the tasks are learned sequentially, the setting is called lifelong learning.

2.3.1 Multi-Task Learning

Multi-task learning (MTL) setting is quite different from domain adaptation or ZSL as usually we have access to labeled data in all problems. Hence, the goal is not to transfer knowledge unidirectionally from some source tasks with abundant labeled data to some other target tasks, where we face labeled data scarcity. The goal is to identify and use relations and similarities between the tasks and transfer knowledge across all tasks bidirectionally to improve generalization error for all tasks. The tasks can be regression, classification, or reinforcement learning tasks. Usually, the same type of tasks is considered in MTL settings.

We formulate MTL for classification and regression tasks, but we will show in chapter 6 that our formulation is applicable to reinforcement learning tasks as well. A naive approach is to assume that in Eq. (2.1), parameterize all models by assuming $h^{(u)}(\cdot) = h(\cdot)$. We can then train all models by minimizing the average risk over all task:

$$\min_{\theta^{(1)},\ldots,\theta^{(U)}} \sum_{u=1}^{U} \frac{1}{U} \mathcal{L}^{(u)}(f_{\theta^{(u)}}^{(u)}(\boldsymbol{X}^{(u)}), \boldsymbol{Y}^{(u)}) \; , \tag{2.4}$$

where $\theta^{(u)}$'s are learnable model parameters, usually selected to be (deep) neural networks. This formalism enforces $\psi^{(u)}(p(\boldsymbol{y}|\boldsymbol{x})) = \psi(p(\boldsymbol{y}|\boldsymbol{x})$ in the shared embedding space for all tasks. Despite the simplicity, this formulation is in particular effective for NLP applications [90], where the shared embedding can be interpreted as a semantic meaning space that transcends vocabulary of languages.

In an MTL setting, usually $u \gg 1$ and hence the tasks are likely diverse. If we use the formulation of Eq. (2.4) on diverse tasks, coupling all tasks can degrade performance compared to learning single tasks individually. This can occur as the tasks are enforced to have the same distribution in the embedding space, while they may be unrelated. This phenomenon is known as the problem of *negative transfer* in MTL literature. To allow for more diversity across the tasks, Tommasi et al. [246] generalized the formalism of Eq. (2.4) by considering two orthogonal subspaces for each task. One of these spaces is assumed to be shared across the tasks, while the other is a task-specific space that captures variations across the tasks. Since for each task, these two spaces are orthogonal, task-specific knowledge and shared-knowledge naturally are divided. This will reduce negative knowledge transfer. This formalism also can address multi-view problems. Broadly speaking, multi-view learning can be formulated as a special case for MTL where each data view is a task and corresponds across the views is captured point-wise by the training data.

Another group of MTL algorithms model task diversity by allowing the mapping functions $\psi^{(u)}(p(\boldsymbol{y}|\boldsymbol{x}))$ to be different. For the case of linear models, i.e., $\boldsymbol{y} = \boldsymbol{w}^\top \boldsymbol{x}$, the GO-MTL algorithm assumes that $\psi^{(u)}(\cdot) = \psi(\cdot)$, $\psi^{(u)}\boldsymbol{x} = \boldsymbol{L}^\top \boldsymbol{x}$, where $\boldsymbol{L} \in \mathbb{R}^{d \times k}$, and $h^{(u)}(\boldsymbol{x}) = g((\boldsymbol{s}^{(u)})\top \boldsymbol{x})$, where $\boldsymbol{s}^{(u)} \in \mathbb{R}^k$ and is a nonlinear function such as softmax to allow classification [110]. In other words, it is assumed that data points for all tasks are mapped into row space of a dictionary that is shared across all tasks. This transform on its own is not helpful but if the task-specific vectors $\boldsymbol{s}^{(u)}$ are enforced to be sparse, then data for each task is going to be mapped to a subspace formed by few rows of the matrix $\boldsymbol{L}$. As a result, if two similar tasks then would share the same rows and hence tasks with similar distributions are grouped. As a result, their distributions are enforced to be similar indirectly, and negative transfer can be mitigated. This process can be implemented by enforcing the vectors $\boldsymbol{s}^{(u)}$ to have minimal ℓ_1-norm. Doing so, Eq. (2.1) would reduce to:

$$\min_{\boldsymbol{L}\boldsymbol{s}^{(1)},\ldots,\boldsymbol{s}^{(u)}} \sum_{u=1}^{U} \frac{1}{U} \sum_{i} \ell\big(g((\boldsymbol{s}^{(u)})^\top \boldsymbol{L}^\top \boldsymbol{x}_i^{(u)}), \boldsymbol{x}_i^{(u)}\big) + \alpha \|\boldsymbol{s}^{(u)}\|_1 + \beta \|\boldsymbol{L}\|_{\mathrm{F}}^2 \ , \qquad (2.5)$$

where $\| \cdot \|_{\mathrm{F}}^2$ denotes the Frobenius norm that controls model complexity, and α and β are regularization parameters. Eq. (2.1) is a biconvex problem for convex $\ell(\cdot)$ and can be solved by alternating iterations over the variables. The Go-MTL algorithm has been extended to handle non-linear tasks by considering deep models [139, 141].

Most RL methods require a significant amount of time and data to learn effective policies for complex tasks such as playing Atari games. MTL method can help to improve the performance of RL tasks by identifying skills that are effective across the tasks. Teh et al. [242] address MTL within RL by considering that a shared cross-tasks policy exists, called distilled policy. The task-specific policies are regularized to have minimal KL-divergence distance with the distilled policy, which enforces the distilled policy to capture actions that are helpful for all tasks with high probabilities. The distilled policy and task-specific policies are parameterized by deep networks that share their output in the action space. Experiments on complex RL tasks demonstrate that MTL helps to learn more stable and robust policies in a shorter time period.

2.3.2 Lifelong Learning

In a lifelong machine learning (LML) setting [211], consecutive tasks are learned sequentially. Upon receiving data for the current tasks, the task is learned, the newly obtained knowledge is accumulated to a repository of knowledge, and the LML agent advances to learn the next task. The goal is to learn the current task by transferring knowledge from previous experiences, gained from learning past tasks. Since the previous tasks may be encountered at any time, performance across all tasks seen so far must be optimized. Ideally, the lifelong learning agent should scale effectively to large numbers of tasks over its lifetime.

Building upon the Go-MTL formulation, ELLA solves Eq. (2.5) in a lifelong learning setting [211]. For this purpose, a second-order Taylor expansion of each individual loss function around the single task optimal parameter $\tilde{\boldsymbol{\theta}}^{(t)}$ is used to approximate the risk terms. This would simplify Eq. (2.5) as:

$$\min_{\boldsymbol{L}\boldsymbol{s}^{(1)},\ldots,\boldsymbol{s}^{(T)}} \sum_{t=1}^{T} \frac{1}{T} \|\boldsymbol{L}\boldsymbol{s}^{(t)} - \tilde{\boldsymbol{\theta}}^{(t)}\|_{\Gamma^{(t)}}^2 + \alpha\|\boldsymbol{s}^{(t)}\|_1 + \beta\|\boldsymbol{L}\|_{\mathrm{F}}^2 \,, \tag{2.6}$$

where $\Gamma^{(t)}$ is the Hessian matrix for individual loss terms and $\|\boldsymbol{v}\|_A^2 = \boldsymbol{v}^\top \boldsymbol{A}\boldsymbol{v}$. To solve Eq. (2.6) in an online scheme, a sparse coefficient $\boldsymbol{s}^{(t)}$ is only updated when the corresponding current task is learned at each time step. This process reduces the MTL objective to a sparse coding problem to solve for $\boldsymbol{s}^{(t)}$ in the shared dictionary $\boldsymbol{L}$. The shared dictionary is then updated using the task parameters learned so far to accumulate the learned knowledge. This procedure makes LML feasible and improves learning speed by two to three orders of magnitude. ELLA algorithm can also address reinforcement learning tasks in LML setting [7]. The idea is to approximate the expected return function for an RL task using the second-order Taylor expansion around the task-specific optimal policy and enforce the policies to be sparse in a shared dictionary domain. The resulting problem is an instance of Eq. (2.6), which can be addressed using ELLA.

Lifelong learning methods have also been developed using deep models. Deep nets have been shown to be very effective for MTL, but an important problem for lifelong learning with deep neural network models is to address *catastrophic forgetting* catastrophic forgetting. Catastrophic forgetting occurs when obtained knowledge about the current task interferes with what has been learned before. As a result, the network forgets past obtained knowledge when new tasks are learned in an LML setting. Rannen et al. [176] address this challenge for classification tasks by training a shared encoder that maps the data for all tasks into a shared embedding space. Task-specific classifiers are trained to map the encoded data from the shared encoding space into the label spaces of the tasks. Additionally, a set of task-specific auto-encoders are trained with the encoded data as their input. When a new task is learned, trained auto-encoder for past tasks are used to reconstruct features learned for the new task and then prevent them from changing to avoid forgetting. As a result, memory requirement grows linearly in terms of learnable parameters of the auto-encoders. The number of these learnable parameters is considerably less than the parameters that we need to store all the past task data. Another approach to address this challenge is to replay data points from past tasks during training a network on new tasks. This process is called *experience replay* which regularizes the network to retain distribution of past tasks. In other words, experience replay recasts the lifelong learning setting into a multi-task learning setting for which catastrophic forgetting does not occur. Experience replay can be implemented by storing a subset of data points for past tasks, but this would require a memory buffer to store data. As a result, implementing experience replay is challenging when memory constraints exist. Building upon the success of generative models, experience replay can be implemented without any need for a memory buffer by appending the main deep network with a structure that can generate pseudo-data points for the past learned tasks. To this end, we can enforce the tasks to share a common distribution in a shared embedding space. Since the model is generative, we can use samples from this distribution to generate for all past tasks when the current task is being learned. Shin et al. [225] use adversarial learning to mix the distributions of all tasks in the embedding. As a result, the generator network is able to generate pseudo-data points for past tasks.

We address cross-task knowledge transfer in Part II in chapters 5 through 6. As mentioned, chapter 5 addresses ZSL in a sequential task learning setting. In chapter 6, we address catastrophic forgetting for this setting, where deep nets are base models. In chapter 7, we address domain adaptation in a lifelong learning setting, i.e., adapting a model to generalize well on new tasks using few labeled data points without forgetting the past.

2.4 CROSS-AGENT KNOWLEDGE TRANSFER

Most ML algorithms consider a single learning agent, which has centralized access to problem data. However, in many real-world applications, multiple (virtual) agents must collectively solve a set of problems because data is distributed among them. For example, data may only be partially accessible by each learning agent, local data processing can be inevitable, or data communication to a central server may be costly or time-consuming due to limited bandwidth. Cross-agent knowledge transfer is an important tool to address the emerging challenges of these important learning schemes. To model multi-agent learning settings, graphs are suitable models where each node in the graph represents a portion of data or an agent and communication modes between the agents is modeled via edge set (potentially dynamic) of the graph. The challenge is to design a mechanism to optimize the objective functions of individual agents and share knowledge across them over the communication graph without sharing data.

Cross-agent knowledge is a natural setting for RL agents as in many applications; there are many similar RL agents, e.g., personal assistance robots that operate for different people. Since the agents perform similar tasks, the agents can learn collectively and collaboratively to accelerate RL learning speed for each agent. Gupta et al. [75] address cross-agent transfer for two agents with deep models that learn multiple skills to handle RL tasks. The agents learn similar tasks, but their state space, actions space, and transition functions can be different. For example, two different robots are trained to do the same task. The idea is to use the skills that are acquired by both agents and train two deep neural networks to map the optimal policies for each agent into a shared invariant feature space such that the distribution of the optimal policies become similar. Upon learning the shared space, the agents map any acquired new skill into the shared space. Each agent can then benefit from skills that are acquired only by the other agent through tracking the corresponding features for that skill in the shared space and subsequently its own actions. By doing so, each agent can accelerate its learning substantially using skills that are learned by the other agent.

Cross-agent knowledge transfer is more challenging when the agents process time-dependent data. A simple approach to model this case is to assume that in Eq. (2.1), there are K agents and $\mathcal{L}^{(u)}(f^{(u)}(\boldsymbol{X}^{(u)})) = \sum_k \mathcal{L}_k^{(u)}(f_k^{(u)}(\boldsymbol{X}_k^{(u)}))$. In consensus learning scenarios, it is assumed that all agents try to reach consensus on learning a parameter that is shared across the agents. We have addressed this cross-agent knowledge-transfer scenario within an LML scenario [199] in chapter 9.

2.5 CONCLUSIONS

In this chapter, we presented "learning embedding" spaces as a common strategy for transferring knowledge and listed related prior works that benefit from this learning strategy. A major contribution of this book is to present transfer learning through embedding spaces as a common strategy to address the challenges of broad classes of learning scenarios. In particular, in this chapter, we listed the important learning scenarios and setting to categorize our investigations throughout the rest of the thesis. After a brief introduction and familiarity with background works, we explain about our novel ideas in the subsequent chapters to develop algorithms that can address the challenges of each learning scenario.

I

Cross-Domain Knowledge Transfer

In the first part of this book, we focus on knowledge transfer across different domains. We use the term *domain* to refer to the input space of the model that is trained to perform a task. The domains can be from two different data modalities, e.g., heterogeneous domains such as visual and textual domains, or the same modality, e.g., two homogeneous visual domains. The major challenge that is addressed in cross-domain knowledge transfer is to tackle labeled data scarcity. Given the complexity of the current state of the art ML models, i.e., deep networks, addressing this challenge has become more important. The common idea to addressed labeled data scarcity is to transfer knowledge from a related domain, where labeled data is accessible. In this part of the book, we address problems of *zero-shot learning* and *domain adaptation* through learning an embedding space which couples two knowledge domains, in chapter 1 to chapter 3, respectively. In a zero-shot learning setting, we have a multi-class classification problem, where for some classes, no labeled data is accessible. We learn a shared embedding space to couple the visual and semantic domain using seen classes for which labeled data is accessible. In a domain adaptation setting, the two domains share the same classes. Our goal is to find a one-to-one correspondence among the classes across the two domains.

CHAPTER 3

Zero-Shot Image Classification through Coupled Visual and Semantic Embedding Spaces

We focus on zero-shot learning (ZSL) in this chapter. ZSL is a framework to classify instances belonging to unseen target classes based on solely semantic information about these unseen classes. The key challenge in performing zero-shot learning is to map an image into its semantic descriptions, i.e., attributes. This mapping can be learned using the seen source classes in the training stage of ZS via a shared embedding space.

Figure 3.1 present the idea within our broad idea of using an embedding space for transferring knowledge. In this figure, each small circle denotes representation of an image in the embedding space and the bigger circles denote the representations for the semantic description of the classes in the embedding space. If we can use the classes with both labeled images and the semantic descriptions, i.e., classes zebra and puma in Figure 3.1, to learn an embedding which captures semantic similarities, then ZSL is feasible. This means that images that belong to a class should lie close to the semantic description of the class in the embedding space. Classifying images from an unseen class, i.e., tiger class is going to be possible by mapping an image from an unseen class to the embedding space and then searching for the closest class description.

Building upon the above intuition, we propose to use coupled dictionary learning (CDL) as the method to learn a shared embedding to map images to their semantic descriptions in this chapter. The core idea is that the visual features and the semantic attributes of an image can be enforced to share the same sparse representation in an intermediate space. In the ZSL training stage, we use images from seen classes and semantic attributes from seen and unseen classes to learn two dictionaries that can represent the visual and semantic feature vectors of an image sparsely. Upon training the coupled dictionaries, images from unseen

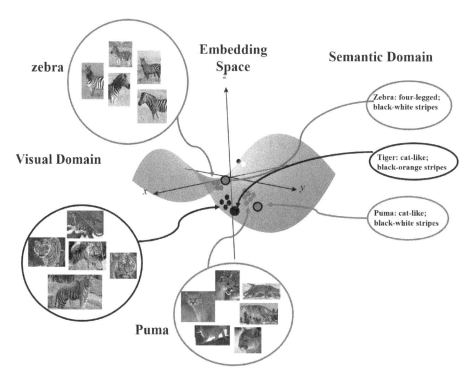

Figure 3.1 Zero-shot learning through an intermediate embedding space: in this figure, the small circles in the embedding space denote representations of images and the bigger circles denote representations of the semantic descriptions for the classes in the embedding space. An image which belongs to an unseen class can be classified by mapping it into the embedding space and then searching for its class by finding the closest semantic description in the embedding space.

classes can be mapped into the attribute space by finding the joint sparse representation using merely the visual data. The image is then classified in the attribute space given semantic descriptions of unseen classes. Results of this chapter have been presented in Refs [107, 200, 106].

3.1 OVERVIEW

Image classification and categorization are two of the most effective and well-studied application areas of machine learning and computer vision. Despite tremendous advances in these areas and development of various algorithms that are as accurate as humans in many applications, most of these approaches are supervised learning algorithms that require a large pool of manually labeled images for decent performance. This amount may be thousands of images, if not tens of thousands of images for deep classifiers, where millions of model parameters need to be learned. Data labeling is becoming more challenging as the numbers of classes are growing and fine-grained classification is becoming more critical. While learning using fully labeled data is practical for some applications, manual labeling of data is economically and time-wise infeasible for many other applications due to complications such as:

- The exponential growth of visual data (e.g., photograph-sharing websites, medical imaging).

- The need for fine-grained multi-class classification (e.g., thousands of classes for animal categorization).

- The persistent and dynamic emergence of new classes (e.g., new products on shopping websites).

- Classes with highly infrequent members.

As a result, current supervised algorithms for image classification suffer from scalability issues in practice. Consequently, it is critical to develop algorithms that can classify objects using few training samples and even from *unseen* classes with no training samples. Such algorithms should classify instances from unseen classes and can incorporate new emerging classes without substantial retraining.

Humans have this remarkable ability to learn enormous numbers of classes from little data. As an example, consider the classification of animal images. It is estimated that as many as one million different species of animals have been identified, with as many as ten thousand new species being discovered annually. This classification problem is a case when ZSL can be extremely helpful. Most people probably have not seen an image of a "tardigrade", nor heard of this species, but we can intuitively demonstrate the potential of ZSL for this class. Consider the following sentence from Wikipedia: "Tardigrades (also known as water bears or moss piglets) are water-dwelling, eight-legged, segmented micro animals". Given this textual description, most humans can easily identify the creature in Figure 3.2 (Left) as a Tardigrade, even though they may have never seen one before. Humans can easily perform this ZSL task by: (1) identifying the semantic features that describe the class *Tardigrade* as "bear-like", "piglet-like", "water-dwelling", "eight-legged", "segmented", and "microscopic animal", (2) parsing the image into its visual attributes (see Figure 3.2), and (3) matching the parsed visual features to the parsed textual information.

Following a similar strategy, ZSL can be implemented in computer vision. The textual features can be parsed into a vector of either predetermined binary attributes e.g., water-dwelling or features extracted from large unlabeled text corpora, e.g., *word2vec* [148] or *glove* [171]. Deep convolutional neural networks (CNNs) [109, 227, 83] can extract visually rich and descriptive features from natural images to parse the visual information. Numerous ZSL algorithms have been developed to learn a mapping between the visual features and semantic attributes using a shared space [162, 4, 230, 159, 114, 292]. In this chapter, we focus on this latter issue of learning the mapping for ZSL, using the novel approach of coupled dictionary learning (CDL) [274] to relate the visual features and the semantic attributes.

CDL was developed in the image processing community to learn two overcomplete dictionaries to couple two feature spaces to address a diverse set of image processing tasks. In many image processing algorithms(e.g., single image super-resolution [179]) there exist two feature spaces (i.e., high- and low-resolution images) and the challenge is that given an instance in one of these spaces (low-resolution image), to find the corresponding instance in the second space (high-resolution image with maximum perceived perceptual quality [280]) or simply find it in a pool of instances. In such applications, it seems natural to assume instances related to the same entity (i.e., high- and low-resolution images) share some type of common aspects. CDL proposes that there exists a single sparse representation for both features that can be recovered using two coupled dictionaries. These two dictionaries can be learned from data. We can use a pool of training data from both feature spaces, and then the learned dictionaries are used to perform desired tasks. CDL has been used to develop algorithms for image super-resolution [274], cross-domain image recognition [87], image fusion [74], image deblurring [206, 266], and lifelong learning [94]. Building upon this progress, our contribution is to use CDL to couple the visual and the semantic spaces to perform zero-shot image classification.

Similarly, upon learning the coupled dictionaries, we can map a given image from an unseen class to the semantic description of the class using the joint-sparse representation, where we can classify the image. Moreover, we incorporate an entropy minimization term into the CDL optimization problem [102] to increase the discriminative power of CDL. Our novel attribute-aware formulation also provides an algorithmic solution to the common domain shift/hubness problem in ZSL [54, 224]. We also provide theoretical analysis on PAC-learnability of our algorithm and finally demonstrate the practicality of the approach through extensive experiments.

3.2 PROBLEM FORMULATION AND TECHNICAL RATIONALE

We are interested in a ZSL setting where semantic information leverages learning unseen classes. We follow Palatucci et al. [162] to formulate ZSL as a two-stage estimation problem. Consider a visual feature metric space $\mathcal{F}$ of dimension p, a semantic metric space $\mathcal{A}$ with dimension of q as well as a class label set $\mathcal{Y}$ with dimension K that ranges over a finite alphabet of size K (images can potentially have multiple memberships in the classes). As an example $\mathcal{F} = \mathbb{R}^p$ for the visual features extracted from a deep CNN and $\mathcal{A} = \{0, 1\}^q$ when a binary code of length q is used to identify the presence/absence of various characteristics in an object [114]. We are given a labeled dataset $\mathcal{D} = \{((\boldsymbol{x}_i, \boldsymbol{z}_i), \boldsymbol{y}_i)\}_{i=1}^N$ of features of seen images and their corresponding semantic attributes, where $\forall i : \boldsymbol{x}_i \in \mathcal{F}, \boldsymbol{z}_i \in \mathcal{A}$, and $\boldsymbol{y}_i \in \mathcal{Y}$. We are also given the unlabeled attributes of unseen classes $\mathcal{D}' = \{\boldsymbol{z}_j', \boldsymbol{y}_j'\}_{j=1}^M$, i.e., we have access to textual information for a wide variety of objects but not have access to the corresponding visual information. Following the standard assumption in ZSL, we also assume that the set of seen and unseen classes are disjoint. The challenge is how to learn a model on the labeled set and transfer the learned knowledge to the unlabeled set. We also assume that the same semantic attributes could not describe two different classes of objects. This assumption ensures that knowing the semantic attribute of an image one can classify that image.

The goal is to learn from the labeled dataset how to classify images of unseen classes indirectly from the unlabeled dataset. For further clarification, consider an instance of ZSL in which features extracted from images of horses and tigers are included in seen visual features $X = [\boldsymbol{x}_1, ..., \boldsymbol{x}_N]$, where $\boldsymbol{x}_i \in \mathcal{F}$, but X does not contain features of zebra images. On the other hand, the semantic attributes contain information of all seen $Z = [\boldsymbol{z}_1, ..., \boldsymbol{z}_N]$ for $\boldsymbol{z}_i \in \mathcal{A}$ and unseen $Z' = [\boldsymbol{z}_1', ..., \boldsymbol{z}_M']$ for $\boldsymbol{z}_j' \in \mathcal{A}$ images including the zebras. The goal is that by learning the relationship between the image features and the attributes "horse-like" and "has stripes" from the seen images, we are able to assign an unseen zebra image to its corresponding attribute.

Within this paradigm, ZSL can be performed by a two-stage estimation. First, the visual features can be mapped to the semantic space and then the label is estimated in the semantic space. More formally, we want to learn the mapping $\phi : \mathcal{F} \to \mathcal{A}$, which relates the visual space and the attribute space. We also assume that $\psi : \mathcal{A} \to \mathcal{Y}$ is the mapping between the semantic space and the label space. The mapping ψ can be as simple as nearest neighbor, assigning labels according to the closest semantic attribute in the semantic attribute space. Having learned this mapping, for an unseen image one can recover the corresponding attribute vector using the image features and then classify the image using a second mapping $y = (\psi \circ \phi)(x)$, where $\circ$ represents function composition. The goal is to introduce a type of bias to learn both mappings using the labeled dataset. Having learned both mappings, ZSL is feasible in the testing stage. Because, if the mapping $\phi(\cdot)$ can map an unseen image close enough to its true semantic features, then intuitively the mapping $\psi(\cdot)$ can still recover the corresponding class label. Following our example, if the function $\phi(\cdot)$ can recover that an unseen image of a zebra is "horse-like" and "has stripes", then it is likely that the mapping $\psi(\cdot)$ can classify the unseen image.

3.2.1 Proposed Idea

The idea of using coupled dictionaries to map data from a given metric space to a second related metric space was first proposed by Yang et al. [275] for single image super-resolution problem [208], where the goal is to generate a high-resolution image with maximum perceptual quality [279, 280] using a single from of low-resolution image. Their pioneering idea is to assume that the high-resolution and corresponding low-resolution patches of the image can be represented with a unique joint sparse vector in two low- and high-resolution dictionaries. The core idea is that in the absence of a high-resolution image and given a low-resolution image, the joint-sparse representation can be computed using sparse signal recovery [57, 185]. The sparse vector is then used to generate the high-resolution image patches using the low-resolution image. They also propose an efficient algorithm to learn the low- and the high-resolution dictionaries using a training set, consisting of both the low- and high-resolution version of natural images. Our goal is to follow the same approach but replacing low- and high-resolution metric spaces with the visual and the semantic spaces, respectively.

As a big-picture to understand our approach, Figure 3.2 captures the gist of our idea based on the work proposed in Ref. [275]. Visual features are extracted via CNNs (left sub-figure). For example, the last fully-connected layer of a trained CNN can be removed, and the rest of the deep net can be used as a feature extractor given an input image. These features have been demonstrated to be highly descriptive and lead to the state of the art performance for many computer vision and image processing tasks [223].

To perform ZSL, we need the textual description of classes, too. Textual descriptions of many classes are cheap to obtain, e.g., Wikipedia. The semantic attributes then can be provided via textual feature extractors like word2vec or potentially via human annotations (right sub-figure). Both the visual features and the semantic attributes are assumed sparsely represented in a shared union of linear subspaces embedding domain using the visual

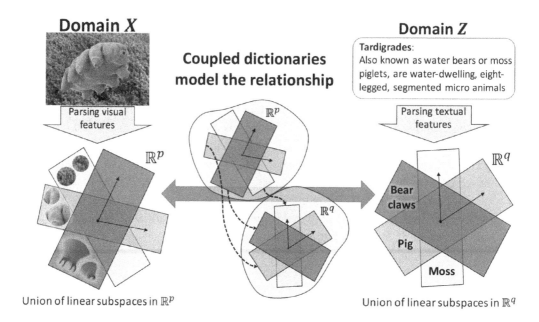

Figure 3.2 A high-level overview of our approach. Left & right: visual and attribute feature extraction and representation using a union of subspaces. We couple the two domains by enforcing features of an image to share the same space representation in this embedding space. Middle: mapping the features in the shared space.

and the attribute dictionaries (left and right sub-figures). The idea here is that the sparse representation vectors for both feature vectors are equal and thus, the visual and the attribute feature spaces are coupled through the joint sparse vector. Thus, one can map an image to its textual description in this space (middle sub-figure).

The intuition from a co-view perspective [281] is that both the visual and the attribute features provide information about the same class or entity, and so each can augment the learning of the other. Each underlying class is common to both views, and so we can find task embeddings that are consistent for both the visual features and their corresponding attribute features. The main challenge is to learn these dictionaries for the visual and the attribute spaces. After training these two dictionaries, zero-shot classification can be performed by mapping images of unseen classes into the attribute space, where classification can be simply done via nearest neighbor or more advanced clustering approaches. Given the coupled nature of the learned dictionaries, an image can be mapped to its semantic attributes by first finding the sparse representation with respect to the visual dictionary and then searching for the semantic descriptions that match with the recovered sparse representation.

Our algorithm is also equipped with a novel entropy minimization regularizer [69], which facilitates the solution to the ZSL problem and addresses the challenge of domain shift for ZSL. Next, the semantic attribute dictionary can be used to recover the attribute vector from the joint sparse representation, which can then be used for classification. We also show that a transductive approach applied to our attribute-aware JD-ZSL formulation provides state-of-the-art or close to state-of-the-art performance on various benchmark datasets.

3.2.2 Technical Rationale

For the rest of our discussion, we assume that $\mathcal{F} = \mathbb{R}^p$, $\mathcal{A} = \mathbb{R}^q$, and $\mathcal{Y} \subset \mathbb{R}^K$. Most ZSL algorithms focus on learning $\phi(\cdot)$ because even using a simple method like nearest neighbor classification for $\psi(\cdot)$ yields descent ZSL performance. The simplest ZSL approach is to assume that the mapping $\phi : \mathbb{R}^p \to \mathbb{R}^q$ is linear, $\phi(\mathbf{x}) = W^T \mathbf{x}$ where $W \in \mathbb{R}^{p \times q}$, and then minimize the regression error $\frac{1}{N} \sum_i \| W^T \mathbf{x}_i - \mathbf{z}_i \|_2^2$ to learn W. Even though a closed-form solution exists for W, the solution contains the inverse of the covariance matrix of X, $(\frac{1}{N} \sum_i (x_i x_i^T))^{-1}$, which requires a large number of data points for accurate estimation. Various regularizations are considered for W to overcome this problem. Decomposition of W as $W = P \Lambda Q$, where $P \in \mathbb{R}^{p \times l}$, $\Lambda \in \mathbb{R}^{l \times l}$, $Q \in \mathbb{R}^{l \times q}$, and $l < min(p, q)$ can also be helpful. Intuitively, P is a right linear operator that projects $\mathbf{x}$'s into a shared low-dimensional subspace, Q is a left linear operator that projects $\mathbf{z}$ into the same shared subspace, and Λ provides a bi-linear similarity measure in the shared subspace. The regression problem can then be transformed into maximizing $\frac{1}{N} \sum_i \mathbf{x}_i^T P \Lambda Q \mathbf{z}_i$, which is a weighted correlation between the embedded $\mathbf{x}$'s and $\mathbf{z}$'s. This is the essence of many ZSL techniques, including Akata et al. [4] and Romera-Paredes et al. [182]. This technique can be extended to nonlinear mappings using kernel methods. However, the choice of kernels remains an open challenge, and usually, other nonlinear models are used.

The mapping $\phi : \mathbb{R}^p \to \mathbb{R}^q$ can be chosen to be highly nonlinear, as in deep nets. Let a deep net be denoted by $\phi(.; \boldsymbol{\theta})$, where $\boldsymbol{\theta}$ represents the synaptic weights and biases. ZSL can then be addressed by minimizing $\frac{1}{N} \sum_i \| \phi(\mathbf{x}_i; \boldsymbol{\theta}) - \mathbf{z}_i \|_2^2$ with respect to $\boldsymbol{\theta}$. Alternatively, one can nonlinearly embed $\mathbf{x}$'s and $\mathbf{z}$'s in a shared metric space via deep nets, $p(\mathbf{x}; \boldsymbol{\theta}_x) : \mathbb{R}^p \to \mathbb{R}^l$ and $q(\mathbf{z}; \theta_z) : \mathbb{R}^q \to \mathbb{R}^l$, and maximize their similarity measure in the embedded space, $\frac{1}{N} \sum_i p(\mathbf{x}_i; \boldsymbol{\theta}_x)^T q(\mathbf{z}_i; \boldsymbol{\theta}_z)$, as in Refs. [120, 287]. This approach might improve performance for particular data sets, but in turn would require more training samples, i.e., we will need more seen classes to train the deep network. Note that this might not be plausible for ZSL because the very reason and motivation to perform ZSL is to learn from as few labeled data points as possible.

By comparing the above approaches, we conclude that nonlinear methods are computationally expensive and require a larger training dataset. On the other hand, linear ZSL algorithms are efficient, but their performances are lower than nonlinear methods. As a compromise, we can model nonlinearities in data distributions as a union of linear subspaces using coupled dictionaries. The relationship between the metric spaces is also reflected in the learned dictionaries. This allows a nonlinear scheme with a computational complexity comparable to linear techniques.

3.3 ZERO-SHOT LEARNING USING COUPLED DICTIONARY LEARNING

In standard dictionary learning, a sparsifying dictionary is learned using a given training sample set $X = [\mathbf{x}_1, ..., \mathbf{x}_N]$ for a particular class of signals [3]. Unlike standard dictionary learning, coupled dictionary learning has been proposed to couple related features from two metric spaces to learn the mapping function between these spaces. Following the same framework, the gist of our approach is to learn the mapping $\phi : \mathbb{R}^p \to \mathbb{R}^q$ through two dictionaries, $D_x \in \mathbb{R}^{p \times r}$ and $D_z \in \mathbb{R}^{q \times r}$ for X and $[Z, Z']$ sets, respectively, where $r > max(p, q)$. The goal is to find a shared sparse representation $\mathbf{a}_i$ for $\mathbf{x}_i$ and $\mathbf{z}_i$, such that $\mathbf{x}_i = D_x \mathbf{a}_i$ and $\mathbf{z}_i = D_z \mathbf{a}_i$, to be used for coupling the semantic and visual features. We first explain how we can train the two dictionaries, and then how can we use these dictionaries to estimate $\phi(\cdot)$.

3.3.1 Training Phase

Standard dictionary learning is based upon minimizing the empirical average estimation error $\frac{1}{N} \|X - D_x A\|_F^2$ on a given training set X, where an additive ℓ_1 regularization penalty term on A enforces sparsity:

$$D_x^*, A^* = \underset{D_x, A}{\text{argmin}} \left\{ \frac{1}{N} \|X - D_x A\|_F^2 + \lambda \|A\|_1 \right\}$$

$$\text{s.t. } \|D_x^{[i]}\|_2^2 \leq 1 \ . \tag{3.1}$$

Here λ is the regularization parameter that controls sparsity level, and $D_x^{[i]}$ is the ith column of D_x. The columns of the dictionary are normalized to obtain a unique dictionary. Alternatively, following the Lagrange multiplier technique, the Frobenius norm of D_x could be used as a regularizer in place of the constraint.

The above problem is not a convex optimization problem; it is biconvex with respect to the variables D_x and A but is convex in each variable alone. As a result, most dictionary learning algorithms use alternation on variables D_x and A to solve Eq. (3.1), leading to the iteration of two separate optimization problems, each solely on one of the variables assuming the other variable to be constant. Upon a suitable initialization, when the dictionary is fixed, Eq. (3.1) reduces to a number of parallel sparse recovery, i.e., LASSO problems which can be solved efficiently [15]. Then, for a fixed A, Eq. (3.1) reduces to a standard quadratically constrained quadratic program (QCQP) problem which can be solved efficiently with iterative methods such as conjugate gradient descent algorithms even for high-dimensional (large p) and huge problems (large r). This alternative procedure on variables is repeated until some convergence criterion is met, e.g., reaching a semi-stationary point.

In our coupled dictionary learning framework, we aim to learn coupled dictionaries D_x and D_z such that they share the sparse coefficients A to represent the seen visual features X and their corresponding attributes Z, respectively. Intuitively this means that visual features for an object have corresponding semantic features. On the other hand, D_z also needs to sparsify the semantic attributes of other (unseen) classes, Z', in order to perform ZSL. Hence, we propose the following optimization problem to learn both dictionaries:

$$D_x^*, A^*, D_z^*, B^* = \underset{D_x, A, D_z, B}{\text{argmin}} \left\{ \frac{1}{Np} \left(\|X - D_x A\|_F^2 + \frac{p\lambda}{r} \|A\|_1 \right) \right.$$

$$\left. + \frac{1}{Nq} \|Z - D_z A\|_F^2 + \frac{1}{Mq} \left(\|Z' - D_z B\|_F^2 + \frac{q\lambda}{r} \|B\|_1 \right) \right\} \tag{3.2}$$

$$\text{s.t.:} \|D_x^{[i]}\|_2^2 \leq 1, \ \|D_z^{[i]}\|_2^2 \leq 1 \ ,$$

Algorithm 1 Coupled Dictionary Learning ($\{X, Z, Z'\}, \lambda, r, itr$)

1: $D_x \leftarrow \text{RandomMatrix}_{p,r},\ D_z \leftarrow \text{RandomMatrix}_{q,r}$
2: $D_z \leftarrow \text{update}(D_x, \{X, Z, Z'\}, \lambda)$ Eq. 3.3
3: $D_x \leftarrow \text{update}(D_z, \{Z\}, \lambda)$ Eq. 3.4

The above formulation combines the dictionary learning problems for X and Z by coupling them via joint-sparse code matrix A, and also enforces D_z to be a sparsifying dictionary for Z' with sparse codes B. Similar to Eq. (3.1), the optimization in Eq. (3.2) is biconvex in (D_x, D_z) and (A, B), i.e., despite being convex in each individual term, it is highly nonconvex in all variables. Inspired by the approach proposed by Yang et al. [274], we use an alternating scheme to update over D_x and D_z for finding a local solution.

First we add the constraints on dictionary atoms in Eq. (3.2) as a penalty term the objective function and solve:

$$\min_{A, D_x} ||X - D_x A||_2^2 + \lambda ||A||_1 + \beta ||D_x||_2^2 \tag{3.3}$$

by alternately solving the LASSO for A and taking gradient steps with respect to D_x. For computational and robustness reasons, we chose to work within a stochastic gradient descent framework, in which we take random batches of rows from X and corresponding rows of A at each iteration to reduce the computational complexity.

Next we solve

$$\min_{B, D_z} ||Z - D_z A||_2^2 + ||Z' - D_z B||_2^2 + \lambda ||B||_1 + \beta ||D_z||_2^2 \ , \tag{3.4}$$

by alternately solving the LASSO for B and taking gradient steps with respect to D_z, (while holding A fixed as the solution found in Eq. (3.3). Here we do not use stochastic batches for B since there are many fewer rows than there were for A.

The learned dictionaries then can be used to perform ZSL using the procedure that we explained. Algorithm 1 summarizes the coupled dictionary learning procedure.

3.3.2 Prediction of Unseen Attributes

In the testing phase, we are only given the extracted features from unseen images, $X' = [\mathbf{x}'_1, ..., \mathbf{x}'_l] \in \mathbb{R}^{p \times l}$ and the goal is to predict their corresponding semantic attributes. We propose two different methods to predict the semantic attributes of the unseen images based on the learned dictionaries in the training phase, namely attribute-agnostic prediction and attribute-aware prediction.

3.3.2.1 Attribute-Agnostic Prediction

The attribute-agnostic (AAg) method is the naive way of predicting semantic attributes from an unseen image $\mathbf{x}'_i$. In the attribute-agnostic formulation, we first find the sparse representation $\boldsymbol{\alpha}_i$ of the unseen image $\mathbf{x}'_i$ by solving the following LASSO problem,

$$\boldsymbol{\alpha}_i = \text{argmin}_{\mathbf{a}} \left\{ \frac{1}{p} ||\mathbf{x}_i - D_x \mathbf{a}||_2^2 + \frac{\lambda}{r} ||\mathbf{a}||_1 \right\} \ . \tag{3.5}$$

and its corresponding attribute is estimated by $\hat{z}_i = D_z \boldsymbol{\alpha}_i$. We call this formulation attribute-agnostic because the sparse coefficients are found without any information from the attribute space. However, given that the attributes of the unseen classes are given, we can improve this base-line estimate. We use AAg as a baseline to demonstrate the effectiveness of the attribute-aware prediction.

3.3.2.2 Attribute-Aware Prediction

In the attribute-aware (AAw) formulation we would like to find the sparse representation $\boldsymbol{\alpha}_i$ to not only approximate the input visual feature, $\mathbf{x}'_i \approx D_x \boldsymbol{\alpha}_i$, but also provide an attribute prediction, $\hat{z}_i = D_z \boldsymbol{\alpha}_i$, that is well resolved in the attribute space. Meaning that ideally $\hat{z}_i = \mathbf{z}'_m$ for some $m \in \{1, ..., M\}$, however since the dictionaries are biased toward seen classes as those classes are used to couple the visual and the textual domains, the dictionaries are biased and the recovered labels are more biased toward the seen classes. This is called the problem of domain shift in ZSL literature. This means that if we bias the recovered sparse vector toward the unseen classes, it is more likely that the correct class label can be recovered. To achieve this, we define the soft assignment of $\hat{z}_i$ to $\mathbf{z}'_m$, denoted by p_m, using the Student's t- distribution as a kernel to measure the similarity between $\hat{z}_i = D_z \boldsymbol{\alpha}_i$ and $\mathbf{z}'_m$,

$$
p_m(\boldsymbol{\alpha}_i) = \frac{\left(1 + \frac{\|D_z \boldsymbol{\alpha}_i - \mathbf{z}'_m\|_2^2}{\rho}\right)^{-\frac{\rho+1}{2}}}{\sum_k \left(1 + \frac{\|D_z \boldsymbol{\alpha}_i - \mathbf{z}'_k\|_2^2}{\rho}\right)^{-\frac{\rho+1}{2}}} , \tag{3.6}
$$

where ρ is the kernel parameter. We chose the t-distribution as it is less sensitive to the choice of kernel parameter, ρ.

Ideally, $p_m(\boldsymbol{\alpha}_i) = 1$ for some $m \in \{1, ..., M\}$ and $p_j(\boldsymbol{\alpha}_i) = 0$ for $j \neq m$. In other words, the ideal soft-assignment $\mathbf{p} = [p_1, p_2, ..., p_M]$ would be one-sparse and have minimum entropy which can be used as an additional informative constraint. This motivates our attribute-aware formulation, which penalizes Eq. 3.5 with the entropy of $\mathbf{p}$.

$$
\boldsymbol{\alpha}_i = \text{argmin}_{\mathbf{a}} \Big\{ \underbrace{\frac{1}{p} \|\mathbf{x}'_i - D_x \mathbf{a}\|_2^2 - \gamma \sum_m p_m(\mathbf{a}) \log(p_m(\mathbf{a}))}_{g(\mathbf{a})} + \frac{\lambda}{r} \|\mathbf{a}\|_1 \Big\} , \tag{3.7}
$$

where γ is the regularization parameter for entropy of the soft-assignment probability vector $\mathbf{p}$, $H_{\mathbf{p}}(\boldsymbol{\alpha})$. The entropy minimization has been successfully used in several works [69, 91] either as a sparsifying regularization or to boost the confidence of classifiers. Such regularization, however, turns the optimization in Eq. (3.7) into a nonconvex problem. However, since $g(\mathbf{a})$ is differentiable and the ℓ_1 norm is continuous (and its proximal operator is simply the soft thresholding operator) we can apply proximal gradient descent [167]. In our implementation we found that gradient descent applied directly to Eq. (3.7) worked fine since Eq. (3.7) is differentiable almost everywhere.

Due to the non-convex nature of the objective function, a good initialization is needed to achieve a sensible solution. Therefore we initialize $\boldsymbol{\alpha}$ from the solution of the attribute-

---

Algorithm 2 Zero-shot Prediction ($\mathbf{x}_i$, λ)

1: Attribute-Agnostic prediction:
2: $\boldsymbol{\alpha}_i \leftarrow \text{argmin}_{\mathbf{a}} \frac{1}{p}\|\mathbf{x}_i - D_x\mathbf{a}\|_2^2 + \frac{\lambda}{r}\|\mathbf{a}\|_1$
3: $\hat{\mathbf{z}}_i = D_z\boldsymbol{\alpha}_i$
4: $\mathbf{z}'_m = \text{argmin}_{\mathbf{z}' \in Z'} \|\mathbf{z}' - \hat{\mathbf{z}}_i\|_2$
5: Attribute-Aware prediction:
6: $\boldsymbol{\alpha}_i \leftarrow \text{argmin}_{\mathbf{a}} \frac{1}{p}\|\mathbf{x}'_i - D_x\mathbf{a}\|_2^2 - \gamma H_{\boldsymbol{p}}(\boldsymbol{\alpha}) + \frac{\lambda}{r}\|\mathbf{a}\|_1$
7: $\hat{\mathbf{z}}_i = D_z\boldsymbol{\alpha}_i$
8: $\mathbf{z}'_m = \text{argmin}_{\mathbf{z}' \in Z'} \|\mathbf{z}' - \hat{\mathbf{z}}_i\|_2$
9: Transducer Prediction
10: Solve 3.7 to predict $\boldsymbol{\alpha}_i$ for all unseen samples.
11: Use label propagation to spread the labels.

---

agnostic formulation and update that solution. Finally the corresponding attributes are estimated by $\hat{z}_i = D_z\boldsymbol{\alpha}_i$, for $i = 1, ..., l$.

3.3.3 From Predicted Attributes to Labels

In order to predict the image labels, one needs to assign the predicted attributes, $\hat{Z} = [\hat{\mathbf{z}}_1, ..., \hat{\mathbf{z}}_l]$, to the M attributes of the unseen classes Z'. This task can be performed in two ways, namely the inductive approach and the transductive approach.

3.3.3.1 Inductive Approach

In the inductive approach, the inference could be performed using the nearest neighbor (NN) approach in which the label of each individual $\hat{\mathbf{z}}_i$ is assigned to be the label of its nearest neighbor $\mathbf{z}'_m$. More precisely,

$$\mathbf{z}'_m = \text{argmin}_{\mathbf{z}' \in Z'}\left\{\|\mathbf{z}' - \hat{\mathbf{z}}_i\|_2\right\}, \tag{3.8}$$

and the corresponding label of $\mathbf{z}'_m$ is assigned to $\hat{\mathbf{z}}_i$. In such an approach, the structure of $\hat{\mathbf{z}}_i$'s is not taken into account. Looking at the t-SNE embedding visualization [133] of $\hat{\mathbf{z}}_i$'s and $\mathbf{z}'_m$'s in Figure 3.3 (b) (details are explained later) it can be seen that NN will not provide an optimal label assignment.

3.3.3.2 Transductive Learning

In the transductive attribute-aware (TAA) method, on the other hand, the attributes for all test images (i.e., unseen) are first predicted to form $\hat{Z} = [\hat{\mathbf{z}}_1, ..., \hat{\mathbf{z}}_L]$. Next, a graph is formed on $[Z', \hat{Z}]$, where the labels for Z' are known and the task is to infer the labels of $\hat{Z}$. Intuitively, we want the data points that are close together to have similar labels. This problem can be formulated as a graph-based semi-supervised label propagation [16, 296].

We follow the work of Zhou et al. [296] and spread the labels of Z' to $\hat{Z}$. More precisely, we form a graph $\mathcal{G}(\mathcal{V}, \mathcal{E})$ where the set of nodes $\mathcal{V} = \{\mathbf{v}\}_1^{M+L} = [\mathbf{z}'_1, ..., \mathbf{z}'_M, \hat{\mathbf{z}}_1, ..., \hat{\mathbf{z}}_L]$, and $\mathcal{E}$ is the set of edges whose weights reflect the similarities between the attributes. Note that the first M nodes are labeled and our task is to use these labels to predict the labels of the rest of the nodes. We use a Gaussian kernel to measure the edge weights between connected nodes, $W_{mn} = exp\{-\|\mathbf{v}_m - \mathbf{v}_n\|^2/2\sigma^2\}$, where σ is the kernel parameter and $W_{ii} = 0$. To construct the graph $\mathcal{G}$ one can utilize efficient k-NN graph construction methods as in Ref. [55], where the assumption is that: a neighbor of a neighbor is more likely to be a neighbor. Let $F \in \mathbb{R}^{M \times (M+L)}$ corresponds to a classification of the nodes, where F_{mn} is the probability of $\mathbf{v}_n$ belonging to the m'th class. Let $Y \in \mathbb{R}^{M \times (M+L)} = [\boldsymbol{I}_{M \times M}, \boldsymbol{0}_{M \times L}]$ represent the initial labels, where $\boldsymbol{I}$ denotes an identity matrix and $\boldsymbol{0}$ denotes a zeros matrix. From a Graph-Signal Processing (GSP) point of view, F is a signal defined on graph $\mathcal{G}$, and one requires this signal to be smooth. Zhou et al. [296] proposed the following optimization to obtain a smooth signal on a graph $\mathcal{G}$ that fits the initial known labels,

$$
\text{argmin}_F \left\{ \frac{1}{2} \left(\sum_{m,n} W_{mn} \| \frac{F_m}{\sqrt{D_{mm}}} - \frac{F_n}{\sqrt{D_{nn}}} \|^2 + \right. \right.
$$
$$
\left. \left. \mu \sum_m \|F_m - Y_m\|^2 \right) \right\} , \tag{3.9}
$$

where $D \in \mathbb{R}^{(M+L) \times (M+L)}$ is the diagonal degree matrix of graph $\mathcal{G}$, $D_{mm} = \sum_n W_{mn}$, and μ is the fitness regularization. Note that the first term in Eq. (3.9) enforces the smoothness of signal F and the second term enforces the fitness of F to the initial labels. The minimization in Eq. (3.9) has the following closed-form solution:

$$
F = \frac{\mu}{1+\mu} \left(\mathbb{I} - \frac{1}{1+\mu}(D^{-\frac{1}{2}}WD^{-\frac{1}{2}}) \right)^{-1} Y . \tag{3.10}
$$

To avoid the matrix inversion in the above formulation, Fujiware et al. [62] proposed to iteratively compute lower and upper-bounds of labeling scores to avoid unnecessary score computation and reduce computational cost. Algorithm 2 summarizes the zero-shot label prediction procedure.

3.4 THEORETICAL DISCUSSION

In this section, we establish PAC-learnability of the proposed algorithm. Our goal is to provide a PAC-style generalization error bound for the proposed ZSL algorithm. The goal is to establish conditions under which our ZSL algorithm can identify instances from unseen classes. We use the framework developed by Palatucci et al. [162], to derive this bound. The core idea is that if we are able to recover the semantic attributes of a given image with high accuracy, then the correct label can be recovered with high probability as well. Note that three probability events are involved in the probability event of predicting an unseen class label correctly, denoted by P_t:

1. Given a certain confidence parameter δ and the error parameter ϵ, a dictionary can be learned with $M_{\epsilon,\delta}$ samples. We denote this event by $\mathcal{D}_\epsilon$. Hence $P(\mathcal{D}_\epsilon) = 1 - \delta$ and $\mathbb{E}(\|\boldsymbol{x} - D\boldsymbol{a}\|_2^2) \leq \epsilon$, where $\mathbb{E}(\cdot)$ denotes statistical expectation.

2. Given the event $\mathcal{D}_\epsilon$ (learned dictionaries), the semantic attribute can be estimated with high probability. We denote this event by $\mathcal{S}_\epsilon | \mathcal{D}_\epsilon$.

3. Given the event $\mathcal{S}_\epsilon | \mathcal{D}_\epsilon$, the true label can be predicted. We denote this event by $\mathcal{T} | \mathcal{S}_\epsilon$ and so $P(\mathcal{T} | \mathcal{S}_\epsilon) = 1 - \zeta$.

Therefore, the event P_t can be expressed as the following probability decoupling by multiplying the above probabilities:

$$P_t = P(\mathcal{D}_\epsilon) P(\mathcal{S}_\epsilon | \mathcal{D}_\epsilon) P(\mathcal{T} | \mathcal{S}_\epsilon) \ . \tag{3.11}$$

Our goal is: given the desired values for confidence parameters ζ and δ for the two ZSL stages, i.e., $P(\mathcal{D}_\epsilon) = 1 - \delta$ and $P(\mathcal{T} | \mathcal{S}_\epsilon) = 1 - \zeta$, we compute the necessary ϵ for that level of prediction confidence as well as $P(\mathcal{S}_\epsilon | \mathcal{D}_\epsilon)$. We also need to compute the number of required training samples to secure the desired errors. Given $P(\mathcal{T} | \mathcal{S}_\epsilon) = 1 - \zeta$, we compute ϵ and the conditional probability $P(\mathcal{S}_\epsilon | \mathcal{D}_\epsilon)$.

To establish the error bound, we need to compute the maximum error in predicting the semantic attributes of a given image, for which we still can predict the correct label with high probability. Intuitively, this error depends on the geometry of $\mathcal{A}$ and probability distribution of semantic attributes of the classes in this space, $\mathcal{P}$. For example, if semantic attributes of the two classes are very close, then error tolerance for those classes will be less than two classes with distant attributes. To model this intuition, we focus our analysis on nearest neighbor label recovery. Let $\hat{z}$ denote the predicted attribute for a given image by our algorithm. Let $d(\hat{z}, z') : \mathbb{R}^q \times \mathbb{R}^q \to \mathbb{R}$ denote the distance between this point and another point in the semantic space. We denote the distribution function for this distance as $R_{\hat{z}}(t) = P(d(\hat{z}, z') \leq t)$. Let $T_{\hat{z}}$ denote the distance to the nearest neighbor of $\hat{z}$ and $W_{\hat{z}}(t) = P(T_{\hat{z}} \leq t)$ denotes its probability distribution. The latter distribution has been computed by Ciaccia and Patella [43] as:

$$W_{\hat{z}}(t) = 1 - \left(1 - R_{\hat{z}}(t)\right)^n \ , \tag{3.12}$$

where n is the number of points drawn from the distribution $\mathcal{P}$. Note that the function $R_{\hat{z}}(t)$ is an empirical distribution which depends on the distribution of semantic feature space, $\mathcal{P}$, and basically is the fraction of sampled points from $\mathcal{P}$ that are less than some distance t away from $\hat{z}$.

Following the general PAC-learning framework, given a desired probability (confidence) ζ, we want the distance $T_{\hat{z}}$ to be less than the distance of the predicted attribute $\hat{z}$ from the true semantic description of the true class that it belongs to, i.e., or $W_{\hat{z}}(\tau_{\hat{z}}) \leq \zeta$. Now note that since $W_{\hat{z}}(\cdot)$ is a cumulative distribution (never decreasing), $W_{\hat{z}}^{-1}(\cdot)$ is well-defined as $W_{\hat{z}}^{-1}(\zeta) = \text{argmax}_{\tau_{\hat{z}}} [W_{\hat{z}}(\tau_{\hat{z}}) \leq \zeta]$. If $\tau_{\hat{z}} \leq W_{\hat{z}}^{-1}(\zeta)$, then the correct label can be recovered with probability of $1 - \zeta$. Hence, prior to label prediction (which itself is done for a given confidence parameter δ), the semantic attributes must be predicted with true error at most $\epsilon_{max} = W_{\hat{z}}^{-1}(\zeta)$ and we need to ensure that semantic attribute prediction achieves this error bound, that is $\mathbb{E}_z(\|z - D_z a^*\|_2^2) \leq W_{\hat{z}}^{-1}(\zeta)$. To ensure this to happen, we rely on the following theorem on PAC-learnability of the dictionary learning (3.1) derived by Gribonval et al. [71]:

Theorem 3.4.1. *Consider dictionary learning problem in* (3.1), *and the confidence parameter δ ($P(\mathcal{D}_\epsilon) = 1 - \delta$) and the error parameter $\epsilon_{max} = W_{\hat{z}}^{-1}(\zeta)$ in standard PAC-learning* *setting. Then the number of required samples to learn the dictionary $M_{W_{\hat{z}}^{-1},\delta}$ satisfies the following relation:*

$$W_{\hat{z}}^{-1}(\zeta) \geq 3\sqrt{\frac{\beta \log(M_{W_{\hat{z}}^{-1},\delta})}{M_{W_{\hat{z}}^{-1},\delta}}} + \sqrt{\frac{\beta + \log(2/\delta)/8}{M_{\epsilon,\delta}}} \tag{3.13}$$

$$\beta = \frac{pr}{8}max\{1, \log(6\sqrt{8}L)\} ,$$

where L is a constant that depends on the loss function which measures the data fidelity. Given all parameters, Eq. (3.13) can be solved for $M_{W_{\hat{z}}^{-1},\delta}$.

So, according to Theorem 3.4.1 if we use at least $M_{W_{\hat{z}}^{-1},\delta}$ sample images to learn the coupled dictionaries, we can achieve the required error rate $\epsilon_{max} = W_{\hat{z}}^{-1}(\zeta)$. Now we need to determine the probability of recovering the true label in the ZSL regime or $P(\mathcal{S}_\epsilon|\mathcal{D}_\epsilon)$. Note that the core step for predicting the semantic attributes in our scheme is to compute the joint-sparse representation for an unseen image. Also note that Eq. 3.1 can be interpreted as a result of a maximum a posteriori (MAP) inference within Bayesian perspective. This means that from a probabilistic perspective, α's are drawn from a Laplacian distribution and the dictionary D is a Gaussian matrix with elements drawn i.i.d: $d_{ij} \sim \mathcal{N}(0, \epsilon)$. This means that given a drawn dataset, we learn MAP estimate of the Gaussian matrix $[D_x, D_z]^\top$ and then use the Gaussian matrix D_z to estimate a in ZSL regime. To compute the probability of recovering a in this setting, we can rely on the following theorem:

Theorem 3.4.2. *(Theorem 3.1 in [56]): Consider the linear system $\mathbf{x}_i = D_x \mathbf{a}_i + \mathbf{n}_i$ with a sparse solution, i.e., $\|\mathbf{a}_i\|_0 = k$, where $D_x \in \mathbb{R}^{p\times r}$ is a random Gaussian matrix and $\|\mathbf{n}_i\|_2 \leq \epsilon$). Then the unique solution of this system can be recovered by solving Eq. (3.5) with probability of $(1 - e^{p\xi})$ as far as $k \leq c'p\log(\frac{r}{p})$, where c' and ξ are two constant parameters.*

Theorem 3.4.2 suggests that we can use Eq. (3.5) to recover the sparse representation and subsequently unseen attributes with high probability $P(\mathcal{S}_\epsilon|\mathcal{D}_\epsilon) = (1 - e^{p\xi})$. This theorem also suggests that for our approach to work, the existence of a good sparsifying dictionary, as well as rich attribute data, is essential. Therefore, given desired the error parameters $1 - \zeta$ and $1 - \delta$ for the two stages of ZSL algorithm and the error parameter ϵ, the probability event of predicting the correct label for an unseen class can be computed as:

$$P_t = (1 - \delta)(1 - e^{p\xi})(1 - \zeta) , \tag{3.14}$$

which concludes our proof on PAC-learnability of the algorithm ■

3.5 EXPERIMENTS

We carried out experiments on three benchmark ZSL datasets: AwA, SUN, and CUB dataset (we used both versions of the AwA dataset in our experiments). We empirically evaluated the resulting performance against the existing state of the art ZSL algorithms.

Datasets: We conducted our experiments on three benchmark datasets namely: the Animals with Attributes (AwA1) [114] and (AwA2) [264], the Scene UNderstanding (SUN) attribute [170], and the Caltech-UCSD-Birds 200-2011 (CUB) bird [252] datasets.

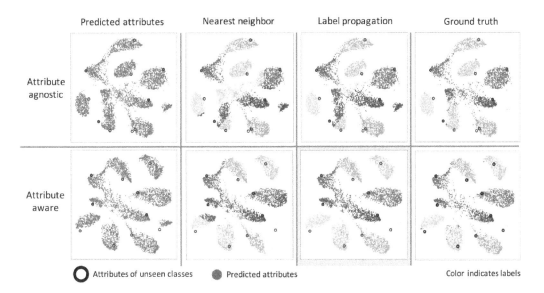

Figure 3.3 Attributes predicted from the input visual features for the unseen classes of images for AWA1 dataset using our attribute-agnostic and attribute-aware formulations respectively in the top and bottom rows. The nearest neighbor and label propagation assignment of the labels together with the ground truth labels are visualized. It can be seen that the attribute-aware formulation, together with the label propagation scheme overcomes the hubness and domain shift problems, enclosed in yellow margins. Best viewed in color.

The Animals with Attributes (AwA1) dataset is a coarse-grained dataset containing 30475 images of 50 types of animals with 85 corresponding attributes for these classes. Semantic attributes for this dataset are obtained via human annotations. The images for the AWA1 dataset are not publicly available; therefore, we use the publicly available features of dimension 4096 extracted from a VGG19 convolutional neural network, which was pre-trained on the ImageNet dataset. Following the conventional usage of this dataset, 40 classes are used as source classes to learn the model, and the remaining ten classes are used as target (unseen) classes to test the performance of zero-shot classification. The major disadvantage of AwA1 dataset is that only extracted features are available for this dataset. The AwA2 dataset developed recently to compensate for this weakness by providing the original images. The AWA2 dataset has a similar structure with the same 50 animal classes and 85 attributes, but with 37,322 images. Because the original images are available, one can use alternative deep net structures for feature extraction.

The Scene UNderstanding (SUN) dataset is a fine-grained dataset and contains 717 classes of different scene categories with 20 images per category (14,340 images total). Each image is annotated with 102 attributes that describe the corresponding scene. There are two general approaches that has been used in the literature to split this dataset into training and testing sets. Following [292], 707 classes are used to learn the dictionaries, and the remaining ten classes are used for testing. Following the second approach [114], we used 645 classes to learn the dictionaries, and the remaining 72 classes are used for testing.

Both splits are informative because together help to understand the effect of the training set size on ZSL performance.

The Caltech-UCSD-Birds (CUB200) dataset is a fine-grained dataset containing 200 classes of different types of birds with 11,788 images. There are 312 attributes and boundary segmentation for each image of the dataset. The attributes are obtained via human annotation. The dataset is divided into four almost equal folds, where three folds are used to learn the model, and the fourth fold is used for testing.

For each dataset, except for AwA1 (where images are not available), we use features extracted by the final layer before classification of VGG19 [227], Inception [239], ResNet [83], and DenseNet [89]. For AwA1, AwA2, and CUB200-2011 the networks were trained on ImageNet [109]. For SUN, they were trained on Places [295].

Tuning parameters: Our experiments show that the regularization parameters λ, ρ, γ as well as the number of dictionary atoms r need to be tuned for maximal performance. We simply used the standard k-fold cross-validation to search for the optimal parameters for each dataset. After splitting the datasets accordingly into training, validation, and testing sets, we used performance on the validation set for tuning the parameters in a brute-force search. We used the common evaluation metric in ZSL, flat hit@K classification accuracy, to measure the performance. This means that a test image is said to be classified correctly if it is classified among the top K predicted labels. We report hit@1 rate to measure ZSL image classification performance and hit@3 and hit@5 for image retrieval performance.

Results: Each experiment is performed ten times, and the mean is reported in Table 3.1 (please check the last pages of this chapter). For the sake of transparency and to provide the complete picture to the reader, we included results for the AAg formulation using nearest neighbor, the AAw using nearest neighbor, and AAw using the transductive approach, denoted as transductive attribute-aware (TAAw) formulation. As can be seen, while the AAw formulation significantly improves the AAg formulation, adding the transductive approach (i.e., label propagation on predicted attributes) to the AAw formulation further boosts the classification accuracy, as also shown in Figure 3.3. These results also support the logic behind our approach that: (1) the attribute aware optimization always boosts the performance by addressing domain shift problem, and (2) the transductive prediction of labels leads to a secondary boost in performance of our method by reducing the hubness effect. Finally, for completeness hit@3 and hit@5 rates measure image retrieval performance for our algorithm. This result demonstrates that ZSL can be used for image retrieval.

Figure 3.3 demonstrates the 2D t-SNE embedding for predicted attributes and actual class attributes of the AWA1 dataset. It can be seen that our algorithm can cluster the dataset in the attribute space. The actual attributes are depicted by colored circles with black edges. The first column of Figure 3.3 demonstrates the attribute prediction for AAg and AAw formulations. We also see that the entropy regularization in AAw formulation improves the clustering quality, decreases data overlap, and reduces the domain shift problem. The nearest neighbor label assignment is shown in the second column, which demonstrates the domain shift and hubness problems with NN label assignment in the attribute space. The third column of Figure 3.3 shows the transductive approach in which a label propagation is performed on the graph of the predicted attributes. Note that the label propagation addresses the domain shift and hubness problem and when used with the AAw formulation provides significantly better zero-shot classification accuracy.

Method / Feature	AAg (3.5)	AAw (3.6)	TAAw	AAg(hit@3)	AAw(hit@3)	TAAw(hit@3)	AAg(hit@5)	AAw(hit@5)	TAAw(hit@5)
AwA1 Dataset									
VGG19	77.30	79.48	89.35	96.05	96.54	97.52	98.56	98.67	98.51
AwA2 Dataset									
VGG19	41.68	45.54	69.93	74.80	78.62	88.77	91.36	92.56	93.34
Inception	39.05	47.61	71.72	82.15	84.58	97.12	90.64	92.08	97.66
ResNet50	43.55	47.81	81.99	80.09	83.32	94.76	92.92	93.91	95.37
DenseNet161	40.72	43.47	78.14	77.08	80.17	98.09	94.63	95.89	98.44
CUB									
VGG19	35.29	40.62	48.41	60.52	67.67	67.75	72.14	74.44	78.57
Inception	35.32	40.31	49.65	51.17	55.52	63.78	67.05	71.37	75.33
ResNet50	24.81	29.79	44.19	48.22	56.52	67.03	58.93	66.69	75.60
DenseNet161	28.91	33.55	51.03	51.51	59.57	73.13	61.06	68.25	79.63
SUN Dataset (645/72 Split)									
VGG19	42.36	45.69	48.40	57.50	61.48	67.50	71.94	75.76	82.01
Inception	55.66	56.02	57.03	80.10	80.65	81.18	87.06	87.22	87.72
ResNet50	44.60	45.49	53.09	70.13	70.76	75.06	79.53	79.81	81.79
DenseNet161	42.76	43.48	51.22	68.24	68.76	74.65	77.71	78.40	81.35
SUN Dataset (707/10 Split)									
VGG19	85.50	89.25	91.00	93.95	96.50	98.05	97.15	98.05	98.50
Inception	83.30	83.80	84.95	96.80	96.80	96.95	98.85	98.85	98.80
ResNet50	76.10	83.60	84.60	93.20	97.35	97.10	96.70	96.95	99.05
DenseNet161	74.65	75.10	86.65	93.05	93.05	97.30	96.60	96.70	99.25

Table 3.1 Zero-shot classification and image retrieval results for the coupled dictionary learning algorithm.

Method		SUN	CUB	AwA1
Romera-Paredes and Torr [182]		82.10	-	75.32
Zhang and Saligrama [292][†]		82.5	30.41	76.33
Zhang and Saligrama [293][†]		83.83	42.11	80.46
Bucher, Herbin, and Jurie [26][†]		84.41	43.29	77.32
Xu et al. [271][†]		83.5	53.6	84.5
Li et al. [125] [†]		-	61.79	87.22
Ye and Guo [278][†]		85.40	57.14	85.66
Ding, Shao, and Fu [53][†]		86.0	45.2	82.8
Wang and Chen [256][†]		-	42.7	79.8
Kodirov, Xiang, and Gong [103][†]		91.0	61.4	84.7
Ours	AAg (3.5)	85.5	35.29	77.30
Ours	AAw (3.6)	89.3	40.62	79.48
Ours	Transductive AAw (TAAw)	91.00	48.41	89.35

Table 3.2 Zero-shot classification results for four benchmark datasets: all methods use VGG19 features trained on the ImageNet dataset, and the original continuous (or binned) attributes provided by the datasets. Here, † indicates that the results are extracted directly from the referred paper, ‡ indicates that the results are reimplemented with VGG19 features, and " -" indicates that the results are not reported.

Method		SUN	CUB	AwA2
Romera-Paredes and Torr [182][†]		18.7	44.0	64.5
Norouzi et al. [159][†]		51.9	36.2	63.3
Mensink et al. [147][†]		47.9	40.8	61.8
Akata et al. [5][†]		56.1	50.1	66.7
Lampert et al. [113][†]		44.5	39.1	60.5
Changpinyo et al. [31] [†]		62.7	54.5	72.9
Bucher, Herbin, and Jurie [26][†]		-	43.3	77.3
Xian et al. [263][†]		-	45.5	71.9
Bucher et al. [27][†]		56.4	60.1	55.3
Zhang and Saligrama [292][†]		-	30.4	76.3
Ours	AAg (3.5)	55.7	35.3	39.1
Ours	AAw (3.6)	56.0	40.3	47.6
Ours	Transductive AAw (TAAw)	57.0	49.7	71.7

Table 3.3 Zero-shot classification results for three benchmark datasets: all methods use Inception features trained on the ImageNet dataset, and the original continuous (or binned) attributes provided by the datasets. Here "-" indicates that the results are not reported.

Performance comparison results using VGG19 and GoogleNet extracted features are summarized in Tables 3.2 and 3.3, as these features have been used in the literature extensively. Note that in Table 3.3 we used AwA2 in order to be able to extract the ResNet and GoogleNet features. As pointed out by Xian et al. [264] the variety of used image features (e.g., various DNNs and various combinations of these features) as well as the variation of used attributes (by, e.g., word2vec, human annotation), and different data splits make direct comparison with the ZSL methods in the literature very challenging. In Tables 3.2 and 3.3 we provide a fair comparison of our JDZSL performance to the recent methods in the literature. All compared methods use the same visual features and the same attributes (i.e., the continuous or binned) provided in the dataset. Tables 3.2 and 3.3 provide a comprehensive explanation of the shown results. Note that our method achieves state-of-the-art or close to state-of-the-art performance. Note that our approach leads to better and comparable performance in all three datasets, which include zero-shot scene and object recognition tasks. More importantly, while the other methods can perform well on a specific dataset, our algorithm leads to competitive performance on all the three datasets.

3.6 CONCLUSIONS

A ZSL formulation is developed which models the relationship between visual features and semantic attributes via coupled dictionaries that sparsify the visual and the semantic features. We established the PAC-learnability of our method and demonstrated that while a classic coupled dictionary learning approach suffers from the domain shift problem, an entropy regularization scheme can help with this phenomenon and provide superior zero-shot performance. In addition, we demonstrated that a transductive approach toward assigning labels to the predicted attributes could boost the performance considerably and lead to state-of-the-art zero-shot classification. Finally, we compared our method to the state of the art approaches in the literature and demonstrated its competitiveness on benchmark datasets. An important limitation of coupled dictionary learning is that the learning scheme is not end-to-end, i.e., we need preprocessed features. The reason is that dictionary learning on unprocessed natural images is computationally infeasible. In the next two chapters, we discuss how deep neural networks can be used to couple two visual domains in an end-to-end data-driven training framework.

CHAPTER 4

Learning a Discriminative Embedding for Unsupervised Domain Adaptation

In the previous chapter, we considered the problem of zero-shot learning, where the goal was to transfer knowledge from the semantic domain to the visual domain. Although the focus was to solve a classification problem, data scarcity was a challenge for a subset of classes and knowledge transfer was performed within the same classification problem.

In this chapter and the next chapter, we focus on the problem of domain adaptation (DA). In a domain adaptation learning scenario, usually, two domains from the same data modality are considered, e.g., two visual domains or two textual domains. In contrast to ZSL setting, we solve a classification problem in each domain. The two domains are related as both classification problems share the same classes. We face the problem of labeled data scarcity in a domain, i.e., the target domain, which makes training a good model infeasible. The solution idea is to transfer knowledge from the other related domain, i.e., the source domain, where labeled data is easy to obtain. Learning a shared discriminate and domain-agnostic embedding space can help to transfer knowledge from the source domain to the target domain as classification can be supervised via labeled data from solely the source domain.

Figure 4.1 visualizes this idea to tackle domain adaptation. In this figure, we have two ternary classification problems in the domains of natural and infrared images as the source and the target domain, respectively. In the domain of natural images, it is easy to generate labeled data, but in the domain of infrared images, we face labeled data scarcity. The idea is that if we can map the images from these two domains into a shared embedding space such that similar classes lie close by in the embedding space, then a classifier that is trained using labeled data of the source domain would generalize well in the target domain. The major challenging is to learn a function that can map the data points from both domains to the shared embedding space such that the corresponding classes lie close by in the embedding space.

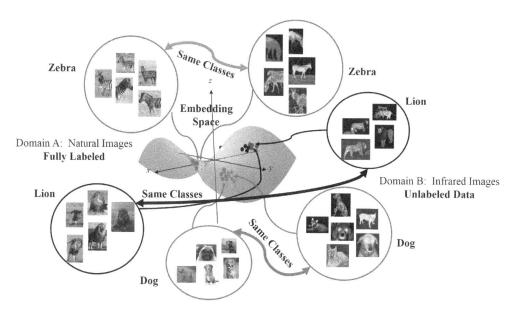

Figure 4.1 Domain adaptation through an intermediate embedding space: in this figure, the darker circles in the embedding space denote representations of images for the source domain, and the lighter circles denote representations of images for the target domain. If the distribution of both domains are aligned in the embedding space such that the same classes lie closely in the embedding space, then a classifier that works well on the source domain would generalize well in the target domain.

In this chapter, we learn such an embedding for *unsupervised domain adaptation* unsupervised domain adaptation (UDA), where we have no labeled data in the target domain. We tackle challenges of UDA by minimizing the discrepancy between the distributions of the source and the target domains in the embedding space. More specifically, we develop an algorithm for adapting a semantic segmentation model that is trained using a labeled source domain to generalize well in an unlabeled target domain. Although we focus on image semantic segmentation, our framework can be easily extended to classification setting [191]. Existing UDA algorithms require access to both the source domain labeled data and the target domain unlabeled data for training a domain agnostic semantic segmentation model. Relaxing this constraint enables a user to adapt pretrained models to generalize in a target domain, without requiring access to source data. To this end, we learn a prototypical distribution for the source domain in an intermediate embedding space. This distribution encodes the abstract knowledge that is learned from the source domain. We then use this distribution for aligning the target domain distribution with the source domain distribution in the embedding space. We provide theoretical analysis and explain conditions under which our algorithm is effective. Experiments on benchmark adaptation task demonstrate our method achieves competitive performance even compared with joint UDA approaches. Results of this chapter have been presented in reference [233].

4.1 INTRODUCTION

Image segmentation is an essential computer vision ability for delivering technologies such as autonomous driving [291] and automatic object tracking [257]. Advances in deep learning have led to the development of image segmentation algorithms with close to human-level performance [282]. However, this success is conditioned on the availability of large and high-quality manually annotated datasets to satisfy the required sample complexity bounds for training generalizable deep neural networks. As a result, data annotation is a major bottleneck to address the problem of *domain shift*, where *domain discrepancy* exists between the distributions of training and testing domains [132] and the trained model needs to be adapted to generalize again after being fielded. This is particularly important in continual learning [225], where the goal is to enable a learning agent to learn new domains autonomously. Retraining the model from scratch is not a feasible solution for continual learning because manual data annotation is an expensive and time-consuming process for image segmentation, e.g., as much as 1.5 hours for a single image of the current benchmark datasets [46]. A practical alternative is to adapt the trained model using only unannotated data.

The problem of model adaptation for image segmentation has been studied extensively in the unsupervised domain adaptation (UDA) framework. The goal in UDA is to train a model for an unannotated target domain by transferring knowledge from a secondary related source domain in which annotated data is accessible or easier to generate, e.g., a synthetically generated domain knowledge transfer can be achieved by extracting domain-invariant features from the source and the target domains to address domain discrepancy. As a result, if we train a classifier using the source domain features as its input, the classifier will generalize on the target domain since the distributions of features are indistinguishable. Distributional alignment can be achieved by matching the distributions at different levels of abstraction, including appearance [85, 214], feature [85, 155], output [290] levels.

A large group of the existing UDA algorithms for image segmentation use adversarial learning for extracting domain-invariant features [131, 24, 85, 155, 213, 214, 51]. Broadly speaking, a domain discriminator network can be trained to distinguish whether an input data point comes from the source or the target domain. This network is fooled by a feature generator network which is trained to make the domains similar at its output. Adversarial training [68] of these two networks leads to learning a domain-agnostic embedding space. A second class of UDA algorithms directly minimize suitable loss functions that enforce domain alignment [262, 290, 64, 63, 288, 119, 277]. Adversarial learning requires delicate optimization initialization, architecture engineering, and careful selection of hyper-parameters to be stable [209]. In contrast, defining a suitable loss function for direct domain alignment may not be trivial.

Domain adaptation is a well-explored topic in the literature but a major limitation of existing UDA algorithms is that domain alignment can be performed only if the source and the target domain data are accessible concurrently. However, the source annotated data may not be necessarily accessible during the model adaptation phase in a continual learning scenario. In this chapter, we focus on a more challenging, yet more practical model adaptation scenario. We consider that a pretrained model is given and the goal is to adapt this model to generalize well in a target domain using solely unannotated target domain data. Our algorithm can be considered as an improvement over using an off-the-shelf pre-trained model naively by benefiting from the unannotated data in the target domain. This is a step toward lifelong image segmentation ability [93, 203]. Our algorithm also relaxes the necessity of sharing training data across the domains when the source domain data is private [232].

Our idea is to learn a prototypical distribution that encodes the abstract knowledge, learned for image segmentation using the source domain annotated data. The prototypical distribution is used for aligning the distributions across the two domains in an embedding space. We also provide theoretical analysis to justify the proposed model adaptation algorithm and determine the conditions under which our algorithm is effective. Finally, we provide experiments on the GTA5→Cityscapes and SYNTHIA→Cityscapes benchmark domain adaptation image segmentation tasks to demonstrate that our method is effective and leads to competitive performance, even when compared against existing UDA algorithms.

4.2 RELATED WORK

We discuss related work on domain adaptation and semantic segmentation, focusing on direct distribution alignment.

4.2.1 Semantic Segmentation

Traditional semantic segmentation algorithms use hand-engineered extracted features which are fed into a classifier [226, 245], where the classifier is trained using supervised learning. In contrast, current state of the art approaches use convolutional neural networks (CNNs) for feature extraction [127]. A base CNN subnetwork is converted into a fully-convolutional network (FCN) for feature extraction and then is combined with a classifier subnetwork to form an end-to-end classifier. The whole pipeline is trained in an end-to-end deep supervised learning training scheme. Due to large size of learnable parameters of the resulting semantic segmentation network, a huge pixel-level manually annotated dataset is required for training.

We can use weakly supervised annotation such as using bounding boxes to reduce manual annotation cost [169, 165], but even obtaining weakly annotated data for semantic segmentation can be time-consuming. Additionally, a trained model using weakly annotated datasets may not generalize well during testing. Another approach for relaxing the need for manually annotated datasets is to use synthetic datasets which are generated using computer graphics [184, 46]. These datasets can be annotated automatically. But a trained model using synthetic datasets might not generalize well to real-world data due to the existence of domain shift problem [214]. Unsupervised domain adaptation is developed to address this problem.

4.2.2 Domain Adaptation

Domain adaptation methods reduce domain discrepancy by aligning distributions using annotated data in a target domain and unannotated data in a target domain. A group of UDA methods use a shared cross-domain encoder to map data into a shared embedding space and train the encoder by minimizing a probability distance measure across the two domains at its output. The Wasserstein distance (WD) [48, 18] is an example of such

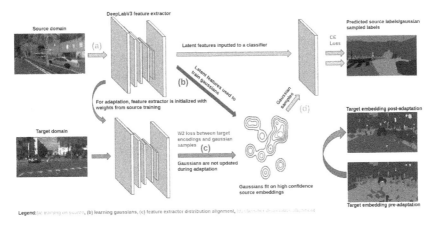

Figure 4.2 Diagram of the proposed model adaptation approach (best seen in color): (a) initial model training using the source domain labeled data, (b) estimating the prototypical distribution as a GMM distribution in the embedding space, (c) domain alignment is enforced by minimizing the distance between the prototypical distribution samples and the target unlabeled samples, (d) domain adaptation is enforced for the classifier module to fit correspondingly to the GMM distribution.

measures which captures higher-order statistics. Damodaran et al. [18] demonstrate that using WD leads to performance improvement over methods that rely on matching lower-order statistics [128, 235]. In this work, we rely on the Sliced Wasserstein Distance (SWD) variant of WD [119] for domain alignment. SWD has a closed form solution and can be computed more efficiently than WD.

Current UDA methods assume that the source and the target domain data are accessible concurrently during domain alignment. However, since usually a model is already pre-trained on the source domain, it is beneficial if we can adapt it using the target domain unannotated data. This model adaptation setting been explored for non-deep models [58, 95, 261], but these works cannot be extended to semantic segmentation tasks. In this work, we benefit from prototypical distributions to align two distributions indirectly. The core idea is that the image pixels that belong to each semantic class form a data cluster in a shared embedding space [187]. The centroid for this cluster is called class prototype. Recently, UDA has been addressed by aligning the prototype pairs across two domains [164, 32, 191]. Inspired by these works, we extend the notion of class prototypes to prototypical distributions in the embedding space. A prototypical distribution for image segmentation is a multimodal distribution that encodes the knowledge learned from the source domain. Our work is based on enforcing the two domains to share a similar prototypical distribution in the embedding space.

4.3 PROBLEM FORMULATION

Consider an image domain X^s and a semantic segmentation model $f_\theta(\cdot) : X^s \to Y^s$ with learnable parameters θ which receives an input image $x^s \in X^s$ and predicts pixel-wise category labels $y^s \in Y^s$. The goal is to train the model such that the expected error, i.e., true risk, between the prediction and the ground truth is minimized, i.e., $\theta^* = \arg\min_{\theta}\{\mathbb{E}_{\boldsymbol{x}^s \sim P_S(\boldsymbol{X})^s}(\mathcal{L}(f_{\theta}(\boldsymbol{x}^s), \boldsymbol{y}^s))\}$, where $P_S(\boldsymbol{X}^s)$ and $\mathcal{L}(\cdot)$ denote the input data distribution and a suitable loss function, respectively. In practice, we use Empirical Risk Minimization (ERM) and the cross-entropy loss for solving for the optimal semantic segmentation model:

$$\hat{\boldsymbol{\theta}} = \arg\min_{\boldsymbol{\theta}}\{\frac{1}{N}\sum_{i=1}^{N}\mathcal{L}_{ce}(f_{\theta}(\boldsymbol{x}^s), \boldsymbol{y}^s)\}\mathcal{L}_{ce} = -\sum_{k=1}^{K}\sum_{h=1}^{H\times W} y_{ijk}\log(p_{ijk}), \qquad (4.1)$$

where N and K denote the training dataset size and the number of semantic categories. H and W denote the input image height and width, respectively. Also, $\boldsymbol{y}_{ij} = [y_{ijk}]_{k=1}^{K}$ is a one-hot vector that denotes the ground-truth semantic labels and $\boldsymbol{p}_{ij} = [p_{ijk}]_{k=1}^{K}$ is a probability vector of the predicted category probabilities by the model, i.e., a softmax layer is used as the last model layer. In practice, the model is fielded after training for testing and we do not store the source samples. If N is large enough and the base model is complex enough, the ERM-trained model will generalize well on unseen samples, drawn from the distribution $P_S(\boldsymbol{X}^s)$.

Now, consider that after training, we want to employ the source-trained model in a target domain $\boldsymbol{X}^t$ with the distribution $P_T(\boldsymbol{X}^t)$, where $P_T(\boldsymbol{X}^t) \neq P_S(\boldsymbol{X}^s)$. Note that this situation emerges naturally in continual learning [225, 204] when data distribution changes over time. Within domain adaptation learning setting, this means that the target domain is encountered sequentially after learning the source domain. Due to existing distributional discrepancy, the source-trained model $f_{\hat{\theta}}$ will have poor generalization capability on the target domain. Our goal is to improve the model generalization by adapting the model such that the source and the target domains share a similar distribution in an embedding space. Following the state-of-the-art semantic segmentation models [127], we consider a deep network as the base model $f_{\theta}(\cdot)$. This network is decomposed into a deep CNN encoder $\phi_{\boldsymbol{u}}(\cdot) : \mathbb{R}^{H\times W} \to \mathbb{R}^P$, a category-wise CNN decoder $\psi_{\boldsymbol{v}}(\cdot) : \mathbb{R}^P \to \mathbb{R}^{H\times W\times K}$, and a pixel-level classifier subnetwork $h_{\boldsymbol{w}}(\cdot) : \mathcal{Z} \subset \mathbb{R}^K \to \mathbb{R}^K$ such that $f_{\theta} = h_{\boldsymbol{w}} \circ \psi_{\boldsymbol{v}} \circ \phi_{\boldsymbol{u}}$, where $\boldsymbol{\theta} = (\boldsymbol{w}, \boldsymbol{v}, \boldsymbol{u})$. In this decomposition, $\mathcal{Z}$ denotes the shared cross-domain embedding space. If we adapt the base trained model $f_{\hat{\theta}}$ such that the domain discrepancy is minimized, i.e., the distance between the distributions $\psi(\phi(p_S(\boldsymbol{X}^s))$ and $\psi(\phi(p_T(\boldsymbol{X}^t))$ is minimized in the embedding space, then the source-trained classifier $h_{\hat{\boldsymbol{w}}}$ will generalize on both domains. Most UDA algorithms benefit from this approach to address annotated data scarcity in the target domain but all assume that the source samples are accessible for model adaptation. Since this makes computing the distance between the distributions $\psi(\phi(p_S(\boldsymbol{X}^s))$ and $\psi(\phi(p_T(\boldsymbol{X}^t))$ feasible, solving UDA reduces to aligning these distributions. Note, however, $\psi(\phi(p_T(\boldsymbol{X}^t))$ cannot be computed directly in our learning framework due to absence of source samples and we need to estimate this distribution.

4.4 PROPOSED ALGORITHM

Figure 4.2 presents a high-level visual description our approach. Our solution is based on aligning the source and the target distributions via an intermediate prototypical distribution in the embedding space. Since the last layer of the classifier is a softmax layer, we can treat the classifier as a maximum *a posteriori* (MAP) estimator. This composition implies that if after training, the model can generalize well in the target domain, it must transform the source input distribution into a multimodal distribution $p_J(z)$ with K separable components in the embedding space (see Figure 4.2 (a)). Each mode of this distribution represents one of the K semantic classes. This prototypical distribution emerges as a result of model training because the classes should become separable in the embedding space for a generalizable softmax classifier. Recently, this property have been used for UDA [164, 32], where the means for distribution modes are considered as the class prototype. The idea for UDA is to align the domain-specific prototypes for each class to enforce distributional alignment across the domains. Our idea is to adapt the trained model using the target unlabeled data such that in addition to the prototypes, the source-learned prototypical distribution does not change after adaptation. As a result, the classifier subnetwork will still generalize in the target domain because its input distribution has been consolidated.

We model the prototypical distribution $p_J(z)$ as a Gaussian mixture model (GMM) with k components:

$$p_J(z) = \sum_{j=1}^{k} \alpha_j \mathcal{N}(z|\mu_j, \Sigma_j), \tag{4.2}$$

where α_j denotes mixture weights, i.e., prior probability for each semantic class. For each component, μ_j and Σ_j denote the mean and co-variance of the Gaussian (see Figure 4.2 (b)).

The empirical version of the prototypical distribution is accessible by the source domain samples $\{(\psi_v(\phi_v(x_i^s)), y_i^s)\}_{i=1}^{N}$ which we use for estimating the parameters. Note that since the labels are accessible in the source domain, we can estimate the parameters of each component independently via MAP estimation. Additionally, since p_{ijk} denotes the confidence of the classifier for the estimated semantic label for a given pixel. We can choose a threshold τ and compute the parameters using samples for which $p_{ijk} > \tau$ to cancel the effect of misclassified samples that would act as outliers. Let S_j denote the support set for class j in the training dataset for which $p_{ijk} > \tau$, i.e., $S_j = \{(x_i^s, y_i^s) \in \mathcal{D}_S | \arg\max \hat{y}_i^s = j, p_{ijk} > \tau\}$. Then, the MAP estimates for the distribution parameters would be:

$$\hat{\alpha}_j = \frac{|S_j|}{\sum_{j=1}^{N} |S_j|}, \quad \hat{\mu}_j = \sum_{(x_i^s, y_i^s) \in S_j} \frac{1}{|S_j|} \psi_u(\phi_v(x_i^s)),$$

$$\hat{\Sigma}_j = \frac{1}{|S_j|} \sum_{(x_i^s, y_i^s) \in S_j} \left(\psi_u(\phi_v(x_i^s)) - \hat{\mu}_j\right)^\top \left(\phi_v(\phi_v(x_i^s)) - \hat{\mu}_j\right). \tag{4.3}$$

We take advantage of the prototypical distributional estimate in Eq.(4.3) as a surrogate for the source domain distribution to align the source and the target domain distribution in the absence of the source samples. We can adapt the model such that the encoder transforms the target domain distribution into the prototypical distributional in the embedding space. We use the prototypical distributional estimate and draw random samples to generate a labeled pseudo-dataset: $\mathcal{D}_\mathcal{P} = (\mathbf{Z}_\mathcal{P}, \mathbf{Y}_\mathcal{P})$, where $\mathbf{Z}_\mathcal{P} = [z_1^p, \ldots, z_{N_p}^p] \in \mathbb{R}^{K \times N_p}$, $\mathbf{Y}_\mathcal{P} = [y_1^p, \ldots, y_{N_p}^p] \in \mathbb{R}^{K \times N_p}$, $z_i^p \sim \hat{p}_J(z)$. To improve the quality of the pseudo-dataset, we use the classifier sub-network prediction on drawn samples z^p to select samples with $h_w(z^p) > \tau$. After generating the pseudo-dataset, we solve the following optimization

---

Algorithm 3 $\text{MAS}^3 \, (\lambda, \tau)$

1: **Initial Training**:
2:   **Input:** source domain dataset $\mathcal{D}_\mathcal{S} = (\boldsymbol{X}_\mathcal{S}, \boldsymbol{Y}_\mathcal{S})$,
3:     **Training on Source Domain:**
4:     $\hat{\theta}_0 = (\hat{\boldsymbol{w}}_0, \hat{\boldsymbol{v}}_0 \hat{\boldsymbol{u}}_0) = \arg\min_\theta \sum_i \mathcal{L}(f_\theta(\boldsymbol{x}_i^s), \boldsymbol{y}_i^s)$
5:   **Prototypical distribution Estimation:**
6:     Use Eq. (4.3) and estimate $\alpha_j, \boldsymbol{\mu}_j$, and Σ_j
7: **Model Adaptation**:
8:   **Input:** target dataset $\mathcal{D}_\mathcal{T} = (\boldsymbol{X}_\mathcal{T})$
9:   **Pseudo-Dataset Generation:**
10:     $\mathcal{D}_\mathcal{P} = (\mathbf{Z}_\mathcal{P}, \mathbf{Y}_\mathcal{P}) =$
11:       $([\boldsymbol{z}_1^p, \ldots, \boldsymbol{z}_N^p], [\boldsymbol{y}_1^p, \ldots, \boldsymbol{y}_N^p])$, where:
12:       $\boldsymbol{z}_i^p \sim \hat{p}_J(\boldsymbol{z}), 1 \leq i \leq N_p$
13:       $\boldsymbol{y}_i^p = \arg\max_j \{h_{\hat{\boldsymbol{w}}_0}(\boldsymbol{z}_i^p)\}, p_{ip} > \tau$
14: **for** $itr = 1, \ldots, ITR$ **do**
15:   draw random batches from $\mathcal{D}_\mathcal{T}$ and $\mathcal{D}_\mathcal{P}$
16:   Update the model by solving Eq. (4.4)
17: **end for**

---

problem to align the source and the target distributions indirectly in the embedding:

$$\arg\min \boldsymbol{u}, \boldsymbol{v}, \boldsymbol{w} \Big\{ \frac{1}{N_p} \sum_{i=1}^{N_p} \mathcal{L}_{ce}(h_{\boldsymbol{w}}(\boldsymbol{z}_i^{(p)}), y_i^{(p)}) + \\ + \lambda D(\psi_{\boldsymbol{v}}(\phi_{\boldsymbol{v}}(p_\mathcal{T}(\boldsymbol{X}_\mathcal{T}))), \hat{p}_J(\boldsymbol{Z}_\mathcal{P})) \Big\}, \tag{4.4}$$

where $D(\cdot, \cdot)$ denotes a probability distribution metric to enforce alignment of the target domain distribution with the prototypical distribution in embedding space and λ is a trade-off parameter between the two terms (see Figure 4.2 (c)).

The first term in Eq. (4.4) is to update the classifier such that it keeps its generalization power on the prototypical distribution. The second term is a matching loss term used to update the model such that the target domain distribution is matched to the prototypical distribution in the embedding space. Given a suitable probability metric, Eq. (4.4) can be solved using standard deep learning optimization techniques.

The major remaining question is selecting a proper probability metric to compute $D(\cdot, \cdot)$. Note that the original target distribution is not accessible and hence we should select a metric that can be used to compute the domain discrepancy via the observed target domain data samples and the drawn samples from the prototypical distribution. Additionally, the metric should be smooth and easy to compute to make it suitable for gradient-based optimization that is normally used to solve Eq. (4.4). In this work, we use SWD [173]. Wasserstein Distance (WD) has been used successfully for domain alignment in the UDA literature [18, 195, 269, 123, 191]. SWD is a variant of WD that can be computed more efficiently [119]. SWD benefits from the idea of slicing by projecting high-dimensional probability distributions into their marginal one-dimensional distributions. Since one-dimensional WD has a closed-form solution, WD between these marginal distributions can be computed fast. SWD approximates WD as a summation of WD between a number of random one-dimensional projections:

$$D(\hat{p}_J, p_T) \approx \frac{1}{L} \sum_{l=1}^{L} \sum_{i=1}^{M} |\langle \gamma_l, z_{p_l[i]}^p \rangle - \langle \gamma_l, \psi(\phi(\mathbf{x}_{t_l[i]}^t)) \rangle|^2 \tag{4.5}$$

where $\gamma_l \in \mathbb{S}^{f-1}$ is uniformly drawn random sample from the unit f-dimensional ball $\mathbb{S}^{f-1}$, and $p_l[i]$ and $t_l[i]$ are the sorted indices for the prototypical and the target domain samples, respectively. We utilize Eq. (4.5) to solve Eq. (4.4).

Our solution for source-free model adaptation, named Model Adaptation for Source-Free Semantic Segmentation (MAS^3), is described conceptually in Figure 4.2 and the corresponding algorithmic solution is given in Algorithm 3.

4.5 THEORETICAL ANALYSIS

We analyze our algorithm within standard PAC-learning and prove that Algorithm 3 optimizes an upper-bound of the expected error for the target domain under certain conditions.

Consider that the hypothesis space within PAC-learning is the set of classifier sub-networks $\mathcal{H} = \{h_{\boldsymbol{w}}(\cdot)|h_{\boldsymbol{w}}(\cdot) : \mathcal{Z} \rightarrow \mathbb{R}^k, \boldsymbol{w} \in \mathbb{R}^W\}$. Let $e_{\mathcal{S}}$ and $e_{\mathcal{T}}$ denote the true expected error of the optimal domain-specific model from this space on the source and target domain respectively. We denote the joint-optimal model with $h_{\boldsymbol{w}^*}$. This model has the minimal combined source and target expected error $e_{\mathcal{C}}(\boldsymbol{w}^*)$, i.e., $\boldsymbol{w}^* = \arg\min_{\boldsymbol{w}} e_{\mathcal{C}}(\boldsymbol{w}) = \arg\min_{\boldsymbol{w}}\{e_{\mathcal{S}} + e_{\mathcal{T}}\}$. In other words, it is a model with the best performance for both domains.

Since we process the observed data points from these domains, let $\hat{\mu}_{\mathcal{S}} = \frac{1}{N} \sum_{n=1}^{N} \delta(\psi(\phi_{\boldsymbol{v}}(\boldsymbol{x}_n^s)))$ and $\hat{\mu}_{\mathcal{T}} = \frac{1}{M} \sum_{m=1}^{M} \delta(\psi(\phi_{\boldsymbol{v}}(\boldsymbol{x}_m^t)))$ denote the empirical source and the empirical target distributions in the embedding space that are built using the observed data points. Similarly, let $\hat{\mu}_{\mathcal{P}} = \frac{1}{N_p} \sum_{q=1}^{N_p} \delta(\boldsymbol{z}_n^q)$ denote the empirical prototypical distribution which is built using the generated pseudo-dataset.

Finally, note that when fitting the GMM and generating the pseudo-dataset, we only included those data points and pseudo-data points for which the model is confident about their predicted labels. For this reason, we can conclude that $\tau = \mathbb{E}_{\boldsymbol{z} \sim p_J(\boldsymbol{z})}(\mathcal{L}(h(\boldsymbol{z}), h_{\hat{\boldsymbol{w}}_0}(\boldsymbol{z}))$.

Theorem 4.5.1. *Consider that we generate a pseudo-dataset using the prototypical distribution and update the model for sequential UDA using algorithm 3. Then, the following holds:*

$$e_{\mathcal{T}} \leq e_{\mathcal{S}} + W(\hat{\mu}_{\mathcal{S}}, \hat{\mu}_{\mathcal{P}}) + W(\hat{\mu}_{\mathcal{T}}, \hat{\mu}_{\mathcal{P}}) + (1 - \tau) + e_{\mathcal{C}'}(\boldsymbol{w}^*)$$
$$+ \sqrt{(2\log(\frac{1}{\xi})/\zeta)}(\sqrt{\frac{1}{N}} + \sqrt{\frac{1}{M}} + 2\sqrt{\frac{1}{N_p}}), \tag{4.6}$$

where $W(\cdot, \cdot)$ denotes the WD distance and ξ is a constant which depends on the loss function $\mathcal{L}(\cdot)$.

Proof: Our proof is based on the following theorem by Redko et al. [178] which relates the performance of a trained model in a target domain to its performance to the source domain.

Theorem 4.5.2. *Under the assumptions described in our framework, assume that a model is trained on the source domain, then for any $d' > d$ and $\zeta < \sqrt{2}$, there exists a constant number N_0 depending on d' such that for any $\xi > 0$ and $\min(N, M) \geq \max(\xi^{-(d'+2)}, 1)$ with probability at least $1 - \xi$, the following holds:*

$$
\begin{aligned}
e_{\mathcal{T}} \leq &e_{\mathcal{S}} + W(\hat{\mu}_{\mathcal{T}}, \hat{\mu}_{\mathcal{S}}) + e_{\mathcal{C}}(\boldsymbol{w}^*) + \\
&\sqrt{(2\log(\frac{1}{\xi})/\zeta)}(\sqrt{\frac{1}{N}} + \sqrt{\frac{1}{M}}).
\end{aligned}
\tag{4.7}
$$

Theorem 4.5.2 provides an upperbound for the performance of the model on the target domain in terms of the source true expected error and the distance between the source and the target domain distributions when measured in WD distance. We use Theorem 4.5.2 to deduce Theorem 4.5.1. Following Redko et al. [178], our analysis has been preformed for the case of binary classifier but it can be conveniently extended.

Note that we use the confidence parameter τ to ensure that we only select the pseudo-data points for which the model is confident. Hence, the probability of predicting incorrect labels for the pseudo-data points by the classifier model is $1 - \tau$. We define the following difference for a given pseudo-data point:

$$
|\mathcal{L}(h_{\boldsymbol{w}_0}(\boldsymbol{z}_i^p), \boldsymbol{y}_i^p) - \mathcal{L}(h_{\boldsymbol{w}_0}(\boldsymbol{z}_i^p), \hat{\boldsymbol{y}}_i^p)| = \begin{cases} 0, & \text{if } \boldsymbol{y}_i^p = \hat{\boldsymbol{y}}_i^p. \\ 1, & \text{otherwise.} \end{cases}
\tag{4.8}
$$

Now using Jensen's inequality and by applying the expectation operator with respect to the target domain distribution in the embedding space, i.e., $\psi(\phi(P_{\mathcal{T}}(\boldsymbol{X}^t)))$, on both sides of above error function, we can deduce:

$$
\begin{aligned}
|e_{\mathcal{P}} - e_{\mathcal{T}}| &\leq \\
\mathbb{E}_{\boldsymbol{z}_i^p \sim \psi(\phi(P_{\mathcal{T}}))} &(|\mathcal{L}(h_{\boldsymbol{w}_0}(\boldsymbol{z}_i^p), \boldsymbol{y}_i^p) - \mathcal{L}(h_{\boldsymbol{w}_0}(\boldsymbol{z}_i^p), \hat{\boldsymbol{y}}_i^p)|) \leq \\
(1 - \tau). &
\end{aligned}
\tag{4.9}
$$

Using Eq. (4.9) we can deduce the following:

$$
\begin{aligned}
e_{\mathcal{S}} + e_{\mathcal{T}} = e_{\mathcal{S}} + e_{\mathcal{T}} + e_{\mathcal{P}} - e_{\mathcal{P}} \leq e_{\mathcal{S}} + e_{\mathcal{P}} + |e_{\mathcal{T}} - e_{\mathcal{P}}| \leq \\
e_{\mathcal{S}} + e_{\mathcal{P}} + (1 - \tau).
\end{aligned}
\tag{4.10}
$$

Eq. (4.10) is valid for all $\boldsymbol{w}$, so by taking infimum on both sides of Eq. (4.10) and using the definition of the joint-optimal model, we deduce the following:

$$
e_C(\boldsymbol{w}^*) \leq e_{C'}(\boldsymbol{w}) + (1 - \tau).
\tag{4.11}
$$

Now consider Theorem 2 for the source and target domains and apply Eq. (4.11) on Eq.(4.7), then we conclude:

$$
\begin{aligned}
e_{\mathcal{T}} \leq &e_{\mathcal{S}} + W(\hat{\mu}_{\mathcal{T}}, \hat{\mu}_{\mathcal{S}}) + e_{C'}(\boldsymbol{w}^*) + (1 - \tau) \\
&+ \sqrt{(2\log(\frac{1}{\xi})/\zeta)}(\sqrt{\frac{1}{N}} + \sqrt{\frac{1}{M}}),
\end{aligned}
\tag{4.12}
$$

where $e_{\mathcal{C}'}$ denotes the joint-optimal model true error for the source and the pseudo-dataset.

Now we apply the triangular inequality twice in Eq. (4.12) on considering that the WD is a metric, we deduce:

$$\begin{aligned} W(\hat{\mu}_{\mathcal{T}}, \hat{\mu}_{\mathcal{S}}) &\leq W(\hat{\mu}_{\mathcal{T}}, \mu_{\mathcal{P}}) + W(\hat{\mu}_{\mathcal{S}}, \mu_{\mathcal{P}}) \leq \\ W(\hat{\mu}_{\mathcal{T}}, \hat{\mu}_{\mathcal{P}}) &+ W(\hat{\mu}_{\mathcal{S}}, \hat{\mu}_{\mathcal{P}}) + 2W(\hat{\mu}_{\mathcal{P}}, \mu_{\mathcal{P}}). \end{aligned} \tag{4.13}$$

We then use Theorem 1.1 in the work by Bolley et al. [20] and simplify the term $W(\hat{\mu}_{\mathcal{P}}, \mu_{\mathcal{P}})$.

Theorem 4.5.3. *(Theorem 1.1 by Bolley et al. [20]): consider that $p(\cdot) \in \mathcal{P}(\mathcal{Z})$ and $\int_{\mathcal{Z}} \exp(\alpha \|\boldsymbol{x}\|_2^2) dp(\boldsymbol{x}) < \infty$ for some $\alpha > 0$. Let $\hat{p}(\boldsymbol{x}) = \frac{1}{N} \sum_i \delta(\boldsymbol{x}_i)$ denote the empirical distribution that is built from the samples $\{\boldsymbol{x}_i\}_{i=1}^N$ that are drawn i.i.d from $\boldsymbol{x}_i \sim p(\boldsymbol{x})$. Then for any $d' > d$ and $\xi < \sqrt{2}$, there exists N_0 such that for any $\epsilon > 0$ and $N \geq N_o \max(1, \epsilon^{-(d'+2)})$, we have:*

$$P(W(p, \hat{p}) > \epsilon) \leq \exp(-\frac{-\xi}{2} N \epsilon^2) \tag{4.14}$$

This relation measures the distance between the estimated empirical distribution and the true distribution when measured by the WD distance.

We can use both Eq. (4.13) and Eq. (4.14) in Eq. (4.12) and conclude Theorem 4.5.1 as stated:

$$\begin{aligned} e_{\mathcal{T}} \leq &e_{\mathcal{S}} + W(\hat{\mu}_{\mathcal{S}}, \hat{\mu}_{\mathcal{P}}) + W(\hat{\mu}_{\mathcal{T}}, \hat{\mu}_{\mathcal{P}}) + (1 - \tau) + e_{\mathcal{C}'}(\boldsymbol{w}^*) \\ &+ \sqrt{(2\log(\frac{1}{\xi})/\zeta)}(\sqrt{\frac{1}{N}} + \sqrt{\frac{1}{M}} + 2\sqrt{\frac{1}{N_p}}), \end{aligned} \tag{4.15}$$

Theorem 4.5.1 justifies effectiveness of our algorithm. We observe that MAS^3 algorithm minimizes the upperbound expressed in Eq. (4.6). The source expected risk is minimized through the initial training on the source domain. The second term in Eq. (4.6) is minimized because we deliberately fit a GMM distribution on the source domain distribution in the embedding space. Note that minimizing this term is conditionally possible when the source domain distribution can be approximated well with a GMM distribution. However, similar constraints exists for all the parametric methods in statistics. Additionally, since we use a softmax in the last layer, this would likely happen because the classes should become separable for a generalizable model to be trained. The third term in the Eq. (4.6) upperbound is minimized as the second terms in Eq. (4.4). The fourth term is a constant term depending on the threshold we use and can be small if $\tau \approx 1$. Note that when selecting the source distribution samples for fitting the Gaussian distribution, if we set τ too close to 1, we may not have sufficient samples for accurate estimation of GMM and hence the second term may increase. Hence, there is a trade-off between minimizing the second and the fourth terms in Eq. (4.6). The term $e_{\mathcal{C}'}(\boldsymbol{w}^*)$ will be small if the domains are related, i.e., share the same classes and the base model can generalize well in both domains, when trained in the presence of sufficient labeled data from both domains. In other words, aligning the distributions in the embedding must be a possibility for our algorithm to work. This is a condition for all UDA algorithms to work. Finally, the last term in Eq. (4.6) is a constant term similar to most PAC-learnability bounds and can be negligible if sufficiently large source and target datasets are accessible and we generate a large pseudo-dataset.

4.6 EXPERIMENTAL VALIDATION

We validate our algorithm using two benchmark domain adaptation tasks and compare it against existing algorithms.

4.6.1 Experimental Setup

Datasets and evaluation metrics: We validate MAS^3 on the standard GTA5 [180]$\rightarrow$ Cityscapes [46] and the SYNTHIA [184]$\rightarrow$ Cityscapes benchmark UDA tasks for semantic segmentation.

GTA5 consists of 24,966 1914×1052 image instances.

SYNTHIA consists of 9,400 1280×760 image instances.

Cityscapes is a real-world dataset consisting of a training set with 2,957 instances and a validation set, used as testing set, with 500 instances of images with size 2040×1016.

The GTA5 and SYNTHIA datasets are used as source domains and after training the model, we adapt it to generalize in the Cityscapes dataset as the target domain. To use a shared cross-domain encoder, we resize all images to 1024×512 size. This can be considered as a preprocessing step using a domain-specific mapping.

Evaluation: Following the literature, we report the results on the Cityscapes validation set and use the category-wise and the mean intersection over union (IoU) to measure segmentation performance [86]. Note that while GTA5 has the same 19 category annotations as Cityscapes, SYNTHIA has 16 common category annotations. For this reason and following the literature, we report the results on the shared cross-domain categories for each task.

Comparison with the State-of-the-art Methods: To the best of our knowledge, there is no prior source-free model adaptation algorithm for performance comparison. For this reason, we compare MAS^3 against UDA algorithms based on joint-training due to proximity of these works to our learning setting. In our comparison, we have included both pioneer and recent UDA image segmentation method to be representative of the literature. We have compared our performance against the adversarial learning-based UDA methods: GIO-Ada [37], ADVENT [251], AdaSegNet [247], TGCF-DA+SE [42], PCEDA [276], and CyCADA [85]. We have also included methods that are based on direct distributional matching which are more similar to MAS^3: FCNs in the Wild [86], CDA [290], DCAN [262], SWD [119], Cross-City [38].

4.6.2 Results

Quantitative performance comparison:

SYNTHIA→Cityscapes: We report the quantitative results in Table 4.1. We note that despite addressing a more challenge learning setting, MAS^3 outperforms most of the UDA methods. Recently developed UDA methods based on adversarial learning outperform our method but we note that these methods benefit from a secondary type of regularization in addition to probability matching. Overall, MAS^3 performs reasonably well even compared with these UDA methods that need source samples. Additionally, MAS^3 has the best performance for some important categories, e.g., traffic light.

GTA5→Cityscapes: Quantitative results for this task are reported in Table 4.2. We observe a more competitive performance for this task but the performance comparison trend

Method	Adv.	road	sidewalk	building	traffic light	traffic sign	vegetation	sky	person	rider	car	bus	motorcycle	bicycle	mIoU
Source Only (VGG16)	N	6.4	17.7	29.7	0.0	7.2	30.3	66.8	51.1	1.5	47.3	3.9	0.1	0.0	20.2
FCNs in the Wild	N	11.5	19.6	30.8	0.1	11.7	42.3	68.7	51.2	3.8	54.0	3.2	0.2	0.6	22.9
CDA	N	65.2	26.1	74.9	3.7	3.0	76.1	70.6	47.1	8.2	43.2	20.7	0.7	13.1	34.8
DCAN	N	9.9	30.4	70.8	6.70	23.0	76.9	73.9	41.9	16.7	61.7	11.5	10.3	38.6	36.4
SWD	N	83.3	35.4	82.1	12.2	12.6	83.8	76.5	47.4	12.0	71.5	17.9	1.6	29.7	43.5
Cross-City	Y	62.7	25.6	78.3	1.2	5.4	81.3	81.0	37.4	6.4	63.5	16.1	1.2	4.6	35.7
GIO-Ada	Y	78.3	29.2	76.9	10.8	17.2	81.7	81.9	45.8	15.4	68.0	15.9	7.5	30.4	43.0
ADVENT	Y	67.9	29.4	71.9	0.6	2.6	74.9	74.9	35.4	9.6	67.8	21.4	4.1	15.5	36.6
AdaSegNet	Y	78.9	29.2	75.5	0.1	4.8	72.6	76.7	43.4	8.8	71.1	16.0	3.6	8.4	37.6
TGCF-DA+SE	Y	90.1	48.6	80.7	3.2	14.3	82.1	78.4	54.4	16.4	82.5	12.3	1.7	21.8	46.6
PCEDA	Y	79.7	35.2	78.7	10.0	28.9	79.6	81.2	51.2	25.1	72.2	24.1	16.7	50.4	48.7
MAS^3 (Ours)	N	75.1	49.6	70.9	14.1	25.3	72.7	76.7	48.5	19.9	65.3	17.6	6.8	39.0	44.7

Table 4.1 Model adaptation comparison results for the SYNTHIA→Cityscapes task. We have used DeepLabV3 [35] as the feature extractor with a VGG16 [227] backbone. The first row presents the source-trained model performance prior to adaptation to demonstrate effect of initial knowledge transfer from the source domain.

Method	Adv.	road	sidewalk	building	wall	fence	pole	traffic light	traffic sign	vegetation	terrain	sky	person	rider	car	truck	bus	train	motorcycle	bicycle	mIoU
Source Only (VGG16)	N	25.9	10.9	50.5	3.3	12.2	25.4	28.6	13.0	78.3	7.3	63.9	52.1	7.9	66.3	5.2	7.8	0.9	13.7	0.7	24.9
FCNs in the Wild	N	70.4	32.4	62.1	14.9	5.4	10.9	14.2	2.7	79.2	21.3	64.6	44.1	4.2	70.4	8.0	7.3	0.0	3.5	0.0	27.1
CDA	N	74.9	22.0	71.7	6.0	11.9	8.4	16.3	11.1	75.7	13.3	66.5	38.0	9.3	55.2	18.8	18.9	0.0	16.8	14.6	28.9
DCAN	N	82.3	26.7	77.4	23.7	20.5	20.4	30.3	15.9	80.9	25.4	69.5	52.6	11.1	79.6	24.9	21.2	1.30	17.0	6.70	36.2
SWD	N	91.0	35.7	78.0	21.6	21.7	31.8	30.2	25.2	80.2	23.9	74.1	53.1	15.8	79.3	22.1	26.5	1.5	17.2	30.4	39.9
CyCADA	Y	85.2	37.2	76.5	21.8	15.0	23.8	22.9	21.5	80.5	31.3	60.7	50.5	9.0	76.9	17.1	28.2	4.5	9.8	0.0	35.4
ADVENT	Y	86.9	28.7	78.7	28.5	25.2	17.1	20.3	10.9	80.0	26.4	70.2	47.1	8.4	81.5	26.0	17.2	18.9	11.7	1.6	36.1
AdaSegNet	Y	86.5	36.0	79.9	23.4	23.3	23.9	35.2	14.8	83.4	33.3	75.6	58.5	27.6	73.7	32.5	35.4	3.9	30.1	28.1	42.4
TGCF-DA+SE	Y	90.2	51.5	81.1	15.0	10.7	37.5	35.2	28.9	84.1	32.7	75.9	62.7	19.9	82.6	22.9	28.3	0.0	23.0	25.4	42.5
PCEDA	Y	90.2	44.7	82.0	28.4	28.4	24.4	33.7	35.6	83.7	40.5	75.1	54.4	28.2	80.3	23.8	39.4	0.0	22.8	30.8	44.6
MAS^3 (Ours)	N	75.5	53.7	72.2	20.5	24.1	30.5	28.7	37.8	79.6	36.9	78.7	49.6	16.5	77.4	26.0	42.6	18.8	15.3	49.9	43.9

Table 4.2 Domain adaptation results for different methods for the GTA5→Cityscapes task.

is similar. These results demonstrate that although the motivation in this work is source-free model adaptation, MAS^3 can also be used as a joint-training UDA algorithm.

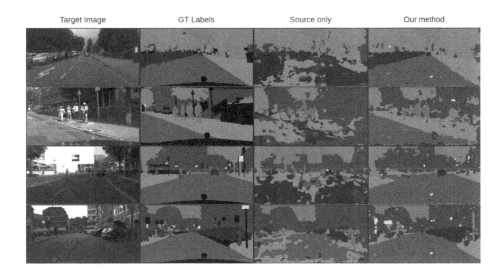

Figure 4.3 Qualitative performance: examples of the segmented frames for SYNTHIA→Cityscapes using the MAS^3 method. Left to right: real images, manually annotated images, source-trained model predictions, predictions based on our method.

Qualitative performance validation:

In Figure 4.3, we have visualized exemplar frames for the Cityscapes dataset for the GTA5→Cityscapes task which are segmented using the model prior and after adaptation along with the ground-truth (GT) manual annotation for each image. Visual observation demonstrates that our method is able to significantly improve image segmentation from the source-only segmentation to the post-adaptation segmentation, noticeably on sidewalk, road, and car semantic classes for the GTA5-trained model.

Effect of alignment in the embedding space:

To demonstrate that our solution implements what we anticipated, we have used UMAP [146] visualization tool to reduce the dimension of the data representations in the embedding space to two for 2D visualization. Figure 4.4 represents the samples of the prototypical distribution along with the target domain data prior and after adaptation in the embedding space for the GTA5→Cityscapes task. Each point in Figure 4.4 denotes a single data point and each color denotes a semantic class cluster. Comparing Figure 4.4 (b) and Figure 4.4 (c) with Figure 4.4 (a), we can see that the semantic classes in the target domain have become much more well-separated and more similar to the prototypical distribution after model adaptation. This means that domain discrepancy has been reduced using MAS^3 and the source and the target domain distributions are aligned indirectly as anticipated using the intermediate prototypical distribution in the embedding space.

(a) GMM samples   (b) Pre-adaptation   (c) Post-adaptation

Figure 4.4 Indirect distribution matching in the embedding space: (a) drawn samples from the GMM trained on the SYNTHIA distribution, (b) representations of the Cityscapes validation samples prior to model adaptation (c) representation of the Cityscapes validation samples after domain alignment.

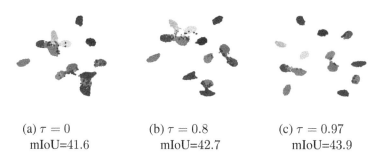

(a) $\tau = 0$ (b) $\tau = 0.8$ (c) $\tau = 0.97$
mIoU=41.6   mIoU=42.7   mIoU=43.9

Figure 4.5 Ablation experiment to study effect of τ on the GMM learnt in the embedding space: (a) all samples are used; adaptation mIoU=41.6, (b) a portion of samples is used; adaptation mIoU=42.7, (c) samples with high model-confidence are used; adaptation mIoU=43.9.

4.6.3 Ablation Study

A major advantage of our algorithm over methods based on adversarial learning is its simplicity in depending on a few hyper-parameters. We note that the major algorithm-specific hyper-parameters are λ and τ. We observed in our experiments that MAS^3 performance is stable with respect to the trade-off parameter λ value. This is expected because in Eq. (4.4), the $\mathcal{L}_{ce}$ loss term is small from the beginning due to prior training on the source domain. We investigated the impact of the confidence hyper-parameter τ value. Figure 4.5 presents the fitted GMM on the source prototypical distribution for three different values of τ. As it can be seen, when $\tau = 0$, the fitted GMM clusters are cluttered. As we increase the threshold τ and use samples for which the classifier is confident, the fitted GMM represents well-separated semantic classes which increases knowledge transfer from the source domain. This experiments also empirically validates what we deduced about importance of τ using Theorem 1.

4.7 CONCLUSIONS

In this chapter, we developed an algorithm for adapting an image segmentation model to generalize in new domains after training using solely unlabeled data. Our algorithm is based on using an intermediate multi-modal prototypical distribution to minimize the distributional cross-domain discrepancy in a shared embedding space. We estimate the prototypical distribution as a parametric GMM distribution. Experiments on benchmark tasks demonstrate our algorithm is effective and leads to competitive performance, even when compared to UDA algorithms that are based on joint-domain model training. A major limitation of the MAS^3 algorithm is that a single deep encoder is shared across the two domains. This means that we learn and use the same features for two domains. If the two domains are quite related, using shared features is a good idea. However, if the domains are distant, we may need to learn different features. In the next chapter, we remove this limitation and propose a domain adaptation algorithm to transfer knowledge across two domains with more domain gap.

CHAPTER 5

Few-Shot Image Classification through Coupled Embedding Spaces

In the previous chapter, we investigated the problem of domain adaptation in the domain of natural images, i.e., electro-optical (EO) images. In this chapter, we investigate the domain adaptation problem when the data modality of the two domains is different. Our formulation is a general framework, but we focus on knowledge transfer from the EO domain as the source domain to the Synthetic Aperture Radar (SAR) domain as the target domain. This is a practical manifestation of our framework for few-shot domain adaptation. In contrast to the UDA framework, we have access to a few labeled data points in the target domain in a few-shot domain adaptation learning setting. Unlike the EO domain, labeling the SAR domain data is a lot more challenging, and for various reasons using crowdsourcing platforms is not feasible for labeling the SAR domain data. As a result, training deep networks using supervised learning is more challenging in the SAR domain.

We present a new framework to train a deep neural network for classifying Synthetic Aperture Radar (SAR) images by eliminating the need for a huge labeled dataset. Similar to the previous chapter, our idea is based on transferring knowledge from a related EO domain problem as the source domain, where labeled data is easy to obtain. We transfer knowledge from the EO domain through learning a shared invariant cross-domain embedding space that is also discriminative for classification. However, since the two domains are not homogeneous, and the domain gap is considerable, a shared encoder is not a good solution to match the distributions. Instead, we train two deep encoders that are coupled through their last layer to map data points from the EO and the SAR domains to the shared embedding space such that the distance between the distributions of the two domains is minimized in the latent embedding space. Similar to the previous chapter, we use the Sliced Wasserstein Distance (SWD) to measure and minimize the distance between these two distributions. Additionally, we use a limited number of SAR label data points to match the distributions class-conditionally. As a result of this training procedure, a classifier trained from the embedding space to the label space using mostly the EO data would generalize well on the SAR domain. We provide theoretical analysis to demonstrate why our approach is effective and validate our algorithm on the problem of ship classification in the SAR domain by comparing against several other learning competing approaches. Results of this chapter have been presented in Refs. [105, 194, 197, 196].

5.1 OVERVIEW

Historically and prior to the emergence of machine learning, most imaging devices were designed first to generate outputs that are interpretable by humans, mostly natural images. As a result, the dominant visual data that is collected even nowadays is the electro-optical (EO) domain data. Digital EO images are generated by a planar grid of sensors that detect and record the magnitude and the color of reflected visible light from the surface of an object in the form of a planner array of pixels. Naturally, most machine learning algorithms that are developed for automation, also process EO domain data as their input. Recently, the area of EO-based machine learning and computer vision has made significant advances in developing classification and detection algorithms with a human-level performance for many applications. In particular, the reemergence of neural networks in the form of deep Convolutional Neural Networks (CNNs) has been crucial for this success. The major reason for the outperformance of CNNs over many prior classic learning methods is that the time consuming and unclear procedure of feature engineering in classic machine learning and computer vision can be bypassed when CNN's are trained. CNN's are able to extract abstract and high-quality discriminative features for a given task automatically in a blind end-to-end supervised training scheme, where CNN's are trained using a huge labeled dataset of images. Since the learned features are task-dependent, often lead to better performance compared to engineered features that are usually defined for a broad range of tasks without considering the specific structure of the data, e.g., wavelet, DFT, SIFT, etc.

Despite a wide range of applicability of EO imaging, it is also naturally constrained by limitations of the human visual sensory system. In particular, in applications such as continuous environmental monitoring and large-scale surveillance [108], and earth remote sensing [135], continuous imaging at extended time periods and independent of the weather conditions is necessary. EO imaging is not suitable for such applications because imaging during the night and cloudy weather is not feasible. In these applications, using other imaging techniques that are designed for imaging beyond the visible spectrum is inevitable. Synthetic Aperture Radar (SAR) imaging is a major technique in this area that is highly effective for remote sensing applications. SAR imaging benefits from radar signals that can propagate in occluded weather and at night. Radar signals are emitted sequentially from a moving antenna, and the reflected signals are collected for subsequent signal processing to generate high-resolution images irrespective of the weather conditions and occlusions. While both the EO and the SAR domain images describe the same physical world and often SAR data is represented in a planner array form similar to an EO image, processing EO and SAR data and developing suitable learning algorithms for these domains can be quite different. In particular, replicating the success of CNN's in supervised learning problems of the SAR domain is more challenging. This is because training CNNs is conditioned on the availability of huge labeled datasets to supervise blind end-to-end learning. Until quite recently, generating such datasets was challenging and expensive. Nowadays, labeled datasets for the EO domain tasks are generated using crowdsourcing labeling platforms such as Amazon Mechanical Turk, e.g., ImageNet [50]. In a crowdsourcing platform, a pool of participants with common basic knowledge for labeling EO data points, i.e., natural images, is recruited. These participants need minimal training and in many cases, are not even compensated for their time and effort. Unlabeled images are presented to each participant independently, and each participant selects a label for each given image. Upon collecting labels from several people from the pool of participants, collected labels are aggregated according to the skills and reliability of each participant to increase labeling accuracy [192]. Despite being very effective for generating high quality labeled large dataset for EO domains, for various reasons using crowdsourcing platforms for labeling SAR datasets is not feasible:

- Preparing devices for collecting SAR data, solely for generating training datasets is much more expensive compared to EO datasets [136]. In many cases, EO datasets can even be generated from the Internet using existing images that are taken by commercial cameras. In contrast, SAR imaging devices are not commercially available and usually are expensive to operate and only are operated by governments, e.g., satellites.

- SAR images are often classified data because for many applications, the goal is surveillance and target detection. This issue makes access to SAR data heavily regulated and limited to certified cleared people. For this reason, while SAR data is consistently collected, only a few datasets are publicly available, even for research purposes. This limits the number of participants who can be hired to help with processing and labeling.

- Despite similarities, SAR images are not easy to interpret by an average untrained person. For this reason, labeling SAR images needs trained experts who know how to interpret SAR data. This is in contrast with tasks within the EO domain images, where ordinary people can label images by minimal training and guidance [219]. This challenge makes labeling SAR data more expensive as only professional trained people can perform labeling SAR data.

- Continuous collection of SAR data is common in SAR applications. As a result, the distribution of data is likely to be non-stationery. Hence, even if a high-quality labeled dataset is generated, the data would become unrepresentative of the current distribution over extended time intervals. This would obligate persistent data labeling to update a trained model, which, as explained above, is expensive [92].

As a result of the above challenges, generating labeled datasets for the SAR domain data is in general difficult. In particular, given the size of most existing SAR datasets, training a CNN leads to overfitted models as the number of data points are considerably less than the required sample complexity of training a deep network [36, 222]. When the model is overfitted, naturally it will not generalize well on test sets. In other words, we face situations in which the amount of accessible labeled SAR data is not sufficient for training deep neural networks that extract useful features. In the machine learning literature, challenges of learning in this scenario have been investigated within transfer learning [163]. The general idea that we focus on is to transfer knowledge from a secondary domain to reduce the amount of labeled data that is necessary to train a model. Building upon prior works in the area of transfer learning, several recent works have used the idea of knowledge transfer to address challenges of SAR domains [92, 136, 286, 258, 116, 222]. The common idea in these works is to transfer knowledge from a secondary related problem, where labeled data is easy and cheap to obtain. For example, the second domain can be a related task in the EO domain or a task generated by synthetic data. Following this line of work, our goal in this chapter is to tackle the challenges of learning in SAR domains when the labeled data is scarce. This particular setting of transfer learning is also called domain adaptation in machine learning literature. In this setting, the domain with labeled data scarcity is called the target domain, and the domain with sufficient labeled data is called the target domain. We develop a method that benefits from cross-domain knowledge transfer from a related task in EO domains as the source domain to address a task in SAR domains as the target domain. More specifically, we consider a classification task with the same classes in two domains, i.e., SAR and EO. This is a typical situation for many applications, as it is common to use both SAR and EO imaging. We consider a domain adaptation setting, where we have sufficient labeled data points in the source domain, i.e., EO. We also have access to abundant data points in the target domain, i.e., EO, but only a few labeled data points are labeled. This setting is called semi-supervised domain adaptation in the machine learning literature [154].

Several approaches have been developed to address the problem of domain adaptation. A common technique for cross-domain knowledge transfer is encoded data points of the two related domains in a domain-invariant embedding space such that similarities between the tasks can be identified and captured in the shared space. As a result, knowledge can be transferred across the domains in the embedding space through correspondences that are captured between the domains in the shared space. The key challenge is how to find such an embedding space. We model the shared embedding space as the output space of deep encoders. We couple two deep encoders to map the data points from the two domains into a shared embedding space as their outputs such that both domains would have similar distributions in this space. If both domains have similar class-conditional probability distributions in the embedding space, then if we train a classifier network using only the source-domain labeled data points from the shared embedding to the label space, it will also generalize well on the target domain test data points [178]. This goal can be achieved by training the deep encoders as two deterministic functions using training data such that the empirical distribution discrepancy between the two domains is minimized in the shared output of the deep encoders with respect to some probability distribution metric[250, 70].

Our contribution is to propose a novel semi-supervised domain adaptation algorithm to transfer knowledge from the EO domain to the SAR domain using the above explained procedure. We train the encoder networks by using the Sliced-Wasserstein Distance (SWD) [174] to measure and then minimize the discrepancy between the source and the target domain distributions. There are two major reasons for using SWD. First, SWD is an effective metric for the space of probability distributions that can be computed efficiently. Second, SWD is non-zero even for two probability distributions with non-overlapping supports. As a result, it has non-vanishing gradients, and first-order gradient-based optimization algorithms can be used to solve optimization problems involving SWD terms [104, 178]. This is important as most optimization problems for training deep neural networks are solved using gradient-based methods, e.g., stochastic gradient descent (SGD). The above procedure might not succeed because while the distance between distributions may be minimized, they may not be aligned class-conditionally. We use the few accessible labeled data points in the SAR domain to align both distributions class-conditionally to tackle the class matching challenge [102]. We demonstrate theoretically why our approach is able to train a classifier with generalizability on the target SAR domain. We also provide experimental results to validate our approach in the area of maritime domain awareness, where the goal is to understand activities that could impact the safety and the environment. Our results demonstrate that our approach is effective and leads to state-of-the-art performance against common approaches that are currently used in the literature.

5.2 RELATED WORK

Recently, several prior works have addressed classification in the SAR domain in the label-scarce regime. Huang et al. [92] use an un supervised learning approach to generate discriminative features. Given that generating unlabeled SAR data is easier, their idea is to train a deep autoencoder using a large pool of unlabeled SAR data. Upon training the autoencoder, features extracted in the middle-layer of the autoencoder capture difference across different classes and can be used for classification. For example, the trained encoder sub-network of the autoencoder can be concatenated with a classifier network, and both would be fine-tuned using the labeled portion of data to map the data points to the label space. In other words, the deep encoder is used as a task-dependent feature extractor.

Hansen et al. [136] proposed to transfer knowledge using synthetic SAR images which are easy to generate and are similar to real images. Their idea is to generate a simulated dataset for a given SAR problem based on simulated object radar reflectivity. Upon generating the synthetic labeled dataset, it can be used to train a CNN network prior to presenting the real data. The pre-trained CNN then can be used as an initialization for the real SAR domain problem. Due to the pretraining stage and similarities between the synthetic and the read data, the model can be thought of a better initial point and hence fine-tuned using fewer real labeled data points. Zhang et al. [286] propose to transfer knowledge from a secondary source SAR task, where labeled data is available. Similarly, a CNN network can be pre-trained on the task with labeled data and then fine-tuned on the target task.

Lang et al. [116] use an automatic identification system (AIS) as the secondary domain for knowledge transfer. AIS is a tracking system for monitoring movement of ships that can provide labeling information. Shang et al. [222] amend a CNN with an information recorder. The recorder is used to store spatial features of labeled samples, and the recorded features are used to predict labels of unlabeled data points based on spatial similarity to increase the number of labeled samples.

Finally, Weng et al. [258] use an approach more similar to our framework. Their proposal is to transfer knowledge from EO domain using VGGNet as a feature extractor in the learning pipeline, which itself has been pretrained on a large EO dataset. Despite being effective, the common idea of these past works is mostly using a deep network that is pretrained using a secondary source of knowledge, which is then fine-tuned using few labeled data points on the target SAR task. Hence, knowledge transfer occurs as a result of selecting a better initial point for the optimization problem using the secondary source.

We follow a different approach by recasting the problem as a domain adaptation (DA) problem [70], where the goal is to adapt a model trained on the source domain to generalize well in the target domain. Our contribution is to demonstrate how to transfer knowledge from EO imaging domain in order to train a deep network for the SAR domain. The idea is to use a related EO domain problem with abundant labeled data when training a deep network on a related EO problem with abundant labeled data and simultaneously adapt the model considering that only a few labeled SAR data points are accessible. In our training scheme, we enforce the distributions of both domains to become similar within a mid-layer of the deep network.

Domain adaptation has been investigated in the computer vision literature for a broad range of application for the EO domain problems. The goal in domain adaptation is to train a model on a source data distribution with sufficient labeled data such that it generalizes well on a different, but related target data distribution, where labeling the data is challenging. Despite being different, the common idea of DA approaches is to preprocess data from both domains or at least the target domain such that the distributions of both domains become similar after preprocessing. As a result, a classifier which is trained using the source data can also be used on the target domain due to similar post-processing distributions. We consider that two deep convolutional neural networks preprocess data to enforce both EO and SAR domains data to have similar probability distributions. To this end, we couple two deep encoder sub-networks with a shared output space to model the embedding space. This space can be considered as an intermediate embedding space between the input space from each domain and the label space of a classifier network that is shared between the two domains. These deep encoders are trained such that the discrepancy between the source and the target domain distributions is minimized in the shared embedding space, while overall classification is supervised mostly via the EO domain labeled data. This procedure can be done via adversarial learning [68], where the distributions are matched indirectly. We can also formulate an optimization problem with probability matching objective to match the distributions directly [48]. We use the latter approach for in our approach. Similar to the previous chapter, we use the Sliced Wasserstein Distance (SWD) to measure and minimize the distance between the probability distributions. Our rationale for the selection is explained in the previous chapter.

5.3 PROBLEM FORMULATION AND RATIONALE

Let $\mathcal{X}^{(t)} \subset \mathbb{R}^d$ denote the domain space of SAR data. Consider a multiclass SAR classification problem with k classes in this domain, where i.i.d data pairs are drawn from the joint probability distribution, i.e., $(\boldsymbol{x}_i^t, \boldsymbol{y}_i^t) \sim q_T(\boldsymbol{x}, \boldsymbol{y})$ which has the marginal distribution $p_T(\boldsymbol{x})$ over $\mathcal{X}^{(t)}$. Here, a label $\boldsymbol{y}_i^t \in \mathcal{Y}$ identifies the class membership of the vectorized SAR image $\boldsymbol{x}_t^i$ to one of the k classes. We have access to $M \gg 1$ unlabeled images $\mathcal{D}_\mathcal{T} = (\boldsymbol{X}_\mathcal{T} = [\boldsymbol{x}_1^t, \ldots, \boldsymbol{x}_M^t]) \in \mathbb{R}^{d \times M}$ in this target domain. Additionally, we have access to O labeled images $\mathcal{D}'_\mathcal{T} = (\boldsymbol{X}'_\mathcal{T}, \boldsymbol{Y}'_\mathcal{T})$, where $\boldsymbol{X}'_\mathcal{S} = [\boldsymbol{x}_1^{'t}, \ldots, \boldsymbol{x}_O^{'t}] \in \mathbb{R}^{d \times O}$ and $\boldsymbol{Y}'_\mathcal{S} = [\boldsymbol{y}_1^{'t}, \ldots, \boldsymbol{y}_O^{'t}] \subset \mathbb{R}^{k \times O}$ contains the corresponding one-shot labels. The goal is to train a parameterized classifier $f_\theta : \mathbb{R}^d \to \mathcal{Y} \subset \mathcal{R}^k$, i.e., a deep neural network with weight parameters θ, on this domain by solving for the optimal parameters using labeled data. Given that we have access to only few labeled data points and considering model complexity of deep neural networks, training the deep network such that it generalizes well using solely the SAR labeled data is not feasible as training would lead to overfitting on the few labeled data points such that the trained network would generalize poorly on test data points. As we discussed, this is a major challenge to benefit from deep learning in the SAR domain.

To tackle the problem of label scarcity, we consider a domain adaptation scenario. We assume that a related source EO domain problem exists, where we have access to sufficient labeled data points such that training a generalizable model is feasible. Let $\mathcal{X}^{(s)} \subset \mathbb{R}^{d'}$ denotes the EO domain $\mathcal{D}_S = (\boldsymbol{X}_S, \boldsymbol{Y}_S)$ denotes the dataset in the EO domain, with $\boldsymbol{X}_S \in \mathcal{X} \subset \mathbb{R}^{d' \times N}$ and $\boldsymbol{Y}_S \in \mathcal{Y} \subset \mathbb{R}^{k \times N}$ ($N \gg 1$). Note that since we consider the same cross-domain classes, we are considering the same classification problem in two domains. In other words, the relation between the two domains is the existence of the same classes that are sensed by two types EO and SAR sensory systems. This cross-domain similarity is necessary for making knowledge transfer feasible. In other words, we have a classification problem with bi-modal data, but there is no point-wise correspondence across the data modals, and in most data points in one of them are unlabeled. We assume the source samples are drawn i.i.d. from the source joint probability distribution $q_S(\boldsymbol{x}, \boldsymbol{y})$, which has the marginal distribution p_S. Note that despite similarities between the domains, the marginal distributions of the domains are different. Given that extensive research and investigation has been done in EO domains, we hypothesize that finding such a labeled dataset is likely feasible or labeling such an EO data is easier than labeling more SAR data points. Our goal is to use the similarity between the EO and the SAR domains and benefit from the unlabeled SAR data to train a model for classifying SAR images using the knowledge that can be learned from the EO domain.

Since we have access to sufficient labeled source data, training a parametric classifier for the source domain is a straightforward supervised learning problem. Usually, we solve for an optimal parameter to select the best model from the family of parametric functions f_θ. We can solve for an optimal parameter by minimizing the average empirical risk on the training labeled data points, i.e., Empirical Risk Minimization (ERM):

$$\hat{\theta} = \arg \min_\theta \hat{e}_\theta = \arg \min_\theta \frac{1}{N} \sum_{i=1}^{N} \mathcal{L}(f_\theta(\boldsymbol{x}_i^s), \boldsymbol{y}_i^s) \ , \tag{5.1}$$

where $\mathcal{L}$ is a proper loss function (e.g., cross entropy loss). Given enough training data points, the empirical risk is a suitable surrogate for the real risk function:

$$e = \mathbb{E}_{(\boldsymbol{x}, \boldsymbol{y}) \sim p_S(\boldsymbol{x}, \boldsymbol{y})}(\mathcal{L}(f_\theta(\boldsymbol{x}), \boldsymbol{y})) \ , \tag{5.2}$$

which is the objective function for Bayes optimal inference. This means that the learned classifier would generalize well on data points if they are drawn from p_S. A naive approach to transfer knowledge from the EO domain to the SAR domain is to use the classifier that is trained on the EO domain directly in the target domain. However, since distribution discrepancy exists between the two domains, i.e., $p_S \neq p_T$, the trained classifier on the source domain $f_{\hat{\theta}}$, might not generalize well on the target domain. Therefore, there is a need for adapting the training procedure for $f_{\hat{\theta}}$. The simplest approach which has been used in most prior works is to fine-tune the EO classifier using the few labeled target data points to employ the model in the target domain. This approach would add the constraint of $d = d'$ as the same input space is required to use the same network across the domains. Usually, it is easy to use image interpolation to enforce this condition, but information may be lost after interpolation. We want to use a more principled approach and remove the condition of $d = d'$. Additionally, since SAR and EO images are quite different, the same features, i.e., features extracted by the same encoder, may not be as equally good for both domains. More importantly, when fine-tuning is used, unlabeled data is not used. However, unlabeled data can be used to determine the data structure. We want to take advantage of the unlabeled SAR data points. Unlabeled data points are accessible and provide additional information about the SAR domain marginal distribution.

Figure 5.1 presents a block diagram visualization of our framework. In the figure, we have visualized images from two related real world SAR and EO datasets that we have used in the experimental section. The task is to classify ship images. Notice that SAR images are confusing for the untrained human eye, while EO ship/no-ship images can be distinguished by minimal inspection. This suggests that as we discussed before, SAR labeling is more challenging, and labeling SAR data requires expertise. In our approach, we consider the EO deep network $f_{\theta}(\cdot)$ to be formed by a feature extractor $\phi_v(\cdot)$, i.e., convolutional layers of the network, which is followed by a classifier sub-network $h_w(\cdot)$, i.e., fully connected layers of the network, that inputs the extracted feature and maps them to the label space. Here, w and v denote the corresponding learnable parameters for these sub-networks, i.e., $\theta = (w, v)$. This decomposition is synthetic but helps to understand our approach. In other words, the feature extractor sub-network $\phi_v : \mathcal{X} \to \mathcal{Z}$ maps the data points into a discriminative embedding space $\mathcal{Z} \subset \mathbb{R}^f$, where classification can be done easily by the classifier sub-network $h_w : \mathcal{Z} \to \mathcal{Y}$. The success of deep learning stems from optimal feature extraction, which converts the data distribution into a multimodal distribution, which makes class separation feasible. Following the above, we can consider a second encoder network $\psi_u(\cdot) : \mathbb{R}^d \to \mathbb{R}^f$, which maps the SAR data points to the same target embedding space at its output. Similar to the previous chapter, the idea that we want to explore is based on training ϕ_v and ψ_u such that the discrepancy between the source distribution $p_{\mathcal{S}}(\phi(x))$ and target distribution $p_{\mathcal{T}}(\phi(x))$ is minimized in the shared embedding space, modeled as the shared output space of these two encoders. As a result of matching the two distributions, the embedding space becomes invariant with respect to the domain. In other words, data points from the two domains become indistinguishable in the embedding space, e.g., data points belonging to the same class are mapped into the same geometric cluster in the shared embedding space as depicted in Figure 5.1. Consequently, even if we train the classifier sub-network using solely the source labeled data points, it will still generalize well when target data points are used for testing. The key question is how to train the encoder sub-networks such that the embedding space becomes invariant. We need to adapt the standard supervised learning in Eq. (5.1) by adding additional terms that enforce cross-domain distribution matching.

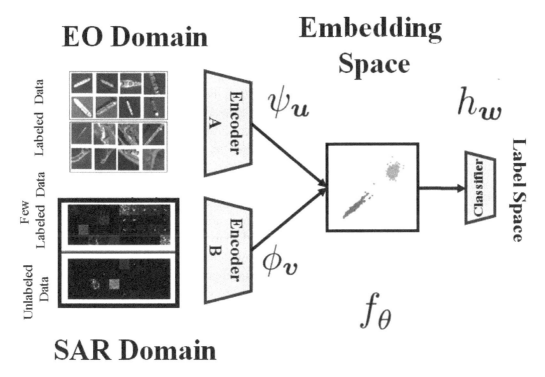

Figure 5.1 Block diagram architecture of the proposed framework for transferring knowledge from the EO to the SAR domain. The encoder networks are domain-specific, but their outputs are shared and fed into the shared classifier sub-networks.

5.4 PROPOSED SOLUTION

In our solution, the encoder sub-networks need to be learned such that the extracted features in the encoder output are discriminative. Only then, the classes become separable for the classifier sub-network (see Figure 5.1). This is a direct result of supervised learning for EO encoder. Additionally, the encoders should mix the SAR and the EO domains such that the embedding becomes domain-invariant. As a result, the SAR encoder is indirectly enforced to be discriminative for the SAR domain. We enforce the embedding to be domain-invariant by minimizing the discrepancy between the distributions of both domains in the embedding space. Following the above, we can formulate the following optimization problem for computing the optimal values for v, u, and w:

$$
\min_{v,u,w} \frac{1}{N} \sum_{i=1}^{N} \mathcal{L}\big(h_w(\phi_v(x_i^s)), y_i^s\big) + \frac{1}{O} \sum_{i=1}^{O} \mathcal{L}\big(h_w(\psi_u(x_i^{'t})), y_i^{'t}\big)
$$

$$
+ \lambda D\big(\phi_v(p_{\mathcal{S}}(X_{\mathcal{S}})), \psi_u(p_{\mathcal{T}}(X_{\mathcal{T}}))\big) + \eta \sum_{j=1}^{k} D\big(\phi_v(p_{\mathcal{S}}(X_{\mathcal{S}})|C_j), \psi_u(p_{\mathcal{T}}(X_{\mathcal{T}}')|C_j)\big) ,
$$

$$(5.3)$$

where $D(\cdot, \cdot)$ is a discrepancy measure between the probabilities, and λ and η are trade-off parameters. The first two terms in Eq. (5.3) are standard empirical risks for classifying the EO and SAR labeled data points, respectively. The third term is the cross-domain unconditional probability matching loss. We match the unconditional distributions as the SAR data is mostly unlabeled. The matching loss is computed using all available data points from both domains to learn the learnable parameters of encoder sub-networks and the classifier sub-network is simultaneously learned using the labeled data from both domains. Finally, the last term is Eq. (5.3) is added to enforce semantic consistency between the two domains by matching the distributions class-conditionally. This term is important for knowledge transfer. To clarify this point, note that the domains might be aligned such that their marginal distributions $\phi(p_{\mathcal{S}}(\boldsymbol{X}_{\mathcal{S}}))$ and $\psi(p_{\mathcal{T}}(\boldsymbol{X}_{\mathcal{T}}))$ have minimal discrepancy, while the distance between $\phi(q_{\mathcal{S}}(\cdot,\cdot))$ and $\psi(q_{\mathcal{T}}(\cdot,\cdot))$ is not minimized. This means that the classes may not have been aligned correctly, e.g., images belonging to a class in the target domain may be matched to a wrong class in the source domain or, even worse, images from multiple classes in the target domain may be matched to the cluster of another class of the source domain. In such cases, the classifier will not generalize well on the target domain as it has been trained to be consistent with the spatial arrangement of the source domain in the embedding space. This means that if we merely minimize the distance between $\phi(p_{\mathcal{S}}(\boldsymbol{X}_{\mathcal{S}}))$ and $\psi(p_{\mathcal{T}}(\boldsymbol{X}_{\mathcal{T}}))$, the shared embedding space might not be a consistently discriminative space for both domains in terms of classes. As we discussed in the previous chapter, the challenge of class-matching is a known problem in domain adaptation, and several approaches have been developed to address this challenge [129]. In the previous chapter, we could overcome this challenge by using pseudo-data points, but since we have more domain gap and the encoder networks are domain-specific, that idea is not applicable in this chapter. Instead, the few labeled data points in the target SAR domain can be used to match the classes consistently across both domains. We use these data points to compute the fourth term in Eq. (5.3). This term is added to match class-conditional probabilities of both domains in the embedding space, i.e., $\phi(p_{\mathcal{S}}(\boldsymbol{x}_{\mathcal{S}})|C_j) \approx \psi(p_{\mathcal{T}}(\boldsymbol{x}|C_j)$, where C_j denotes a particular class.

The remaining key question is selecting a proper metric to compute $D(\cdot,\cdot)$ in the last two terms of Eq 5.1. Building upon our method in the previous chapter, we utilize the SWD as the discrepancy measure between the probability distributions to match them in the embedding space (we refer to the previous chapter and our discussion therein). Our proposed algorithm for few-shot SAR image classification (FSC) using cross-domain knowledge transfer is summarized in Algorithm 4. Note that we have added a pretraining step which trains the EO encoder and the shared classifier sub-network solely on the EO domain for better initialization. Since our problem is non-convex, a reasonable initial point is critical for finding a good local solution.

5.5 THEORETICAL ANALYSIS

In order to demonstrate that our approach is effective, we show that transferring knowledge from the EO domain can reduce the real task on the SAR domain. Similar to the previous chapter, our analysis is based on broad results for domain adaptation and is not limited to the case of EO-to-SAR transfer. Again, we rely on the work by Redko et al. [178], where the focus is on using the same shared classifier $h_w(\cdot)$ on both the source and the target domain. This is analogous to our formulation as the classifier network is shared across the domains

---

Algorithm 4 FCS (L, η, λ)

1: **Input:** data

2:

3: $\mathcal{D}_{\mathcal{S}} = (\boldsymbol{X}_{\mathcal{S}}, \boldsymbol{Y}_{\mathcal{S}}); \mathcal{D}_{\mathcal{T}} = (\boldsymbol{X}_{\mathcal{T}}, , \boldsymbol{Y}_{\mathcal{T}}), \mathcal{D}'_{\mathcal{T}} = (\boldsymbol{X}'_{\mathcal{T}}),$

4:

5: **Pre-training**: initialization

6:

7: $\quad \hat{\theta}_0 = (\boldsymbol{w}_0, \boldsymbol{v}_0) = \arg\min_\theta 1/N \sum_{i=1}^{N} \mathcal{L}(f_\theta(\boldsymbol{x}_i^s), \boldsymbol{y}_i^s)$

8:

9: **for** $itr = 1, \ldots, ITR$ **do**

10:

11: $\quad$ **Update** encoder parameters using:

12:

13: $\quad\quad \hat{\boldsymbol{v}}, \hat{\boldsymbol{u}} = \lambda D(\phi_{\boldsymbol{v}}(p_{\mathcal{S}}(\boldsymbol{X}_{\mathcal{S}})), \psi_{\boldsymbol{u}}(p_{\mathcal{T}}(\boldsymbol{X}_{\mathcal{T}})))$

14:

15: $\quad\quad\quad + \eta \sum_j D(\phi_{\boldsymbol{v}}(p_{\mathcal{S}}(\boldsymbol{X}_{\mathcal{S}})|C_j), \psi_{\boldsymbol{v}}(p_{\mathcal{SL}}(\boldsymbol{X}'_{\mathcal{T}})|C_j))$

16:

17: $\quad$ **Update** entire parameters:

18:

19: $\quad\quad \hat{\boldsymbol{v}}, \hat{\boldsymbol{u}}, \hat{\boldsymbol{w}} = \arg\min_{\boldsymbol{w}, \boldsymbol{v}, \boldsymbol{u}} 1/N \sum_{i=1}^{N} \mathcal{L}(h_{\boldsymbol{w}}(\phi_{\boldsymbol{v}}(\boldsymbol{x}_i^s)), \boldsymbol{y}_i^s)$

20:

21: $\quad\quad\quad + 1/O \sum_{i=1}^{O} \mathcal{L}(h_{\boldsymbol{w}}(\psi_{\boldsymbol{u}}(\boldsymbol{x}_i^{'t})), \boldsymbol{y}_i^{'t})$

22:

23: **end for**

---

in our framework. We use similar notions. The hypothesis class is the set of all model $h_w(\cdot)$ that are parameterized by θ, and the goal is to select the best model from the hypothesis class. For any member of this hypothesis class, the true risk on the source domain is denoted by $e_{\mathcal{S}}$ and the true risk on the target domain with $e_{\mathcal{T}}$. Analogously, $\hat{\mu}_{\mathcal{S}} = \frac{1}{N} \sum_{n=1}^{N} \delta(\boldsymbol{x}_n^s)$ denote the empirical marginal source distribution, which is computed using the training samples and $\hat{\mu}_{\mathcal{T}} = \frac{1}{M} \sum_{m=1}^{M} \delta(\boldsymbol{x}_m^t)$ similarly denotes the empirical target distribution. In this setting, conditioned on availability of labeled data on both domains, we can train a model jointly on both distributions. Let h_{w^*} denote such an ideal model that minimizes the combined source and target risks $e_{\mathcal{C}}(w^*)$:

$$w^* = \arg\min_w e_{\mathcal{C}}(w) = \arg\min_w \{e_{\mathcal{S}} + e_{\mathcal{T}}\} . \tag{5.4}$$

This term is small if the hypothesis class is complex enough and given sufficient labeled target domain data, the joint model can be trained such that it generalizes well on both domains. This term is to measure an upper bound for the target risk. For self-containment of this chapter, we reiterate the following theorem by Redko et al. [178] that we use to analyze our algorithm.

Theorem 5.5.1. *Under the assumptions described above for UDA, then for any $d' > d$ and $\zeta < \sqrt{2}$, there exists a constant number N_0 depending on d' such that for any $\xi > 0$*

and $\min(N, M) \geq \max(\xi^{-(d'+2),1})$ *with probability at least* $1 - \xi$ *for all* h_w, *the following holds:*

$$e_{\mathcal{T}} \leq e_{\mathcal{S}} + W(\hat{\mu}_{\mathcal{T}}, \hat{\mu}_{\mathcal{S}}) + e_{\mathcal{C}}(w^*) + \sqrt{(2\log(\frac{1}{\xi})/\zeta)}(\sqrt{\frac{1}{N}} + \sqrt{\frac{1}{M}}) \ . \quad (5.5)$$

Note that although we use SWD in our approach, it has been theoretically demonstrated that SWD is a good approximation for computing the Wasserstein distance [22]:

$$SW_2(p_X, p_Y) \leq W_2(p_X, p_Y) \leq \alpha SW_2^{\beta}(p_X, p_Y) \ , \quad (5.6)$$

where α *is a constant and* $\beta = (2(d+1))^{-1}$ *(see [215] for more details). For this reasons, minimizing the SWD metric enforces minimizing WD.*

The proof for Theorem 5.5.1 is based on the fact that the Wasserstein distance between a distribution μ and its empirical approximation $\hat{\mu}$ using N identically drawn samples can be made small as desired given existence of large enough number of samples N [178]. More specifically, in the setting of Theorem 5.5.1, we have:

$$W(\mu, \hat{\mu}) \leq \sqrt{(2\log(\frac{1}{\xi})/\zeta)}\sqrt{\frac{1}{N}} \ . \quad (5.7)$$

We need this property for our analysis. Additionally, we consider bounded loss functions and consider the loss function is normalized by its upper bound. Interested reader may refer to Redko et al. [178] for more details of the derivation of this property.

As we discussed in the previous chapter, it is important to enforce the third term in the right-hand side of Eq. (5.5) to become small only if such a joint model exists, i.e., the domains are matched class-conditionally. However, as opposed to the previous chapter since the domain gap is considerable, and the domains are non-homogeneous, we cannot use pseudo-labels to tackle these challenges. Instead, the few target labeled data points are used to minimize the joint model. Building upon the above result, we provide the following lemma for our algorithm.

Lemma 5.5.1. *Consider we use the target dataset labeled data in a semi-supervised domain adaptation scenario in the algorithm 4. Then, the following inequality for the target true risk holds:*

$$e_{\mathcal{T}} \leq e_{\mathcal{S}} + W(\hat{\mu}_{\mathcal{S}}, \hat{\mu}_{\mathcal{PL}}) + \hat{e}_{\mathcal{C}'}(w^*) + \sqrt{(2\log(\frac{1}{\xi})/\zeta)}(2\sqrt{\frac{1}{N}} + \sqrt{\frac{1}{M}} + \sqrt{\frac{1}{O}}) \ , \quad (5.8)$$

where $\hat{e}_{\mathcal{C}'}(w^*)$ *denote the empirical risk of the optimally joint model* h_{w^*} *on both the source domain and the target labeled data points.*

Proof: We use μ_{TS} to denote the combined distribution of both domains. The model parameter w^* is trained for this distribution using ERM on the joint empirical distribution formed by the labeled data points for the both source and target domains: $\hat{\mu}_{TS} = \frac{1}{N}\sum_{n=1}^{N} \delta(\boldsymbol{x}_n^s) + \frac{1}{O}\sum_{n=1}^{O} \delta(\boldsymbol{x}_n'^t)$. We note that given this definition and considering the corresponding joint empirical distribution, $p_{ST}(\boldsymbol{x}, \boldsymbol{y})$, it is easy to show that

$e_{\hat{T}S} = \hat{e}_{\mathcal{C}'}(w^*)$. In other words, we can denote the empirical risk for the model as the true risk for the empirical distribution.

$$e_{\mathcal{C}'}(w^*) = \hat{e}_{\mathcal{C}'}(w^*) + \left(e_{\mathcal{C}'}(w^*) - \hat{e}_{\mathcal{C}'}(w^*)\right) \le \hat{e}_{\mathcal{C}'}(w^*) + W(\mu_{TS}, \hat{\mu}_{TS})$$

$$\le \hat{e}_{\mathcal{C}'}(w^*)) + \sqrt{\left(2\log(\frac{1}{\xi})/\zeta\right)}\left(\sqrt{\frac{1}{N}} + \sqrt{\frac{1}{O}}\right) .$$

$$(5.9)$$

We have used the definition of expectation and the Cauchy-Schwarz inequality to deduce the first inequality in Eq. (5.9). We have also used the above mentioned property of the Wasserstein distance in Eq. (5.7) to deduce the second inequality. A combining Eq. (5.9) and Eq. (5.5) yields the desired result, as stated in the Lemma ■

Lemma 5.5.1 explains that our algorithm is effective because it minimizes an upper bound of the risk in the SAR domain. According to Lemma 5.5.1, the most important samples also are the few labeled samples in the target domain as the corresponding term is dominant among the constant terms in Eq. (5.8) (note $O \ll M$ and $O \ll N$). This accords with our intuition. Since these samples are important to circumvent the class matching challenge across the two domains, they carry more important information compared to the unlabeled data.

5.6 EXPERIMENTAL VALIDATION

In this section, we validate our approach empirically. We tested our method in the area of maritime domain awareness on SAR ship detection problem.

5.6.1 Ship Detection in SAR Domain

We tested our approach in the binary problem of ship detection using SAR imaging [219]. This problem arises within maritime domain awareness (MDA) where the goal is monitoring the ocean continually to decipher maritime activities that could impact the safety of the environment. Detecting ships is important in this application as the majority of important activities that are important are related to ships and their movements. Traditionally, planes and patrol vessels are used for monitoring, but these methods are effective only for limited areas and time periods. As the regulated area expands and monitoring period becomes extended, these methods become time consuming and inefficient. To circumvent these limitations, it is essential that we make this process automatic such that it requires minimal human intervention. Satellite imaging is highly effective to reach this goal because large areas of the ocean can be monitored. The generated satellite images can be processed using image processing and machine learning techniques automatically. Satellite imaging has been performed using satellite with both EO and SAR imaging devices. However, only SAR imaging allows continual monitoring during a broad range of weather conditions and during the night. This property is important because illegal activities likely to happen during the night and during occluded weather, human errors are likely to occur. For these reasons, SAR imaging is very important in this area, and hence, we can test our approach on this problem.

When satellite imaging is used, a huge amount of data is generated. However, a large portion of data is not informative because a considerable portion of images contains only the surface of the ocean with no important object of interest or potentially land areas adjacent to the sea. In order to make the monitoring process efficient, classic image processing techniques are used to determine regions of interest in aerial SAR images. A region of interest is a limited surface area, where the existence of a ship is probable. First, land areas are removed, and then ships, ship-like, and ocean regions are identified and then extracted as square image patches. These image patches are then fed into a classification algorithm to determine whether the region corresponds to a ship or not. If a ship detected with suspicious movement activity, then regulations can be enforced.

The dataset that we have used in our experiments is obtained from aerial SAR images of the South African Exclusive Economic Zone [219]. The dataset is preprocessed into 51×51 pixels sub-images. We define a binary classification problem, where each image instance is either contains ships (positive data points), or no-ship (negative data points). The dataset contains 1436 positive examples and 1436 negative sub-images. The labels are provided by experts. We recast the problem as a few-shot learning problem by assuming that only a few of the data points are labeled. To solve this problem using knowledge transfer within our framework, we use the "EO Ships in Satellite Imagery" dataset [78]. The dataset is prepared to automate monitoring port activity levels and supply chain analysis and contains EO images extracted from Planet satellite imagery over the San Francisco Bay area with 4000 RGB 80×80 images. Again, each instance is either a ship image (a positive data point) or no-ship (a negative data point). The dataset is split evenly into positive and negative samples. Instances from both datasets are visualized in Figure 5.1 (left). Note that since these datasets are from extensively different regions, there are no correspondences between images.

5.6.2 Methodology

We consider a deep CNN with two layers of convolutional 3×3 filters as SAR encoder. We use N_F and $2N_F$ filters in these layers, respectively, where N_F is a parameter to be determined. We have used both maxpool and batch normalization layers in these convolutional layers. These layers are used as the SAR encoder sub-network in our framework, ϕ. We have used a similar structure for EO domain encoder, ψ, with the exception of using a CNN with three convolutional layers. The reason is that the EO dataset seems to have more details, and a more complex model can learn information content better. The third convolutional layer has $2N_F$ filters as well. The convolutional layers are followed by a flattening layer and a subsequent shared dense layer as the embedding space with dimension f, which can be tuned as a parameter. After the embedding space layer, we have used a shallow two-layer classifier based on Eq. (5.3). We used TensorFlow for implementation and Adam optimizer [99].

For comparison purpose, we compared our results against the following learning settings:

1) Supervised training on the SAR domain (ST): we just trained a network directly in the SAR domain using the few labeled SAR data points to generate a lower-bound for our approach to demonstrate that knowledge transfer is effective. This approach is also a lower-bound because unlabeled SAR data points and their information content are discarded.

2) Direct transfer (DT): we just directly used the network that is trained on EO data

directly in the SAR domain. In order to do this end, we resized the EO domain to 51×51 pixels so we can use the same shared encoder networks for both domains. As a result, potentially helpful details may be lost. This can be served as a second lower-bound to demonstrate that we can benefit from unlabeled SAR data.

3) Fine-tuning (FT): we used the no transfer network from the previous method, and fine-tuned the network using the few available SAR data points. As discussed before in the "Related Work" section, this is the main strategy that several prior works have used in the literature to transfer knowledge from the EO to the SAR domain and is served to compare against previous methods that use knowledge transfer. The major benefit of our approach is using the information that can be obtained from the unlabeled SAR data points. For this reason, the performance of FT can be served as an ablation study to demonstrate that helpful information is encoded in the unlabeled data.

In our experiments, we used a 90/10 % random split for training the model and testing performance. For each experiment, we report the performance on the SAR testing split to compare the methods. We use the classification accuracy rate to measure performance, and whenever necessary, we used cross-validation to tune the hyper parameters. We have repeated each experiment 20 times and have reported the average and the standard error bound to demonstrate statistical significance in the experiments.

In order to find the optimal parameters for the network structure, we used cross-validation. We first performed a set of experiments to empirically study the effect of dimension size (f) of the embedding space on the performance of our algorithm. Figure 5.2a presents performance on SAR testing set versus dimension of the embedding space when ten SAR labeled data per class is used for training. The solid line denotes the average performance over ten trials, and the shaded region denotes the standard error deviation. We observe that the performance is quite stable when the embedding space dimension changes. This result suggests that because convolutional layers are served to reduce the dimension of input data, if the learned embedding space is discriminative for the source domain, then our method can successfully match the target domain distribution to the source distribution in the embedding. We conclude that for computational efficiency, it is better to select the embedding dimension to be as small as possible. We conclude from Figure 5.2a that increasing the dimension beyond eight is not helpful. For this reason, we set the dimension of the embedding to be eight for the rest of our experiments in this chapter. We performed a similar experiment to investigate the effect of the number of filters N_F on performance. Figure 5.2b presents performance on SAR testing set versus this parameter. We conclude from Figure 5.2b that $N_F = 16$ is a good choice as using more filters in not helpful. We did not use a smaller value for N_F to avoid overfitting when the number of labeled data is less than ten.

5.6.3 Results

Figure 5.3 presents the performance results on the data test split for our method along with the three mentioned methods above, versus the number of labeled data points per class that has been used for the SAR domain. For each curve, the solid line denotes the average performance over all ten trials, and the shaded region denotes the standard error deviation. These results accord with intuition. It can be seen that direct transfer is the least effective

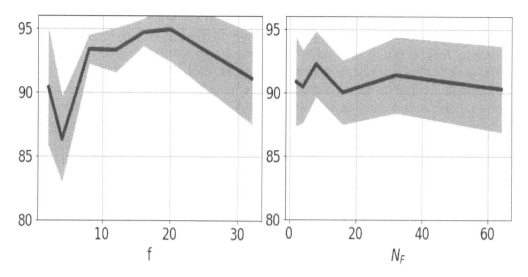

(a) Performance vs Embedding Dimension   (b) Performance vs Number of Filters

Figure 5.2 The SAR test performance versus the dimension of the embedding space and the number of filters.

O	1	2	3	4	5	6	7
Supervised Training	58.5	74.0	79.2	84.1	85.2	84.9	87.2
Fine Tuning	75.5	75.6	73.5	85.5	87.6	84.2	88.5
Direct Transfer	71.5	67.6	71.4	68.5	71.4	71.0	73.1
Ours	86.3	86.3	82.8	94.2	87.8	96.0	91.1

Table 5.1 Comparison results for the SAR test performance.

method as it uses no information from the second domain. Supervised training on the SAR domain is not effective in few-shot learning regime, i.e., its performance is close to chance. Direct transfer method boosts the performance of supervised training in the one-shot regime but after 2–3 labeled samples per class, as expected supervised training overtakes direct transfer. This is the consequence of using more target task data. In other words, direct transfer only helps to test the network on a better initial point compared to the random initialization. Fine-tuning can improve the direct performance, but the only few-shot regime, and beyond few-shot learning regime, the performance is similar to supervised training. In comparison, our method outperforms these methods as we have benefited from SAR unlabeled data points. For a more clear quantitative comparison, we have presented data in Figure 5.3 in Table 5.1 for different number of labeled SAR data points per class, O. It is also important to note that in the presence of enough labeled data in the target domain, supervised training would outperform our method because the network is trained using merely the target domain data.

For having better intuition, Figure 5.4 denotes the Umap visualization [146] of the EO and SAR data points in the learned embedding as the output of the feature extractor encoders. Each point denotes on a data point in the embedding which has been mapped to 2D plane

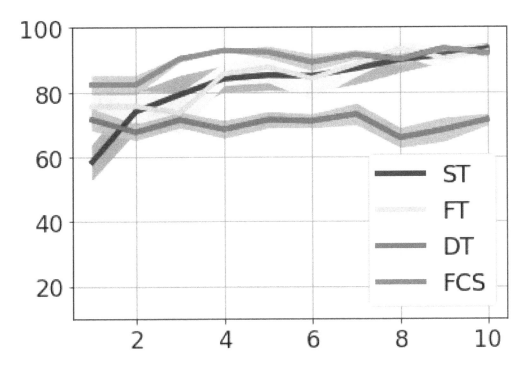

Figure 5.3 The SAR test performance versus the number of labeled data per class. The shaded region denotes the standard error deviation.

for visualization. In this figure, we have used five labeled data points per class in the SAR domain. In Figure 5.4, each color corresponds to one of the classes. In Figures 5.4a and 5.4b, we have used real labels for visualization, and in Figures 5.4c and 5.4d, we have used the predicted labels by networks trained using our method for visualization. In Figure 5.4, the points with brighter red and darker blue colors are the SAR labeled data points that have been used in training. By comparing the top row with the bottom row, we see that the embedding is discriminative for both domains. Additionally, by comparing the left column with the right column, we see that the domain distributions are matched in the embedding class-conditionally, suggesting our framework formulated is Eq. (5.3) is effective. This result suggests that learning an invariant embedding space can be served as a helpful strategy for transferring knowledge even when the two domains are not homogeneous. Additionally, we see that labeled data points are important to determine the boundary between two classes, which suggests that why part of one of the classes (blue) is predicted mistakenly. This observation suggests that the boundary between classes depends on the labeled target data as the network is certain about the labels of these data points, and they are matched to the right source class.

We also performed an experiment to serve as an ablation study for our framework. Our previous experiments demonstrate that the first three terms in Eq. (5.3) are all important for successful knowledge transfer. We explained that the fourth term is important for class-conditional alignment. We solved Eq. (5.3) without considering the fourth term to study its effect. We have presented the Umap visualization [146] of the datasets in the embedding

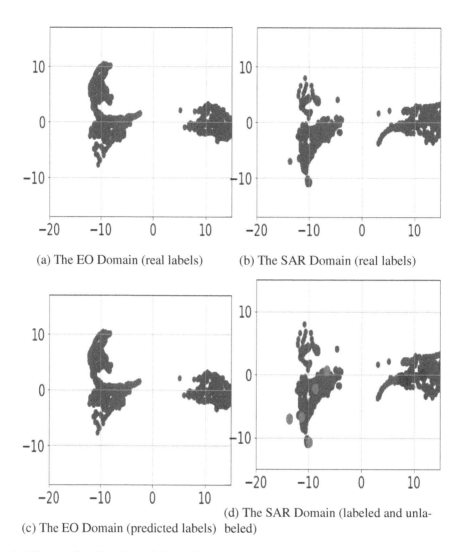

(a) The EO Domain (real labels) (b) The SAR Domain (real labels)

(c) The EO Domain (predicted labels) (d) The SAR Domain (labeled and unlabeled)

Figure 5.4 Umap visualization of the EO versus the SAR dataset in the shared embedding space (best viewed in color).

space for a particular experiment in Figure 5.5. We observe that as expected, the embedding is discriminative for EO dataset and predicted labels are close to the real data labels as the classes are separable. However, despite following a similar marginal distribution in the embedding space, the formed SAR clusters are not class-specific. We can see that in each cluster, we have data points from both classes, and as a result, the SAR classification rate is poor. This result demonstrates that all the terms in Eq. (5.3) are important for the success of our algorithm. We highlight that Figure 5.5 visualizes results of a particular experiment. Note that we observed in some experiments, the classes were matched, even when no labeled target data was used. However, these observations show that the method is not stable. Using the few-labeled data helps to stabilize the algorithm.

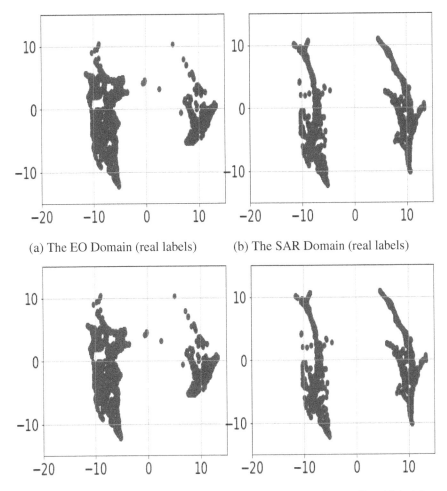

(a) The EO Domain (real labels)   (b) The SAR Domain (real labels)

(c) The EO Domain (predicted labels) (d) The SAR Domain (predicted labels)

Figure 5.5 Umap visualization of the EO versus the SAR dataset for ablation study (best viewed in color).

5.7 CONCLUSIONS

We considered the problem of SAR image classification in the label-scarce regime. We developed an algorithm for training deep neural networks when only few-labeled SAR samples are available. The core idea was to transfer knowledge from a related EO domain problem with sufficient labeled data to tackle the problem of label-scarcity. Due to non-homogeneity of the two domains, two coupled deep encoders were trained to map the data samples from both domains to a shared embedding space, modeled as the output space of the encoders, such that the distributions of the domains are matched. We demonstrated theoretically and empirically effectiveness for the problem of SAR ship classification. It is important to note that despite focusing on EO-to-SAR knowledge transfer, our framework can be applied on a broader range of semi-supervised domain adaptation problems.

The focus in Part I has been on cross-domain knowledge transfer. We considered knowledge transfer scenarios in which transfer is usually unidirectional from a source domain to a target domain, where either labeled data is scarce or obtaining labeled data is expensive. In the next part of this book, we focus on cross-task knowledge transfer, where a group of related tasks is defined in a single domain. Important learning scenarios, including multi-task learning and lifelong machine learning, focus on tackling challenges of cross-task knowledge transfer. Cross-task knowledge transfer can be more challenging because the data for all the tasks might not be accessible simultaneously. However, similar to cross-domain knowledge transfer, we demonstrate that the idea transfer knowledge transfer across several related tasks can be used to couple the tasks in an embedding space, where the task relations are captured.

II

Cross-Task Knowledge Transfer

In Part I of the book, we focused on transferring knowledge across different manifestations of the same ML problem across different domains. The major challenge was to address labeled data scarcity in one of the domains or in some of the classes. In the second part of this book, we focus on **cross-task knowledge transfer**. Sharing information across different ML problems that are defined in the same domain is another area in which we can benefit from knowledge transfer. In this setting, each problem is usually called a *task*, and the goal is to improve learning performance in terms of speed or prediction accuracy against learning the tasks in isolation. This can be done by identifying similarities between the tasks and using them to transfer knowledge. Knowledge transfer between tasks can improve the performance of learned models by learning the inter-task relationships to identify the relevant knowledge to transfer. These inter-task relationships are typically estimated based on training data for each task. When the tasks can be learned simultaneously, the setting is called multi-task learning, while lifelong learning deals with sequential task learning. In a multi-task learning setting, the direction of knowledge transfer is bilateral across any pair of tasks. In contrast, knowledge transfer is uni-directional in a sequential learning setting, where previous experiences are used to learn the current task more efficiently. In Part II, we focus on addressing the challenges of these learning settings by coupling the tasks in a shared embedding space that is shared across the tasks. In chapter 6, we develop a method for zero-shot learning in a sequential learning setting. In chapter 7, we address the challenge of *catastrophic forgetting* for this setting. Chapter 8 focuses on continual concept learning, which can be considered as an extension for homogeneous domain adaptation to a continual learning setting. We will show that the same idea of a shared embedding which we used in Part I, can be used to address the challenges of these learning settings.

CHAPTER 6

Lifelong Zero-Shot Learning Using High-Level Task Descriptors

In this chapter, we focus on addressing zero-shot learning in a lifelong learning scenario. ZSL in this chapter is different from the learning setting that we addressed in chapter 3. In chapter 3, the goal was to learn classes with no labeled data in a multiclass classification problem via transferring knowledge from seen classes with labeled data. In this chapter, our goal is to learn a task with no data via transferring knowledge from other similar tasks that have been learned before and for which labeled data is accessible. These tasks are learned sequentially in a *lifelong machine learning* lifelong machine learning setting. Estimating the inter-task relationships using training data for each task is inefficient in lifelong learning settings as the goal is to learn each consecutive task rapidly from as little data as possible. To reduce this burden, we develop a lifelong learning method based on coupled dictionary learning that utilizes high-level task descriptions to model inter-task relationships. Our idea is similar to chapter 2, but the goal is to couple the space of the tasks descriptors and the task data through these two dictionaries.

Figure 6.1 presents a high-level description of our idea. In this figure, we have two sources of information about each task: task data and high-level descriptors. Our idea is to embed the optimal parameters for the tasks and the corresponding high-level descriptions in the embedding space such that we can map the high-level descriptions to the optimal task parameters. This mapping is learned using the past learned tasks for which we have both data and high-level descriptors. By doing so, an optimal parameter for a particular task can be learned using the high-level descriptions through the shared embedding space. We show that using task descriptors improves the performance of the learned task policies, providing both theoretical justifications for the benefit, and empirical demonstration of the improvement across a variety of learning problems. Given only the descriptor for a new task, the lifelong learner is also able to accurately predict a model for the new task through zero-shot learning using the coupled dictionary, eliminating the need to gather training data before addressing the task.

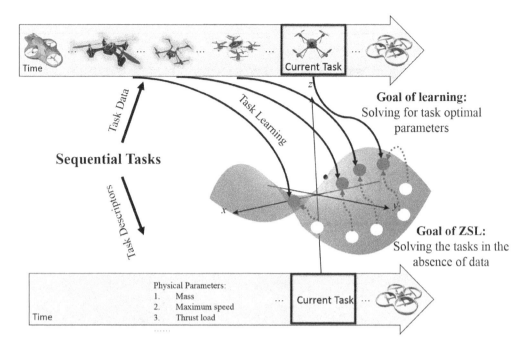

Figure 6.1 Zero-shot learning of sequential tasks using task descriptors through an embedding space: the red circles in the embedding space denote representations of optimal task parameters, and the yellow circles indicate representations of the high-level descriptions for the tasks in the embedding space. If we learn a mapping from the task descriptions to the optimal parameters, denoted by dotted blue arrows, tasks can be learned with no data. It suffices to embed the task descriptions and then use the mapping to find the optimal tasks parameter.

6.1 OVERVIEW

Transfer learning (TL) and multi-task learning (MTL) methods reduce the amount of experience needed to train individual task models by reusing knowledge from other related tasks. This transferred knowledge can improve the training speed and model performance, as compared to learning the tasks in isolation following the classical machine learning pipeline. TL and MTL techniques typically select the relevant knowledge to transfer by modeling inter-task relationships using a shared representation, based on training data for each task [13, 8, 19, 141]. Despite benefits over single-task learning, this process requires sufficient training data for each task to identify these relationships before knowledge transfer can succeed and improve generalization performance. This need for data is especially problematic in learning systems that are expected to rapidly learn to handle new tasks during real-time interaction with the environment: when faced with a new task, the learner would first need to gather data on the new task before bootstrapping a model via transfer, consequently delaying how quickly the learner could address the new task.

Consider instead the human ability to bootstrap a model for a new task rapidly, given *only* a *high-level task description*—before obtaining experience on the actual task. For example, viewing only the image on the box of a new IKEA chair, we can immediately identify previous related assembly tasks and begin formulating a plan to assemble the chair. Additionally, after assembling multiple IKEA chairs, assembling new products become meaningfully easier. In the same manner, an experienced inverted pole balancing agent may be able to predict the controller for a new pole given its mass and length, prior to interacting with the physical system. These examples suggest that an agent could similarly use high-level task information to bootstrap a model for a new task to learn it more efficiently, conditioned on gaining prior experience.

Inspired by this idea, we explore the use of high-level task descriptions to improve knowledge transfer between multiple machine learning tasks, belonging to a single domain. We focus on lifelong learning scenarios [243, 211], in which multiple tasks arrive consecutively, and the goal is to learn each new task by building upon previous knowledge rapidly. Our approach for integrating task descriptors into lifelong machine learning is general, as demonstrated on applications to reinforcement learning, regression, and classification problems. In reinforcement learning settings, our idea can be compared with the universal value function approximation algorithm by Schaul et al. [217] in that the goal is to generalize the learned knowledge to other unexplored scenarios. Schaul et al. [217] incorporate the goals of an RL learner into the value function so as to allow for generalization over unexplored goals. In contrast, our goal is to learn a mapping from high-level task descriptions into the optimal task parameters that are generally learned using data to learn future tasks without exploration using solely high-level task descriptions. Results of this chapter have been presented in Refs. [193, 94].

Our algorithm, Task Descriptors for Lifelong Learning (TaDeLL), encodes task descriptions as feature vectors that identify each task, treating these descriptors as side information in addition to training data on the individual tasks. The idea of using task features for knowledge transfer has been explored previously by Bonilla et al. [21] in an offline batch MTL setting. Note that "batch learning" in this context refers to offline learning when all tasks are available before processing and is not related to the notion of the batch in the first-order optimization. A similar idea has been used more recently by Sinapov et al. [228] in a computationally expensive method for estimating transfer relationships between pairs of tasks. Svetlik et al. [238] also use task descriptors to generate a curriculum that improves the learning performance in the target task by learning the optimal order in which tasks should be learned. In comparison, our approach operates online over consecutive tasks with the assumption that the agent does not control the order in which tasks are learned.

We use *coupled dictionary learning* to model the inter-task relationships between the task descriptions and the individual task policies in lifelong learning. This can be seen as associating task descriptions with task data across these two different feature spaces. The coupled dictionary enforces the notion that tasks with similar descriptions should have similar policies, but still allows dictionary elements the freedom to accurately represent the different task policies. We connect the coupled dictionaries to the PAC-learning framework, providing theoretical justification for why the task descriptors improve performance. We also demonstrate this improvement empirically.

In addition to improving the task models, we show that the task descriptors enable the learner to accurately predict the policies for unseen tasks given only their description—this process of learning without data on "future tasks" is known as *zero-shot learning*. This capability is particularly important in the online setting of lifelong learning. It enables the system to accurately predict policies for new tasks through transfer from past tasks with data, without requiring the system to pause to gather training data on each future tasks. In particular, it can speed up learning reinforcement learning tasks, where generally learning speed is slow.

Specifically, we provide the following contributions:

● We develop a general mechanism based on **coupled dictionary learning** to incorporate task descriptors into knowledge transfer algorithms that use a factorized representation of the learned knowledge to facilitate transfer [110, 141, 211, 107].

● Using this mechanism, we develop **two algorithms**, for lifelong learning (TaDeLL) and multi-task learning (TaDeMTL), that incorporate task descriptors to improve learning performance. These algorithms are general and apply to scenarios involving classification, regression, and reinforcement learning tasks.

● Most critically, we show how these algorithms can achieve **zero-shot transfer** to bootstrap a model for a novel task, given only the high-level task descriptor.

● We provide **theoretical justification** for the benefit of using task descriptors in lifelong learning and MTL, building on the PAC-learnability of the framework.

● Finally, we demonstrate the empirical effectiveness of TaDeLL and TaDeMTL on **reinforcement learning** scenarios involving the control of dynamical systems, and on prediction tasks in **classification and regression** settings, showing the generality of our approach.

6.2 RELATED WORK

Multi-task learning (MTL) [29] methods often model the relationships between tasks to identify similarities between their datasets or underlying models. There are many different approaches for modeling these task relationships. Bayesian approaches take a variety of forms, making use of common priors [260, 117], using regularization terms that couple task parameters [59, 294], and finding mixtures of experts that can be shared across tasks [11].

Where Bayesian MTL methods aim to find an appropriate bias to share among all task models, transformation methods seek to make one dataset look like another, often in a transfer learning setting. This can be accomplished with distribution matching [19], inter-task mapping [241], or manifold alignment techniques [254, 77].

Both the Bayesian strategy of discovering biases and the shared spaces often used in transformation techniques are implicitly connected to methods that learn shared knowledge representations for MTL. For example, the original MTL framework developed by Caruana [29] and later variations [13] capture task relationships by sharing hidden nodes in neural networks that are trained on multiple tasks. Related work in dictionary learning techniques for MTL [141, 110] factorizes the learned models into a shared latent dictionary over the model space to facilitate transfer. Individual task models are then captured as sparse representations over this dictionary; the task relationships are captured in these sparse codes which are used to reconstruct optimal parameters individual tasks [175, 44].

The Efficient Lifelong Learning Algorithm (ELLA) framework [211] used this same approach of a shared latent dictionary, trained online, to facilitate transfer as tasks arrive consecutively. The ELLA framework was first created for regression and classification [211], and later developed for policy gradient reinforcement learning (PG-ELLA) [7]. Other approaches that extend MTL to online settings also exist [30]. Saha et al. [212] use a task interaction matrix to model task relations online, and Dekel et al. [49] propose a shared global loss function that can be minimized as tasks arrive.

However, *all* these methods use task data to characterize the task relationships—this explicitly requires training on the data from each task in order to perform transfer. Our goal is to adapt an established lifelong learning approach and develop a framework which uses task descriptions to improve performance and allows for zero-shot learning. Instead of relying solely on the tasks' training data, several works have explored the use of high-level task descriptors to model the inter-task relationships in MTL and transfer learning settings. Task descriptors have been used in combination with neural networks [11] to define a task-specific prior and to control the gating network between individual task clusters. Bonilla et al. [21] explore similar techniques for multi-task kernel machines, using task features in combination with the data for a gating network over individual task experts to augment the original task training data. These papers focus on multi-task classification and regression in batch settings where the system has access to the data and features for all tasks, in contrast to our study of task descriptors for lifelong learning over consecutive tasks. We use coupled dictionary learning to link the task description space with the task's parameter space. This idea was originally used in image processing [275] and was recently explored in the machine learning literature [270]. The core idea is that two feature spaces can be linked through two dictionaries, which are coupled by a joint-sparse representation.

In the work most similar to our problem setting, Sinapov et al. [228] use task descriptors to estimate the transferability between each pair of tasks for transfer learning . Given the descriptor for a new task, they identify the source task with the highest predicted transferability and use that source task for a warm start in reinforcement learning (RL). Though effective, their approach is computationally expensive, since they estimate the transferability for every task pair through repeated simulation, which grows quadratically as the number of tasks increase. Their evaluation is also limited to a transfer learning setting, and they do not consider the effects of transfer over consecutive tasks or updates to the transferability model, as we do in the lifelong setting.

Our work is also related to the notion of zero-shot learning that was addressed in chapter 3. Because ZSL in multiclass classification setting also seeks to successfully label out-of- distribution examples, often through means of learning an underlying representation that extends to new tasks and using outside information that appropriately maps to the latent space [162, 230]. For example, the Simple Zero-Shot method by Romera-Paredes and Torr [182] also uses task descriptions. Their method learns a multi-class linear model, and factorizes the linear model parameters, assuming the descriptors are coefficients over a latent basis to reconstruct the models. Our approach assumes a more flexible relationship: that both the model parameters and task descriptors can be reconstructed from separate latent bases that are coupled together through their coefficients. In comparison to our lifelong learning approach, the Simple Zero-Shot method operates in an offline multi-class setting.

6.3 BACKGROUND

Our methods in the previous chapters mostly can address supervised learning setting. In contrast, our proposed framework for lifelong learning with task descriptors supports both supervised learning (classification and regression) and reinforcement learning settings. We briefly review these learning paradigms to demonstrate that despite major differences, reinforcement learning tasks can be formulated similar to supervised learning tasks.

6.3.1 supervised learning

Consider a standard batch supervised learning setting. Let $x \in \mathcal{X} \subseteq \mathbb{R}^d$ be a d-dimensional vector representing a single data instance with a corresponding label $y \in \mathcal{Y}$. Given a set of n sample observations $X = \{x_1, x_2, \ldots, x_n\}$ with corresponding labels $y = \{y_1, y_2, \ldots, y_n\}$, the goal of supervised learning is to learn a function $f_\theta : \mathcal{X} \mapsto \mathcal{Y}$ that labels inputs X with their outputs y and generalizes well to unseen observations.

In **regression** tasks, the labels are assumed to be real-valued (i.e., $\mathcal{Y} = \mathbb{R}$). In **classification** tasks, the labels are a set of discrete classes; for example, in binary classification, $\mathcal{Y} = \{+1, -1\}$. We assume that the learned model for both paradigms f_θ can be parameterized by a vector θ. The model is then trained to minimize the average loss over the training data between the model's predictions and the given target labels:

$$\arg\min_{\theta} \frac{1}{n} \sum_{i=1}^{n} \mathcal{L}\big(f(x_i, \theta), y_i\big) + \mathcal{R}(f_\theta) \ ,$$

where $\mathcal{L}(\cdot)$ is generally assumed to be a convex metric, and $\mathcal{R}(\cdot)$ regularizes the learned model. The form of the model f, loss function $\mathcal{L}(\cdot)$, and the regularization method varies between learning methods. This formulation encompasses a number of parametric learning methods, including linear regression and logistic regression.

6.3.2 Reinforcement Learning

A reinforcement learning (RL) agent selects sequential actions in an environment to maximize its expected return. An RL task is typically formulated as a Markov Decision Process (MDP) $\langle \mathcal{X}, \mathcal{A}, P, R, \gamma \rangle$, where $\mathcal{X}$ is the set of states, and $\mathcal{A}$ is the set of actions that the agent may execute, $P : \mathcal{X} \times \mathcal{A} \times \mathcal{X} \to [0, 1]$ is the state transition probability describing the systems dynamics, $R : \mathcal{X} \times \mathcal{A} \times \mathcal{X} \to \mathbb{R}$ is the reward function, and $\gamma \in [0, 1)$ is the discount assigned to rewards over time. At time step h, the agent is in state $x_h \in \mathcal{X}$ and chooses an action $a \in \mathcal{A}$ according to policy $\pi : \mathcal{X} \times \mathcal{A} \mapsto [0, 1]$, which is represented as a function defined by a vector of control parameters $\theta \in \mathbb{R}^d$. The agents then receive reward r_h according to R and transitions to state x_{h+1} according to P. This sequence of states, actions, and rewards is given as a trajectory $\tau = \{(x_1, a_1, r_1), \ldots, (x_H, a_H, r_H)\}$ over a horizon H. The goal of RL is to find the optimal policy π^* with parameters θ^* that maximizes the expected reward. However, learning an individual task still requires numerous trajectories, motivating the use of transfer to reduce the number of interactions with the environment.

Policy Gradient (PG) methods [237], which we employ as our base learner for RL tasks, are a class of RL algorithms that are effective for solving high dimensional problems with continuous state and action spaces, such as robotic control [172]. PG methods are appealing for their ability to handle continuous state and action spaces, as well as their ability to scale well to high dimensions. The goal of PG is to optimize the expected average return: $\mathcal{J}(\boldsymbol{\theta}) = E\left[\frac{1}{H}\sum_{h=1}^{H} r_h\right] = \int_{\mathbb{T}} p_{\boldsymbol{\theta}}(\boldsymbol{\tau})\mathfrak{R}(\boldsymbol{\tau})d\boldsymbol{\tau}$, where $\mathbb{T}$ is the set of all possible trajectories, the average reward on trajectory $\boldsymbol{\tau}$ is given by $\mathfrak{R}(\boldsymbol{\tau}) = \frac{1}{H}\sum_{h=1}^{H} r_h$, and $p_{\boldsymbol{\theta}}(\boldsymbol{\tau}) = P_0(\boldsymbol{x}_1)\prod_{h=1}^{H} p(\boldsymbol{x}_{h+1} \mid \boldsymbol{x}_h, \boldsymbol{a}_h)\,\pi(\boldsymbol{a}_h \mid \boldsymbol{x}_h)$ is the probability of $\boldsymbol{\tau}$ under an initial state distribution $P_0 : \mathcal{X} \mapsto [0, 1]$. Most PG methods (e.g., episodic REINFORCE [259], PoWER [101], and Natural Actor Critic [172]) optimize the policy by employing supervised function approximators to maximize a lower bound on the expected return of $\mathcal{J}(\boldsymbol{\theta})$, comparing trajectories generated by $\pi_{\boldsymbol{\theta}}$ against those generated by a new candidate policy $\pi_{\tilde{\boldsymbol{\theta}}}$. This optimization is carried out by generating trajectories using the current policy $\pi_{\boldsymbol{\theta}}$, and then comparing the result with a new policy $\pi_{\tilde{\boldsymbol{\theta}}}$. Jensen's inequality can then be used to lower bound the expected return [101]:

$$
\begin{aligned}
\log \mathcal{J}\left(\tilde{\boldsymbol{\theta}}\right) &= \log \int_{\mathbb{T}} p_{\tilde{\boldsymbol{\theta}}}(\boldsymbol{\tau})\,\mathfrak{R}(\boldsymbol{\tau})\,\mathrm{d}\boldsymbol{\tau} \\
&= \log \int_{\mathbb{T}} \frac{p_{\boldsymbol{\theta}}(\boldsymbol{\tau})}{p_{\boldsymbol{\theta}}(\boldsymbol{\tau})}\, p_{\tilde{\boldsymbol{\theta}}}(\boldsymbol{\tau})\,\mathfrak{R}(\boldsymbol{\tau})\,\mathrm{d}\boldsymbol{\tau} \\
&\geq \int_{\mathbb{T}} p_{\boldsymbol{\theta}}(\boldsymbol{\tau})\,\mathfrak{R}(\boldsymbol{\tau}) \log \frac{p_{\tilde{\boldsymbol{\theta}}}(\boldsymbol{\tau})}{p_{\boldsymbol{\theta}}(\boldsymbol{\tau})}\,\mathrm{d}\boldsymbol{\tau} + \text{constant} \\
&\propto -\mathfrak{D}_{\mathrm{KL}}\big(p_{\boldsymbol{\theta}}(\boldsymbol{\tau})\,\mathfrak{R}(\boldsymbol{\tau}) \parallel p_{\tilde{\boldsymbol{\theta}}}(\boldsymbol{\tau})\big) = \mathcal{J}_{\mathcal{L},\boldsymbol{\theta}}\left(\tilde{\boldsymbol{\theta}}\right) \quad ,
\end{aligned}
$$

where $\mathfrak{D}_{\mathrm{KL}}\big(p(\boldsymbol{\tau}) \parallel q(\boldsymbol{\tau})\big) = \int_{\mathbb{T}} p(\boldsymbol{\tau}) \log \frac{p(\boldsymbol{\tau})}{q(\boldsymbol{\tau})}\,\mathrm{d}\boldsymbol{\tau}$. This is equivalent to minimizing the KL divergence between the reward-weighted trajectory distribution of $\pi_{\boldsymbol{\theta}}$ and the trajectory distribution $p_{\tilde{\boldsymbol{\theta}}}$ of the new policy $\pi_{\tilde{\boldsymbol{\theta}}}$.

In our work, we treat the term $\mathcal{J}_{\mathcal{L},\boldsymbol{\theta}}\left(\tilde{\boldsymbol{\theta}}\right)$ similar to the loss function $\mathcal{L}$ of a classification or regression task. Consequently, both supervised learning tasks and RL tasks can be modeled in a unified framework, where the goal is to minimize a convex loss function.

6.3.3 Lifelong Machine Learning

In a lifelong learning setting [243, 211], a learner faces multiple, consecutive tasks and must rapidly learn each new task by building upon its previous experience. The learner may encounter a previous task at any time, and so must optimize performance across all tasks seen so far. A priori, the agent does not know the total number of tasks $T_{\max}$, the task distribution, or the task order.

At time t, the lifelong learner encounters task $\mathcal{Z}^{(t)}$. In our framework, all tasks are either regression problems $\mathcal{Z}^{(t)} = \langle \boldsymbol{X}^{(t)}, \boldsymbol{y}^{(t)}\rangle$, classification problems $\mathcal{Z}^{(t)} = \langle \boldsymbol{X}^{(t)}, \boldsymbol{y}^{(t)}\rangle$, or reinforcement learning problems specified by an MDP $\langle \mathcal{X}^{(t)}, \mathcal{A}^{(t)}, P^{(t)}, R^{(t)}, \gamma^{(t)}\rangle$. Note that we do not mix the learning paradigms and hence, a lifelong learning agent will only face one type of learning task during its lifetime. The agent will learn each task consecutively, acquiring training data (i.e., trajectories or samples) in each task before advancing to

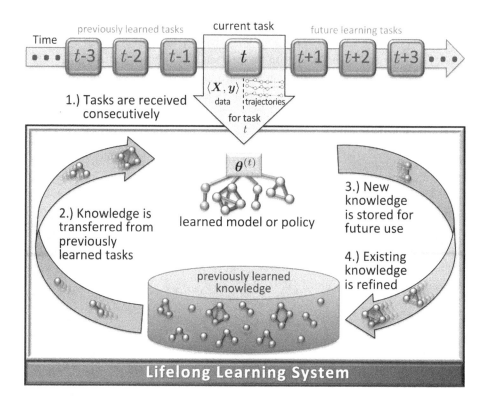

Figure 6.2 The lifelong machine learning process as based on ELLA framework [211]: as a new task arrives, knowledge accumulated from previous tasks is selectively transferred to the new task to improve learning. Newly learned knowledge is then stored for future use.

the next. The agent's goal is to learn the optimal models $\{f^*_{\boldsymbol{\theta}^{(1)}}, \ldots, f^*_{\boldsymbol{\theta}^{(T)}}\}$ or policies $\{\pi^*_{\boldsymbol{\theta}^{(1)}}, \ldots, \pi^*_{\boldsymbol{\theta}^{(T)}}\}$ with corresponding parameters $\{\boldsymbol{\theta}^{(1)}, \ldots, \boldsymbol{\theta}^{(T)}\}$, where T is the number of unique tasks seen so far ($1 \leq T \leq T_{\max}$). Ideally, knowledge learned from previous tasks $\{\mathcal{Z}^{(1)}, \ldots, \mathcal{Z}^{(T-1)}\}$ should accelerate training and improve performance on each new task $\mathcal{Z}^{(T)}$. Also, the lifelong learner should scale effectively to large numbers of tasks, learning each new task rapidly from minimal data. The lifelong learning framework is depicted in Figure 6.2.

The Efficient Lifelong Learning Algorithm (ELLA) [211] and PG-ELLA [7] were developed to operate in this lifelong learning setting for classification/regression and RL tasks, respectively. Both approaches assume the parameters for each task model can be factorized using a shared knowledge base $\boldsymbol{L}$, facilitating transfer between tasks. Specifically, the model parameters for task $\mathcal{Z}^{(t)}$ are given by $\boldsymbol{\theta}^{(t)} = \boldsymbol{L}\boldsymbol{s}^{(t)}$, where $\boldsymbol{L} \in \mathbb{R}^{d \times k}$ is the shared basis over the model space, and $\boldsymbol{s}^{(t)} \in \mathbb{R}^k$ are the sparse coefficients over the basis. This factorization, depicted in Figure 6.3, has been effective for transfer in both lifelong and multi-task learning [110, 141].

Under this assumption, the MTL objective is:

$$\min_{\boldsymbol{L},\boldsymbol{S}} \frac{1}{T} \sum_{t=1}^{T} \left[\mathcal{L}(\boldsymbol{\theta}^{(t)}) + \mu \|\boldsymbol{s}^{(t)}\|_1 \right] + \lambda \|\boldsymbol{L}\|_{\mathsf{F}}^2 \ , \tag{6.1}$$

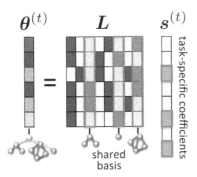

Figure 6.3 The task-specific model (or policy) parameters $\boldsymbol{\theta}^{(t)}$ are factored into a shared knowledge repository $\boldsymbol{L}$ and a sparse code $\boldsymbol{s}^{(t)}$. The repository $\boldsymbol{L}$ stores chunks of knowledge that are useful for multiple tasks, and the sparse code $\boldsymbol{s}^{(t)}$ extracts the relevant pieces of knowledge for a particular task's model (or policy).

where $\boldsymbol{S} = [\boldsymbol{s}^{(1)} \cdots \boldsymbol{s}^{(T)}]$ is the matrix of sparse vectors, $\mathcal{L}$ is the task-specific loss for task $\mathcal{Z}^{(t)}$, and $\| \cdot \|_{\mathsf{F}}$ is the Frobenius norm. The L_1 norm is used to approximate the true vector sparsity of $\boldsymbol{s}^{(t)}$, and μ and λ are regularization parameters. Note that for a convex loss function $\mathcal{L}(\cdot)$, this problem is convex in each of the variables $\boldsymbol{L}$ and $\boldsymbol{S}$. Thus, one can use an alternating optimization approach to solve it in a batch learning setting. To solve this objective in a lifelong learning setting, Ruvolo and Eaton [211] take a second-order Taylor expansion to approximate the objective around an estimate $\boldsymbol{\alpha}^{(t)} \in \mathbb{R}^d$ of the single-task model parameters for each task $\mathcal{Z}^{(t)}$, and update only the coefficients $\boldsymbol{s}^{(t)}$ for the current task at each time step. This process reduces the MTL objective to the problem of sparse coding the single-task policies in the shared basis $\boldsymbol{L}$, and enables $\boldsymbol{S}$ and $\boldsymbol{L}$ to be solved efficiently by the following alternating online update rules that constitute ELLA [211]:

$$\boldsymbol{s}^{(t)} \leftarrow \arg\min_{\boldsymbol{s}} \| \boldsymbol{\alpha}^{(t)} - \boldsymbol{L}\boldsymbol{s} \|_{\boldsymbol{\Gamma}^{(t)}}^2 + \mu \| \boldsymbol{s} \|_1 \tag{6.2}$$

$$\boldsymbol{A} \leftarrow \boldsymbol{A} + (\boldsymbol{s}^{(t)}\boldsymbol{s}^{(t)\top}) \otimes \boldsymbol{\Gamma}^{(t)} \tag{6.3}$$

$$\boldsymbol{b} \leftarrow \boldsymbol{b} + \mathrm{vec}\left(\boldsymbol{s}^{(t)\top} \otimes \left(\boldsymbol{\alpha}^{(t)\top} \boldsymbol{\Gamma}^{(t)} \right) \right) \tag{6.4}$$

$$\boldsymbol{L} \leftarrow \mathrm{mat}\left(\left(\frac{1}{T}\boldsymbol{A} + \lambda \boldsymbol{I}_{kd} \right)^{-1} \frac{1}{T}\boldsymbol{b} \right) , \tag{6.5}$$

where $\|\boldsymbol{v}\|_A^2 = \boldsymbol{v}^\top \boldsymbol{A} \boldsymbol{v}$, the symbol $\otimes$ denotes the Kronecker product, $\boldsymbol{\Gamma}^{(t)}$ is the Hessian of the loss $\mathcal{L}(\boldsymbol{\alpha}^{(t)})$, $\boldsymbol{I}_m$ is the $m \times m$ identity matrix, resulting from Taylor approximation, $\boldsymbol{A}$ is initialized to a $kd \times kd$ zero matrix, and $\boldsymbol{b} \in \mathbb{R}^{kd}$ is initialized to zeros.

This was extended to handle reinforcement learning by Bou Ammar et al. [7] via approximating the RL multi-task objective by first substituting in the convex lower-bound to the PG objective $\mathcal{J}(\boldsymbol{\alpha}^{(t)})$ in order to make the optimization convex.

While these methods are effective for lifelong learning, this approach requires training data to estimate the model for each new task before the learner can solve it. Our key idea is to eliminate this restriction by incorporating task descriptors into lifelong learning, enabling

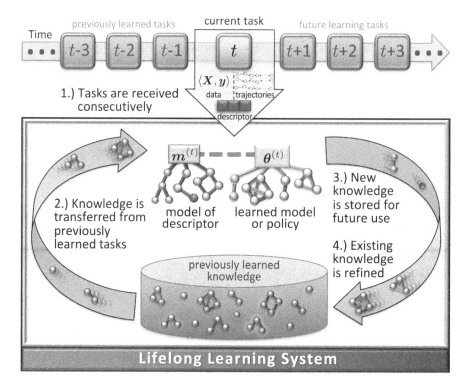

Figure 6.4 The lifelong machine learning process with task descriptions: a model of task descriptors is added into the lifelong learning framework and couple with the learned model. Because of the learned coupling between model and description, the model for a new task can be predicted from the task description.

zero-shot transfer to new tasks. That is, upon learning a few tasks, future task models can be predicted solely using task descriptors.

6.4 LIFELONG LEARNING WITH TASK DESCRIPTORS

6.4.1 Task Descriptors

While most MTL and lifelong learning methods use task training data to model inter-task relationships, high-level descriptions can describe task differences. For example, in multi-task medical domains, patients are often grouped into tasks by demographic data and disease presentation [161]. In control problems, the dynamical system parameters (e.g., the spring, mass, and damper constants in a spring-mass-damper system) describe the task. Descriptors can also be derived from external sources, such as text descriptions [171, 88] or Wikipedia text associated with the task [230].

To incorporate task descriptors into the learning procedure, we assume that each task $\mathcal{Z}^{(t)}$ has an associated descriptor $m^{(t)}$ that is given to the learner upon the first presentation of the task. The learner has no knowledge of future tasks or the distribution of task descriptors. The descriptor is represented by a feature vector $\phi(m^{(t)}) \in \mathbb{R}^{d_m}$, where $\phi(\cdot)$ performs feature extraction and (possibly) a non-linear basis transformation on the features. We make no assumptions on the uniqueness of $\phi(\boldsymbol{m}^{(t)})$, although in general tasks will have different descriptors.[1] In addition, each task also has associated training data $\boldsymbol{X}^{(t)}$ to learn the model; in the case of RL tasks, the data consists of trajectories that are dynamically acquired by the agent through experience in the environment.

We incorporate task descriptors into lifelong learning via sparse coding with a coupled dictionary, enabling the descriptors and learning models to augment each other. This construction improves performance and enables zero-shot lifelong learning. We show how our approach can be applied to regression, classification, and RL tasks.

6.4.2 Coupled Dictionary Optimization

As described previously, many multi-task and lifelong learning approaches have found success with factorizing the policy parameters $\boldsymbol{\theta}^{(t)}$ for each task as a sparse linear combination over a shared basis: $\boldsymbol{\theta}^{(t)} = \boldsymbol{L}\boldsymbol{s}^{(t)}$. In effect, each column of the shared basis $\boldsymbol{L}$ serves as a reusable model or policy component representing a cohesive chunk of knowledge. In lifelong learning, the basis $\boldsymbol{L}$ is refined over time as the system learns more tasks over time. The coefficient vectors $\boldsymbol{S} = [\boldsymbol{s}^{(1)} \ldots \boldsymbol{s}^{(T)}]$ encode the task policies in this shared basis, providing an embedding of the tasks based on how their policies share knowledge.

We make a similar assumption about the task descriptors—that the descriptor features $\phi(\boldsymbol{m}^{(t)})$ can be linearly factorized[2] using a latent basis $\boldsymbol{D} \in \mathbb{R}^{d_m \times k}$ over the descriptor space. This basis captures relationships among the descriptors, with coefficients that similarly embed tasks based on commonalities in their descriptions. From a co-view perspective [281], both the policies and descriptors provide information about the task, and so each can augment the learning of the other. Each underlying task is common to both views, and so we seek to find task embeddings that are consistent for *both* the policies and their corresponding task descriptors. As depicted in Figure 6.5, we can enforce this by coupling the two bases $\boldsymbol{L}$ and $\boldsymbol{D}$, sharing the same coefficient vectors $\boldsymbol{S}$ to reconstruct both the policies and descriptors. Therefore, for task $\mathcal{Z}^{(t)}$,

$$\boldsymbol{\theta}^{(t)} = \boldsymbol{L}\boldsymbol{s}^{(t)} \qquad\qquad \phi(\boldsymbol{m}^{(t)}) = \boldsymbol{D}\boldsymbol{s}^{(t)} \ . \qquad (6.6)$$

To optimize the coupled bases $\boldsymbol{L}$ and $\boldsymbol{D}$ during the lifelong learning process, we employ techniques for coupled dictionary optimization from the sparse coding literature [275], which optimizes the dictionaries for multiple feature spaces that share a joint-sparse representation. Accordingly, coupled dictionary learning allows us to observe an instance in one feature space, and then recover its underlying latent signal in the other feature spaces using the corresponding dictionaries and sparse coding. This notion of coupled dictionary learning has led to high-performance algorithms for image super-resolution [275], allowing the reconstruction of high-res images from low-res samples, and for multi-modal retrieval [298], and cross-domain retrieval [281]. The core idea is that features in two independent subspaces can have the same representation in a third subspace.

---

[1]This raises the question of what descriptive features to use, and how task performance will change if some descriptive features are unknown. We explore these issues in Section 6.8.1.

[2]This is potentially non-linear with respect to $\boldsymbol{m}^{(t)}$, since ϕ can be non-linear.

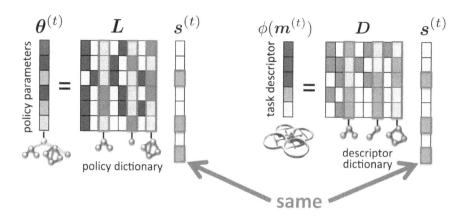

Figure 6.5 The coupled dictionaries of TaDeLL, illustrated on an RL task. Policy parameters $\boldsymbol{\theta}^{(t)}$ are factored into $\boldsymbol{L}$ and $\boldsymbol{s}^{(t)}$ while the task description $\phi(\boldsymbol{m}^{(t)})$ is factored into $\boldsymbol{D}$ and $\boldsymbol{s}^{(t)}$. Because we force both dictionaries to use the same sparse code $\boldsymbol{s}^{(t)}$, the relevant pieces of information for a task become coupled with the description of the task.

Given the factorization in Eq. 6.6, we can re-formulate the multi-task objective (Eq. 6.1) for the coupled dictionaries as

$$\min_{\boldsymbol{L},\boldsymbol{D},\boldsymbol{S}} \frac{1}{T} \sum_t \left[\mathcal{L}\left(\boldsymbol{\theta}^{(t)}\right) + \rho \left\| \phi(\boldsymbol{m}^{(t)}) - \boldsymbol{D}\boldsymbol{s}^{(t)} \right\|_2^2 + \mu \left\| \boldsymbol{s}^{(t)} \right\|_1 \right] + \lambda(\|\boldsymbol{L}\|_{\mathsf{F}}^2 + \|\boldsymbol{D}\|_{\mathsf{F}}^2) ,$$
(6.7)

where ρ balances the model's or policy's fit to the task descriptor's fit.

To solve Eq. 6.7 online, we approximate $\mathcal{L}(\cdot)$ by a second-order Taylor expansion around $\boldsymbol{\alpha}^{(t)}$, the ridge minimizer for the single-task learner:

$$\boldsymbol{\alpha}^{(t)} = \arg\min_{\boldsymbol{\theta}^{(t)}} \mathcal{L}\left(\boldsymbol{\theta}^{(t)}\right) + \mu_s \|\boldsymbol{\theta}^{(t)}\|_2^2 ,$$
(6.8)

where μ_s is a regularization parameter. In reinforcement learning, $\pi_{\boldsymbol{\alpha}^{(t)}}$ is the single-task policy for $\mathcal{Z}^{(t)}$ based on the observed trajectories [7]. In supervised learning, $\boldsymbol{\alpha}^{(t)}$ is the single-task model parameters for $\mathcal{Z}^{(t)}$ [211]. Note that these parameters are computed once, when the current task is learned. Then we can expand $\mathcal{L}\left(\boldsymbol{\theta}^{(t)}\right)$ for each task around $\boldsymbol{\alpha}^{(t)}$ as:

$$\mathcal{L}\left(\boldsymbol{\theta}^{(t)} = \boldsymbol{L}\boldsymbol{s}^{(t)}\right) = \mathcal{L}\left(\boldsymbol{\alpha}^{(t)}\right) + \nabla\mathcal{L}\left(\boldsymbol{\theta}^{(t)}\right)^\top_{\boldsymbol{\theta}^{(t)}=\boldsymbol{\alpha}^{(t)}} \left(\boldsymbol{\alpha}^{(t)} - \boldsymbol{L}\boldsymbol{s}^{(t)}\right) + \left\| \boldsymbol{\alpha}^{(t)} - \boldsymbol{L}\boldsymbol{s}^{(t)} \right\|_{\boldsymbol{\Gamma}^{(t)}}^2 ,$$
(6.9)

where ∇ denotes the gradient operator. Note that $\boldsymbol{\alpha}^{(t)}$ is the minimizer of the function $\mathcal{L}\left(\boldsymbol{\theta}^{(t)}\right)$, and hence $\nabla\mathcal{L}\left(\boldsymbol{\theta}^{(t)}\right)_{\boldsymbol{\theta}^{(t)}=\boldsymbol{\alpha}^{(t)}} = 0$. Also, since $\mathcal{L}\left(\boldsymbol{\alpha}^{(t)}\right)$ is a constant term with respect to the variables. As a result, this procedure leads to a unified simplified formalism that is independent of the learning paradigm (i.e., classification, regression, or RL).

Approximating Eq. 6.7 leads to

$$\min_{L,D,S} \frac{1}{T} \sum_t \left[\left\| \boldsymbol{\alpha}^{(t)} - \boldsymbol{L}\boldsymbol{s}^{(t)} \right\|_{\Gamma^{(t)}}^2 + \rho \left\| \phi(\boldsymbol{m}^{(t)}) - \boldsymbol{D}\boldsymbol{s}^{(t)} \right\|_2^2 + \mu \left\| \boldsymbol{s}^{(t)} \right\|_1 \right] + \lambda(\|\boldsymbol{L}\|_\mathsf{F}^2 + \|\boldsymbol{D}\|_\mathsf{F}^2) .$$

(6.10)

We can merge terms in Eq. 6.10 pair-wise by choosing:

$$\boldsymbol{\beta}^{(t)} = \begin{bmatrix} \boldsymbol{\alpha}^{(t)} \\ \phi(\boldsymbol{m}^{(t)}) \end{bmatrix} \qquad \boldsymbol{K} = \begin{bmatrix} \boldsymbol{L} \\ \boldsymbol{D} \end{bmatrix} \qquad \boldsymbol{A}^{(t)} = \begin{bmatrix} \Gamma^{(t)} & 0 \\ 0 & \rho \boldsymbol{I}_{d_m} \end{bmatrix} ,$$

where 0 is the zero matrix, letting us rewrite (6.10) concisely as

$$\min_{\boldsymbol{K},\boldsymbol{S}} \frac{1}{T} \sum_t \left[\left\| \boldsymbol{\beta}^{(t)} - \boldsymbol{K}\boldsymbol{s}^{(t)} \right\|_{\boldsymbol{A}^{(t)}}^2 + \mu \left\| \boldsymbol{s}^{(t)} \right\|_1 \right] + \lambda \|\boldsymbol{K}\|_\mathsf{F}^2 .$$

(6.11)

This objective can now be solved efficiently online, as a series of per-task update rules given in Algorithm 5, which we call TaDeLL (Task Descriptors for Lifelong Learning). In other words, task descriptors serve as a secondary source of measurements in the sparse recovery problem [205, 207]. When a task arrives, the corresponding sparse vector $\boldsymbol{s}^{(t)}$ is computed, and then the dictionaries are updated. Note that Eq. (6.11) can be decoupled into two optimization problems with similar form on $\boldsymbol{L}$ and $\boldsymbol{D}$, and then $\boldsymbol{L}$ and $\boldsymbol{D}$ can be updated independently using Equations 6.3–6.5, following a recursive construction based on an eigenvalue decomposition. Note that the objective function in Eq. (6.10) is biconvex and hence it can also be solved in an offline setting through alternation on the variables $\boldsymbol{K}$ and $\boldsymbol{S}$, similar to the GO-MTL [110]. At each iteration, one variable is fixed, and the other variable is optimized in an offline setting as denoted in Algorithm 6. This gives rise to an offline version of TaDeLL which we call TaDeMTL (Task Descriptors for Multi-task Learning) algorithm. Note that TaDeMTL has a nested loop and computationally is demanding because at each iteration, sparse vectors for all tasks are recomputed, and the dictionaries are updated from scratch. The major benefit is that TaDeMTL can be thought as an upper-bound for TaDeLL which not only can be used to assess the quality of online performance in the asymptotic regime, but a useful algorithm on its own when online learning is not a priority and accuracy is the priority.

For the sake of clarity, we now explicitly state the differences between using TaDeLL for RL problems and for classification and regression problems. In an RL setting, at each timestep, TaDeLL receives a new RL task and samples trajectories for the new task. We use the single-task policy as computed using a twice-differentiable policy gradient method as $\boldsymbol{\alpha}^{(t)}$. The Hessian $\Gamma^{(t)}$, calculated around the point $\boldsymbol{\alpha}^{(t)}$, is derived according to the particular policy gradient method being used. Bou Ammar et al. [7] derive it for the cases of Episodic REINFORCE and Natural Actor-Critic. The reconstructed $\boldsymbol{\theta}^{(t)}$ is then used as the policy for the task $\mathcal{Z}^{(t)}$.

In the case of classification and regression, at each time step TaDeLL observes a labeled training set $(\boldsymbol{X}^{(t)}, \boldsymbol{y}^{(t)})$ for task $\mathcal{Z}^{(t)}$, where $\boldsymbol{X}^{(t)} \subseteq \mathbb{R}^{n_t \times d}$. For classification tasks, $\boldsymbol{y}^{(t)} \in \{+1, -1\}^{n_t}$, and for regression tasks, $\boldsymbol{y}^{(t)} \in \mathbb{R}^{n_t}$. We then set $\boldsymbol{\alpha}^{(t)}$ to be the parameters of a single-task model trained via classification or regression (e.g., logistic or

---

Algorithm 5 TaDeLL (k, λ, μ)

1: $\boldsymbol{L} \leftarrow$ RandomMatrix$_{d,k}$, $\boldsymbol{D} \leftarrow$ RandomMatrix$_{m,k}$
2: **while** some task $\left(\mathcal{Z}^{(t)}, \phi(\boldsymbol{m}^{(t)}) \right)$ is available **do**
3:     $\mathbb{T}^{(t)} \leftarrow$ collectData($\mathcal{Z}^{(t)}$)
4:     Compute $\boldsymbol{\alpha}^{(t)}$ and $\boldsymbol{\Gamma}^{(t)}$ from $\mathbb{T}^{(t)}$
5:     $\boldsymbol{s}^{(t)} \leftarrow \arg\min_{\boldsymbol{s}} \left\| \boldsymbol{\beta}^{(t)} - \boldsymbol{K s} \right\|^2_{\boldsymbol{A}^{(t)}} + \mu \|\boldsymbol{s}\|_1$
6:     $\boldsymbol{L} \leftarrow$ updateL($\boldsymbol{L}, \boldsymbol{s}^{(t)}, \boldsymbol{\alpha}^{(t)}, \boldsymbol{\Gamma}^{(t)}, \lambda$)   Eq. 6.3–6.5
7:     $\boldsymbol{D} \leftarrow$ updateD($\boldsymbol{D}, \boldsymbol{s}^{(t)}, \phi(\boldsymbol{m}^{(t)}), \rho\boldsymbol{I}_{d_m}, \lambda$)   Eq. 6.3–6.5
8:     **for** $t \in \{1, \dots, T\}$ **do:** $\boldsymbol{\theta}^{(t)} \leftarrow \boldsymbol{L s}^{(t)}$
9: **end while**

Algorithm 6 TaDeMTL (k, λ, μ)

1: $\boldsymbol{L} \leftarrow$ RandomMatrix$_{d,k}$, $\boldsymbol{D} \leftarrow$ RandomMatrix$_{m,k}$
2: $\mathbb{T}^{(t)} \leftarrow$ collectallData($\mathcal{Z}^{(1)}, \dots \mathcal{Z}^{(T)}$)
3: **for** $itr = \{1, \dots, N_{itr}\}$ **do**
4:     **for** $t = \{1, \dots, T\}$ **do**
5:         Compute $\boldsymbol{\alpha}^{(t)}$ and $\boldsymbol{\Gamma}^{(t)}$ from $\mathbb{T}^{(t)}$
6:         $\boldsymbol{s}^{(t)} \leftarrow \arg\min_{\boldsymbol{s}} \left\| \boldsymbol{\beta}^{(t)} - \boldsymbol{K s} \right\|^2_{\boldsymbol{A}^{(t)}} + \mu \|\boldsymbol{s}\|_1$
7:     **end for**
8:     $\boldsymbol{L} \leftarrow$ updateL($\boldsymbol{L}, \boldsymbol{s}^{(t)}, \boldsymbol{\alpha}^{(t)}, \boldsymbol{\Gamma}^{(t)}, \lambda$)   Eq. 6.3–6.5
9:     $\boldsymbol{D} \leftarrow$ updateD($\boldsymbol{D}, \boldsymbol{s}^{(t)}, \phi(\boldsymbol{m}^{(t)}), \rho\boldsymbol{I}_{d_m}, \lambda$)   Eq. 6.3–6.5
10: **end for**
11: **for** $t \in \{1, \dots, T\}$ **do:** $\boldsymbol{\theta}^{(t)} \leftarrow \boldsymbol{L s}^{(t)}$

---

linear regression) on that data set. $\boldsymbol{\Gamma}^{(t)}$ is set to be the Hessian of the corresponding loss function around the single-task solution $\boldsymbol{\alpha}^{(t)}$, and the reconstructed $\boldsymbol{\theta}^{(t)}$ is used as the model parameters for the corresponding classification or regression problem.

6.4.3   Zero-Shot transfer learning

In a lifelong setting, when faced with a new task, the agent's goal is to learn an effective policy for that task as quickly as possible. At this stage, previous multi-task and lifelong learners incurred a delay before they could produce a decent policy since they needed to acquire data from the new task in order to identify related knowledge and train the new policy via transfer.

Incorporating task descriptors enables our approach to predict a policy for the new task immediately, given *only* the descriptor. This ability to perform zero-shot transfer is enabled by the use of coupled dictionary learning, which allows us to observe a data instance in one feature space (i.e., the task descriptor), and then recover its underlying latent signal in the other feature space (i.e., the policy parameters) using the dictionaries and sparse coding.

Algorithm 7 Zero-Shot Transfer to a New Task $\mathcal{Z}^{(t_{new})}$

1: **Inputs:** task descriptor $m^{(t_{new})}$, learned bases L and D
2: $\tilde{s}^{(t_{new})} \leftarrow \arg\min_s \left\| \phi(m^{(t_{new})}) - Ds \right\|_2^2 + \mu \left\| s \right\|_1$
3: $\tilde{\theta}^{(t_{new})} \leftarrow L\tilde{s}^{(t_{new})}$
4: **Return:** $\pi_{\tilde{\theta}^{(t_{new})}}$

Given only the descriptor $m^{(t_{new})}$ for a new task $\mathcal{Z}^{(t_{new})}$, we can estimate the embedding of the task in the latent descriptor space via LASSO on the learned dictionary D:

$$\tilde{s}^{(t_{new})} \leftarrow \arg\min_s \left\| \phi(m^{(t)}) - Ds \right\|_2^2 + \mu \left\| s \right\|_1 \ . \tag{6.12}$$

Since the estimate given by $\tilde{s}^{(t_{new})}$ also serves as the coefficients over the latent policy space L, we can immediately predict a policy for the new task as: $\tilde{\theta}^{(t_{new})} = L\tilde{s}^{(t_{new})}$. This zero-shot transfer learning procedure is given as Algorithm 7.

6.5 THEORETICAL ANALYSIS

This section examines theoretical issues related to incorporating task descriptors into lifelong learning via the coupled dictionaries. We start by proving PAC-learnability of our framework, which is essential for our algorithm to work. We also outline why the inclusion of task features can improve the performance of the learned policies and enable zero-shot transfer to new tasks safely. We then prove the convergence of TaDeLL. A full sample complexity analysis is beyond the scope of our work, and, indeed, remains an open problem for zero-shot learning [182].

6.5.1 Algorithm PAC-learnability

In this section, we establish the PAC-learnability of our algorithm. The goal is to provide bounds on the generalization error given the number of the previously learned tasks. This can help us to compute the number of required learned tasks (i.e., past experience) for the ZSL algorithm to learn future tasks from their descriptors with high probability. We rely on the ZSL framework developed by Palatucci et al. [162]. The core idea is that if we can recover the sparse vector with high accuracy through using the task descriptor, then the task parameters can also be recovered with high probability. Let P_t denote the probability of predicting the task parameters in the ZSL regime. This probability can be decomposed into two probabilities:

1. Given a certain confidence parameter δ and error parameter ϵ, a dictionary can be trained by learning $T_{\epsilon,\delta}$ previous tasks such that for future tasks $\mathbb{E}(\| \beta - Ks \|_2^2) \leq \epsilon$, where $\mathbb{E}(\cdot)$ denotes statistical expectation. We denote this event by $\mathcal{K}_\epsilon$, with $P(\mathcal{K}_\epsilon) = 1 - \delta$. This event denotes that the learned knowledge has been successfully incorporated into the coupled dictionaries and we can rely on this dictionary for ZSL to succeed.

2. Given the event $\mathcal{K}_\epsilon$ (i.e., given the dictionaries learned from previous tasks), the current (future) task sparse vector can be estimated with high probability using task descriptors, enabling us to use it to compute the task parameters. We denote this event by $\mathcal{S}_\epsilon|\mathcal{K}_\epsilon$.

Therefore, since the above two events are independent the event P_t can be expressed as the product of the above probabilities:

$$P_t = P(\mathcal{K}_\epsilon)P(\mathcal{S}_\epsilon|\mathcal{K}_\epsilon) \ . \tag{6.13}$$

Our goal is as follows: given the desired values for the confidence parameter δ (i.e., $P(\mathcal{K}_\epsilon) = 1 - \delta$) and the error parameter ϵ (i.e., $\mathbb{E}(\|\boldsymbol{\beta} - \boldsymbol{K}\boldsymbol{s}\|_2^2) \leq \epsilon$), we compute the minimum number of tasks $T_{\epsilon,\delta}$ that needs to be learned to achieve that level of prediction confidence as well as $P(\mathcal{S}_\epsilon|\mathcal{K}_\epsilon)$ to compute P_t. To establish the error bound, we need to ensure that the coupled dictionaries are learned to a sufficient quality that achieves this error bound. We can rely on the following theorem on PAC-learnability of dictionary learning:

Theorem 6.5.1. *[71] Consider the dictionary learning problem in Eq. (6.11), and the confidence parameter δ ($P(\mathcal{K}_\epsilon) = 1 - \delta$) and the error parameter ϵ in the standard PAC-learning setting. Then, the number of required tasks to learn the dictionary $T_{\epsilon,\delta}$ satisfies the following relation:*

$$\epsilon \geq 3\sqrt{\frac{\beta \log(T_{\epsilon,\delta})}{T_{\epsilon,\delta}}} + \sqrt{\frac{\beta + \log(2/\delta)/8}{T_{\epsilon,\delta}}}$$
$$\beta = \frac{(d + d_m)k}{8} max\{1, \log(6\sqrt{8}\kappa)\} \ , \tag{6.14}$$

where κ is a contestant that depends on the loss function that we use to measure the data fidelity.

Given all parameters, Eq. (6.14) can be solved for $T_{\epsilon,\delta}$. For example, in the asymptotic regime for learned tasks $\epsilon \propto \left(\frac{\log(T_{\epsilon,\delta})}{T_{\epsilon,\delta}}\right)^{0.5}$, and given ϵ we can easily compute $T_{\epsilon,\delta}$.

So, according to Theorem 6.5.1, if we learn at least $T_{\epsilon,\delta}$ tasks to estimate the coupled dictionaries, we can achieve the required error rate ϵ. Now we need to determine the probability of recovering the task parameters in the ZSL regime, given that the learned dictionary satisfies the error bound, or $P(\mathcal{S}_\epsilon|\mathcal{K}_\epsilon)$. For this purpose, the core step in the proposed algorithm is to compute the joint-sparse representation using $\boldsymbol{m}$ and $\boldsymbol{D}$. It is also important to note that Eq. (6.11) has a Bayesian interpretation. We can consider it as a result of a maximum a posteriori (MAP) inference, where the sparse vectors are drawn from a Laplacian distribution and the coupled dictionaries are Gaussian matrices with i.i.d elements, i.e., $d_{ij} \sim \mathcal{N}(0, \epsilon)$. Hence, Eq. (6.11) is an optimization problem resulted from Bayesian inference and hence by solving it, we also learn a MAP estimate of the Gaussian matrix $\boldsymbol{K} = [\boldsymbol{L}, \boldsymbol{D}]^\top$. Consequently, $\boldsymbol{D}$ would be a Gaussian matrix which is used to estimate $\boldsymbol{s}$ in ZSL regime. To compute the probability of recovering the joint-sparse recovery $\boldsymbol{s}$, we can rely on the following theorem for Gaussian matrices [157]:

Theorem 6.5.2. *Consider the linear system* $\beta = \boldsymbol{K}\boldsymbol{s} + \boldsymbol{n}$ *with a sparse solution, i.e.,* $\|\boldsymbol{s}\|_0 = k$, *where* $\boldsymbol{K} \in \mathbb{R}^{d \times k}$ *is a random Gaussian matrix and* $\|\boldsymbol{n}\|_2 \leq \epsilon$, *i.e.,* $\mathbb{E}(\|\beta - \boldsymbol{K}\boldsymbol{s}\|_2^2) \leq \epsilon$. *Then the unique solution of this system can be recovered by solving an* ℓ_1-*minimization with probability of* $(1 - e^{d\xi})$ *as far as* $k \leq c'd \log(\frac{k}{d})$, *where* c' *is a constant that depends on the loss function and noise statistics, and* ξ *is a constant parameter [157].*

Theorem 6.5.2 suggests that in our framework, given the learned coupled dictionaries, we can recover the sparse vector with probability $P(\mathcal{S}_\epsilon|\mathcal{K}_\epsilon) = (1 - e^{(d+d_m)\xi})$ given that $k \leq c'(d_m+d) \log(\frac{k}{d_m+d})$ for a task. This suggests that adding the task descriptors increases the probability of recovering the task parameters from $(1 - e^{d\xi})$ to $(1 - e^{(d+d_m)\xi})$. Moreover, we can use Eq. (6.12) to recover the in the ZSL regime and subsequently unseen attributes with probability $P(\mathcal{S}_\epsilon|\mathcal{K}_\epsilon) = (1 - e^{d_m\xi})$ as far as the corresponding sparse vector satisfies $k \leq c'd_m \log(\frac{k}{d_m})$ to guarantee that the recovered sparse vector is accurate enough to recover the task parameters. This theorem also suggests that the developed framework can only work if a suitable sparsifying dictionary can be learned and also we have access to rich task descriptors. Therefore, given desired error p $1 - \delta$ and error parameter ϵ, the probability event of predicting task parameters in ZSL regime can be computed as:

$$P_t = (1 - \delta)(1 - e^{p\xi}) \ , \tag{6.15}$$

which concludes our proof on PAC-learnability of the algorithm ■

Given the learnability of our model, the next question is whether the proposed dictionary learning algorithm computationally converges to a suitable solution.

6.5.2 Theoretical Convergence of TaDeLL

In this section, we prove the convergence of TaDeLL, showing that the learned dictionaries become increasingly stable as it learns more tasks. We build upon the theoretical results from Bou Ammar et al. [7] and Ruvolo & Eaton [211], demonstrating that these results apply to coupled dictionary learning with task descriptors, and use them to prove convergence.

Let $\hat{g}_T(\text{L})$ represent the sparse coded approximation to the MTL objective, which can be defined as:

$$\hat{g}_T(\boldsymbol{L}) = \frac{1}{T} \sum_{t=1}^{T} \|\boldsymbol{\alpha}^{(t)} - \boldsymbol{L}\boldsymbol{s}^{(t)}\|_{\boldsymbol{\Gamma}^{(t)}}^2 + \mu\|\boldsymbol{s}^{(t)}\|_1 + \lambda\|\boldsymbol{L}\|_F^2 \ .$$

This equation can be viewed as the cost for $\boldsymbol{L}$ when the sparse coefficients are kept constant. Let $\boldsymbol{L}_T$ be the version of the dictionary $\boldsymbol{L}$ obtained after observing T tasks. Given these definitions, we consider the following theorem:

Theorem 6.5.3. *[211]*

1. *The trained dictionary* $\boldsymbol{L}$ *is stabilized over learning with rate:* $\boldsymbol{L}_T - \boldsymbol{L}_{T-1} = O(\frac{1}{T})$

2. $\hat{g}_T(\boldsymbol{L}_T)$ *converges almost surely.*

3. $\hat{g}_T(\boldsymbol{L}_T) - \hat{g}_T(\boldsymbol{L}_{T-1})$ *converges almost surely to zero.*

This theorem requires two conditions:

1. The tuples $\Gamma^{(t)}$, $\alpha^{(t)}$ are drawn i.i.d from a distribution with compact support to bound the norms of L and $s^{(t)}$.

2. For all t, let L_κ be the subset of the dictionary L_t, where only columns corresponding to non-zero element of $s^{(t)}$ are included. Then, all eigenvalues of the matrix $L_\kappa^\top \Gamma^{(t)} L_\kappa$ need to be strictly positive.

Bou Ammar et al. [7] show that both of these conditions are met for the lifelong learning framework given in Eqs. 6.2–6.5. When we incorporate the task descriptors into this framework, we alter $\alpha^{(t)} \to \beta^{(t)}$, $L \to K$, and $\Gamma^{(t)} \to A^{(t)}$. Note both $\beta^{(t)}$ and $A^{(t)}$ are formed by adding deterministic entries and thus can be considered to be drawn i.i.d (because $\Gamma^{(t)}$ and $\alpha^{(t)}$ are assumed to be drawn i.i.d). Therefore, incorporating task descriptors does not violate Condition 1.

To show that Condition 2 holds, if we analogously form K_κ, then the eigenvalues of K_κ are strictly positive because they are either eigenvalues of L (which are strictly positive according to [7]) or the regularizing parameter ρ by definition. Thus, both conditions are met and convergence follows directly from Theorem 6.5.3.

6.5.3 Computational Complexity

In this section, we analyze the computational complexity of TaDeLL. Each update begins with one PG step to update $\alpha^{(t)}$ and $\Gamma^{(t)}$ at a cost of $O(\xi(d, n_t))$, where $\xi()$ depends on the base PG learner and n_t is the number of trajectories obtained for task $\mathcal{Z}^{(t)}$. The cost of updating $L \in \mathbb{R}^{d \times k}$ and $s^{(t)} \in \mathbb{R}^k$ alone is $O(k^2 d^3)$ [211], and so the cost of updating $K \in \mathbb{R}^{(d+d_m) \times k}$ through coupled dictionary learning is $O(k^2(d + d_m)^3)$. This yields an overall per-update cost of $O(k^2(d + d_m)^3 + \xi(d, n_t))$, which is independent of T.

Next, we empirically demonstrate the benefits of TaDeLL on a variety of different learning problems.

6.6 EVALUATION ON REINFORCEMENT LEARNING DOMAINS

We apply TaDeLL to a series of RL problems. We consider the problem of learning a collection of different related systems. For these systems, we use three benchmark control problems and an application to quadrotor stabilization.

6.6.1 Benchmark Dynamical Systems

Spring Mass Damper (SM) The SM system is described by three parameters: the spring constant, mass, and damping constant [211]. The system's state is given by the position and velocity of the mass. The controller applies a force to the mass, attempting to stabilize it to a given position.

Cart Pole (CP) The CP system involves balancing an inverted pendulum by applying a force to the cart [211]. The system is characterized by the cart and pole masses, pole length, and a damping parameter. The states are the position and velocity of the cart and the angle and rotational velocity of the pole.

Bicycle (BK) This system focuses on keeping a bicycle balanced upright as it rolls along a horizontal plane at a constant velocity (see subsection 6.4.2 in Busoniu et al. [28]). The

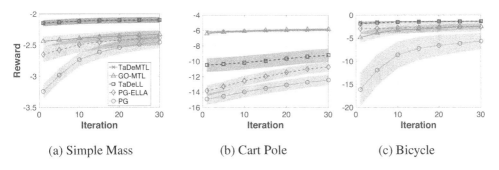

(a) Simple Mass   (b) Cart Pole   (c) Bicycle

Figure 6.6 Performance of multi-task (solid lines), lifelong (dashed), and single-task learning (dotted) on benchmark dynamical systems. (Best viewed in color.)

system is characterized by the bicycle mass, x- and z-coordinates of the center of mass, and parameters relating to the shape of the bike (the wheelbase, trail, and head angle). The state is the bike's tilt and its derivative; the actions are the torque applied to the handlebar and its derivative.

6.6.2   Methodology

In each domain, we generated 40 tasks, each with different dynamics, by varying the system parameters. To this end, we set a maximum value and a minimum value for each task parameter and then generated the systems by uniformly drawing values for the parameters from each parameter range. The reward for each task was taken to be the distance between the current state and the goal. For lifelong learning, tasks were encountered consecutively with repetition, and learning proceeded until each task had been seen at least once. In order to cancel out the effect of the task order, we run each experiment 100 times and report the average performance and standard deviation error. In each experiment, we used the same random task order between methods to ensure a fair comparison. The learners sampled trajectories of 100 steps, and the learning session during each task presentation was limited to 30 iterations. For MTL, all tasks were presented simultaneously. We used Natural Actor Critic [172] as the base learner for the benchmark systems and episodic REINFORCE [259] for quadrotor control. We chose k and the regularization parameters independently for each domain and GO-MTL, ELLA, and PG-ELLA methods to optimize the combined performance of all methods on 20 held-out tasks by using a grid search over ranges $\{10^{-n}|n = 0,\dots,3\}$ for regularization parameters and $\{1,\dots,10\}$ for k, respectively. We set $\rho = mean(diag(\rho^{(t)}))$ to balance the fit to the descriptors and the policies. We measured learning curves based on the final policies for each of the 40 tasks. The system parameters for each task were used as the task descriptor features $\phi(\boldsymbol{m})$; we also tried several non-linear transformations as $\phi(\cdot)$ but found the linear features worked well. Tasks were presented either consecutively (for lifelong) or in batch (for multi-task), using trajectories of 100 steps with each learning session limited to 30 iterations.

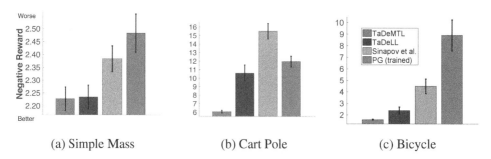

(a) Simple Mass   (b) Cart Pole   (c) Bicycle

Figure 6.7 Zero-shot transfer to new tasks. The figure shows the initial "jumpstart" improvement on each task domain. (Best viewed in color.)

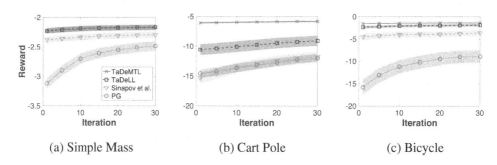

(a) Simple Mass   (b) Cart Pole   (c) Bicycle

Figure 6.8 Learning performance of using the zero-shot policies as warm start initializations for PG. The performance of the single-task PG learner is included for comparison. (Best viewed in color.)

6.6.3 Results on Benchmark Systems

Figure 6.6 compares our TaDeLL approach for lifelong learning with task descriptors to (1) PG-ELLA [7], which does not use task features, (2) GO-MTL [110], the MTL optimization of Eq. 6.1, and (3) single-task learning using PG. For comparison, we also performed an offline MTL optimization of Eq. 6.7 via alternating optimization, and plot the results as TaDeMTL. The shaded regions on the plots denote standard error bars.

We see that task descriptors improve lifelong learning on every system, even driving performance to a level that is unachievable from training the policies from experience alone via GO-MTL in the SM and BK domains. The difference between TaDeLL and TaDeMTL is also negligible for all domains except CP, demonstrating the effectiveness of our online optimization.

To measure zero-shot performance, we generated an additional 40 tasks for each domain, averaging results over these new tasks. We compared our work mainly against Sinapov et al. [228]'s method by using task descriptors as "task features" in that work. To make Sinapov et al. [228]'s method applicable in a lifelong learning setting, we used their method to transfer knowledge from the tasks that have been learned before time t at each time step using a version of their method that uses linear regression to select the source task. Figure 6.7

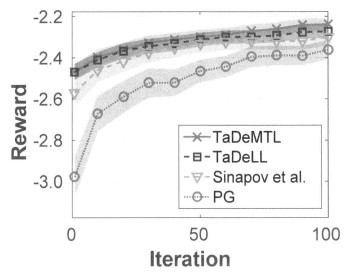

Figure 6.9 Warm start learning on quadrotor control. (Best viewed in color.)

shows that task descriptors are effective for zero-shot transfer to new tasks. We see that our approach improves the initial performance (i.e., the "jumpstart" [240]) on new tasks, outperforming Sinapov et al. [228]'s method and single-task PG, which was allowed to train on the task. We attribute the especially poor performance of Sinapov et al. on CP to the fact that the CP policies differ substantially; in domains where the source policies are vastly different from the target policies, Sinapov et al.'s algorithm does not have an appropriate source to transfer. Their approach is also much more computationally expensive (quadratic in the number of tasks) than our approach (linear in the number of tasks), as shown in Figure 6.15; details of the runtime experiments are included in Section 6.8.2. Figure 6.8 shows that the zero-shot policies can be used effectively as a warm start initialization for a PG learner, which is then allowed to improve the policy.

6.6.4 Application to Quadrotor Control

We also applied our approach to the more challenging domain of quadrotor control, focusing on zero-shot transfer to new stability tasks. To ensure realistic dynamics, we use the model of Bouabdallah and Siegwart [23], which has been verified on physical systems. The quadrotors are characterized by three inertial constants and the arm length, with their state consisting of roll/pitch/yaw and their derivatives.

Figure 6.9 shows the results of our application, demonstrating that TaDeLL can predict a controller for new quadrotors through zero-shot learning that has equivalent accuracy to PG, which had to train on the system. As with the benchmarks, TaDeLL is effective for warm start learning with PG.

Algorithm	Lifelong Learning	Zero-Shot Prediction
TaDeLL	0.131 ± 0.004	0.159 ± 0.005
ELLA	0.152 ± 0.005	N/A
STL	0.73 ± 0.07	N/A

Table 6.1 Regression performance on robot end-effector prediction in both lifelong learning and zero-shot settings: performance is measured in mean squared error.

6.7 EVALUATION ON SUPERVISED LEARNING DOMAINS

In this section, we evaluate TaDeLL on regression and classification domains, considering the problem of predicting the real-valued location of a robot's end-effector and two synthetic classification tasks.

6.7.1 Predicting the Location of a Robot end-effector

We evaluate TaDeLL on a regression domain. We look at the problem of predicting the real-valued position of the end-effector of an 8-DOF robotic arm in 3D space, given the angles of the robot joints. Different robots have different link lengths, offsets, and twists, and we use these parameters as the description of the task, and use the joint angles as the feature representation.

We consider 200 different robot arms and use 10 points as training data per robot. The robot arms are simulated using the Robot Toolbox [47]. The learned dictionaries are then used to predict models for 200 different unseen robots. We measure performance as the mean square error of the prediction against the exact location of the end-effector.

Table 6.1 shows that both TaDeLL and ELLA outperform the single-task learner, with TaDeLL slightly outperforming ELLA. This same improvement holds for zero-shot prediction on new robot arms. To measure the performance of TaDeLL, we computed the single-task learner performance on the new robot using the data which turned out to be 0.70 ± 0.05. Note that we can use STL as a baseline to measure zero-shot prediction quality using our method. Thus STL performance demonstrates that TaDell outperforms STL on new tasks even without using data.

To better understand the relationship of dictionary size to performance, we investigated how learning performance varies with the number of bases k in the dictionary. Figure 6.11 shows this relationship for lifelong learning and zero-shot prediction settings. We observe that TaDeLL performs better with a larger dictionary than ELLA; we hypothesize that difference results from the added difficulty of encoding the representations with the task descriptions. To test this hypothesis, we reduced the number of descriptors in an ablative experiment. Recall that the task has 24 descriptors consisting of a twist, link offset, and link length for each joint. We reduced the number of descriptors by alternatingly removing the subsets of features corresponding to the twist, offset, and length. Figure 6.12 shows the performance of this ablative experiment, revealing that the need for the increased number of bases is particularly related to learning *twist*.

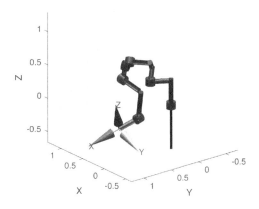

Figure 6.10 Example model of an 8-DOF robot arm.

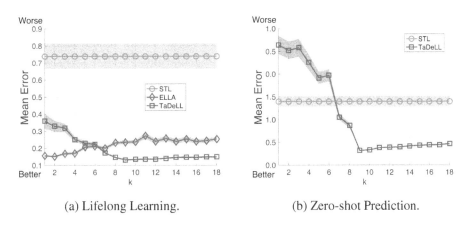

(a) Lifelong Learning.

(b) Zero-shot Prediction.

Figure 6.11 Performance of TaDeLL and ELLA as the dictionary size k is varied for lifelong learning and zero-shot learning. Performance of the single task learner is provided for comparison. In the lifelong learning setting, both TaDeLL and ELLA demonstrate positive transfer that converges to the performance of the single task learner as k is increased. We see that, for this problem, TaDeLL prefers a slightly larger value of k.

6.7.2   Experiments on Synthetic Classification Domains

To better understand the connections between TaDeLL's performance and the structure of the tasks, we evaluated TaDeLL on two synthetic classification domains. The use of synthetic domains allows us to tightly control the task generation process and the relationship between the target model and the descriptor.

The first synthetic domain consists of binary-labeled instances drawn from $\mathbb{R}^8$, and each sample x belongs to the positive class if $x^\top m > 0$. Each task has a different parameter vector m drawn from the uniform distribution $m \in [-0.5, 0.5]$; these vectors m are also used as the task descriptors. Note that by sampling m from the uniform distribution, this

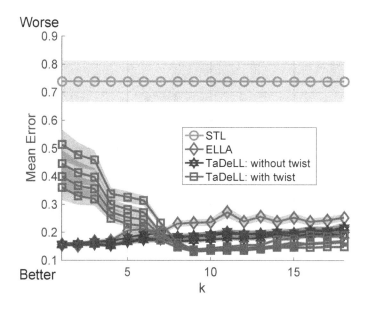

Figure 6.12 An ablative experiment studying the performance of TaDeLL as a function of the dictionary size k, as we vary the subset of descriptors used. The feature consists of twist(t), length(l), and offset(o) variables for each joint. We train TaDeLL using only subsets of the features $\{t, l, o, tl, to, lo, tlo\}$ and we see that the need for a larger k is directly related to learning the *twist*. Subsets that contain twist descriptors are shown in magenta. Trials that do not include twist descriptors are shown in gray. Performance of ELLA and the single-task learner (STL) are provided for comparison. (Best viewed in color.)

Algorithm	Lifelong Learning	Zero-Shot Prediction
TaDeLL	0.926 ± 0.004	0.930 ± 0.002
ELLA	0.814 ± 0.008	N/A
STL	0.755 ± 0.009	N/A

Table 6.2 Classification accuracy on Synthetic Domain 1.

domain violates the assumptions of ELLA that the samples are drawn from a common set of latent features. Each task's data consists of 10 training samples, and we generated 100 tasks to evaluate lifelong learning.

Table 6.2 shows the performance on this Synthetic Domain 1. We see that the inclusion of meaningful task descriptors enables TaDeLL to learn a better dictionary than ELLA in a lifelong learning setting. We also generated an additional 100 unseen tasks to evaluate zero-shot prediction, which is similarly successful.

For the second synthetic domain, we generated L and D matrices, and then generated a random sparse vector $s^{(t)}$ for each task. The true task model is then given by a logistic regression classifier with $\theta^{(t)} = Ls^{(t)}$. This generation process directly follows the assumptions of ELLA and TaDeLL, where D is generated independently. We similarly generate 100 tasks for lifelong learning and another 100 unseen tasks for zero-shot prediction and use

Algorithm	Lifelong Learning	Zero-Shot Prediction
TaDeLL	0.889 ± 0.006	0.87 ± 0.01
ELLA	0.821 ± 0.007	N/A
STL	0.752 ± 0.009	N/A

Table 6.3 Classification accuracy on Synthetic Domain 2.

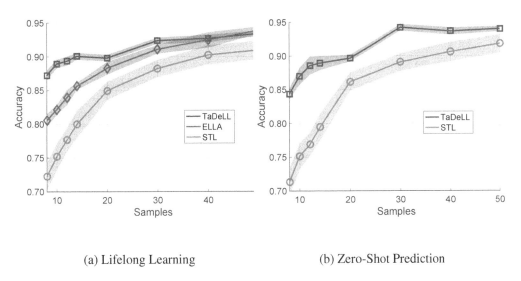

(a) Lifelong Learning   (b) Zero-Shot Prediction

Figure 6.13 Performance versus sample complexity on Synthetic Domain 2.

the true task models to label ten training points per task. In this experiment, we empirically demonstrate that TaDeLL works in the case of this assumption (Table 6.3) in both lifelong learning and zero-shot prediction settings. For comparison, the baseline STL performance using data is equal to 0.762 ± 0.008 and 0.751 ± 0.009, respectively, for these two settings.

We also use this domain to investigate performance versus sample complexity, as we generated varying amounts of training data per task. In Figure 6.13a, we see that TaDeLL is able to improve performance given on a small number of samples, and as expected, its benefit becomes less dramatic as the single-task learner receives sufficient samples. Figure 6.13b shows similar behavior in the zero-shot case.

6.8 ADDITIONAL EXPERIMENTS

Having shown how TaDeLL can improve learning in a variety of settings, we now turn our attention to understanding other aspects of the algorithm. Specifically, we look at the issue of task descriptor selection and partial information, runtime comparisons, and the effect of varying the number of tasks used to train the dictionaries.

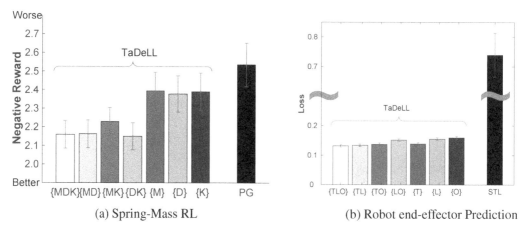

(a) Spring-Mass RL   (b) Robot end-effector Prediction

Figure 6.14 Performance using various subsets of the SM system parameters (mass M, damping constant D, and spring constant K) and Robot system parameters (twist T, link length L, and offset O) as the task descriptors.

6.8.1 Choice of Task Descriptor Features

For RL, we used the system parameters as the task description, and for the robot end-effector prediction, we used the dimensions of the robot. While in these cases, the choice of task descriptor was straightforward, this might not always be the case. It is unclear exactly how the choice of task descriptor features might affect the resulting performance. In other scenarios, we may have only partial knowledge of the system parameters.

To address these questions, we conducted additional experiments on the Spring-Mass (SM) system and robot end-effector problem, using various subsets of the task descriptor features when learning the coupled dictionaries. Figure 6.14a shows how the number and selection of parameters affect performance on the SM domain. We evaluated jumpstart performance when using all possible subsets of the system parameters as the task descriptor features. These subsets of the SM system parameters (mass M, damping constant D, and spring constant K) are shown along the horizontal axis for the task descriptors. Overall, the results show that the learner performs better when using larger subsets of the system parameters as the task descriptors.

The robot task has 24 descriptors consisting of a twist, link offset, and link length for each joint. We group the subset of features describing twist, offset, and length together and examine removing different subsets. Figure 6.14b show that twist is more important than the other features, and again, the inclusion of more features improves performance.

6.8.2 Computational Efficiency

We compared the average per-task runtime of our approach to that of Sinapov et al. [228], the most closely related method to our approach. Since Sinapov et al.'s method requires training transferability predictors between all pairs of tasks, its total runtime grows quadratically with the number of tasks. In comparison, our online algorithm is highly efficient. As shown in Section 6.5.3, the per-update cost of TaDeLL is $O\left(k^2(d+m)^3 + \xi(d, n_t)\right)$. Note that

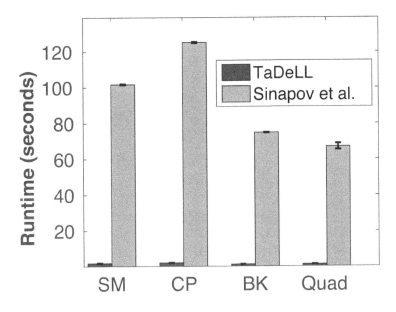

Figure 6.15 Runtime comparison.

this per-update cost is independent of the number of tasks T, giving TaDeLL a total runtime that scales linearly in the number of tasks.

Figure 6.15 shows the per-task runtime for each algorithm based on a set of 40 tasks, as evaluated on an Intel Core I7-4700HQ CPU. TaDeLL samples tasks randomly with replacement and terminates once every task has been seen. For Sinapov et al., we used 10 PG iterations for calculating the warm start, ensuring a fair comparison between the methods. These results show a substantial reduction in computational time for TaDeLL: two orders of magnitude over the 40 tasks.

6.8.3 Performance for Various Numbers of Tasks

Although we have shown in Section 6.5.2 that the learned dictionaries become more stable as the system learns more tasks, we cannot currently guarantee that this will improve the performance of zero-shot transfer. To evaluate the effect of the number of tasks on zero-shot performance, we conducted an additional set of experiments on both the Simple-Mass domain and the robot end-effector prediction domain. Our results, shown in Figure 6.16, reveal that zero-shot performance does indeed improve as the dictionaries are trained over more tasks. This improvement is most stable and rapid in an MTL setting since the optimization over all dictionaries and task policies is run to convergence, but TaDeLL also shows definite improvement in zero-shot performance as T_{max} increases. Since zero-shot transfer involves only the learned coupled dictionaries, we can conclude that the quality of these dictionaries for zero-shot transfer improves as the system learns more tasks.

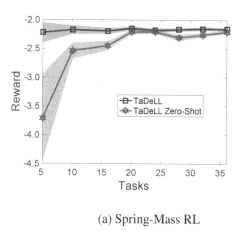

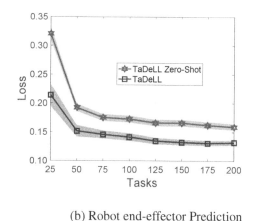

(a) Spring-Mass RL

(b) Robot end-effector Prediction

Figure 6.16 Zero-shot performance as a function of the number of tasks used to train the dictionary. As more tasks are used, the performance of zero-shot transfer improves.

6.9 CONCLUSIONS

We demonstrated that incorporating high-level task descriptors into lifelong learning both improves learning performance and also enables zero-shot transfer to new tasks. The mechanism of using a coupled dictionary to connect the task descriptors with the learned models is relatively straightforward, yet highly effective in practice. Most critically, it provides a fast and simple mechanism to predict the model or policy for a new task via zero-shot learning, given only its high-level task descriptor. This approach is general and can handle multiple learning paradigms, including classification, regression, and RL tasks. Experiments demonstrate that our approach outperforms state of the art and requires substantially less computational time than competing methods.

This ability to rapidly bootstrap models (or policies) for new tasks is critical to the development of lifelong learning systems that will be deployed for extended periods in real environments and tasked with handling a variety of tasks. High-level descriptions provide an effective way for humans to communicate and to instruct each other. The description need not come from another agent; humans often read instructions and then complete a novel task quite effectively. Enabling lifelong learning systems to take advantage of these high-level descriptions provides an effective step toward their practical effectiveness. As shown in our experiments with warm-start learning from the zero-shot predicted policy, these task descriptors can also be combined with training data on the new task in a hybrid approach. Also, while our framework is designed to work for tasks that are drawn from a single domain, an exciting potential direction for future is to extend this work for cross-domain tasks, e.g., balancing tasks of bicycle and spring-mass systems together.

Despite TaDeLL's strong performance, defining what constitutes an effective task descriptor for a group of related tasks remains an open question. In our framework, task descriptors are given, typically as fundamental descriptions of the system. The representation we use for the task descriptors, a feature vector, is also relatively simple. One interesting direction for future work is to develop methods for integrating more complex task descriptors into MTL or lifelong learning. These more sophisticated mechanisms could include natural language descriptions, step-by-step instructions, or logical relationships. Such advance descriptors would likely involve moving beyond the linear framework used in TaDeLL but would constitute an important step toward enabling more practical use of high-level task descriptors in lifelong learning.

In the next chapter, we focus on addressing the challenge of *catastrophic forgetting* catastrophic forgetting in the continual learning setting. Catastrophic forgetting is a phenomenon in machine learning when a model forgets the previously learned tasks when new tasks are learned. In this chapter, tackling catastrophic forgetting is not challenging. The reason is that as more tasks are learned, a better dictionary is learned. To avoid catastrophic forgetting, we can store $\Gamma^{(t)}$ and $\alpha^{(t)}$ and update the estimate for the sparse vector and subsequently the optimal parameter for each learned task using Eq. (6.2). This is possible because the optimal parameters are task-specific. When nonlinear models such as deep neural networks are used as base models, tackling catastrophic forgetting is more challenging because optimal parameters for all the tasks are captures through the weights of the network. These parameters are shared across the tasks, which causes interference. In the next chapter, we will focus on addressing this challenge by coupling the tasks by mapping the tasks into a task-invariant embedding space. Our goal will be to train a model such that the distributions of a number of tasks become similar in a shared embedding space to learn sequential tasks without forgetting.

CHAPTER 7

Complementary Learning Systems Theory for Tackling Catastrophic Forgetting

In the previous chapter, we developed a lifelong learning algorithm to benefit from knowledge transfer to improve learning speed and performance for future tasks. In this chapter, we focus on tackling another challenge for continual learning. Our goal is to learn future tasks such that performance of the ML model that is being continually updated does not degrade on the old tasks. In particular, we consider a deep neural network as the base learner in this chapter. Despite the huge success of deep learning, deep networks are unable to learn effectively in sequential multi-task learning settings as they forget the past learned tasks after learning new tasks. This phenomenon is referred as *catastrophic forgetting* catastrophic forgetting in the literature [145]. Since training deep nets is computationally expensive, the network on past tasks is inefficient. Additionally, it will require storing the data for past tasks which requires a memory buffer. Humans are able to avoid forgetting because various more efficient memory mechanisms are used to retain knowledge about past tasks. Following the broad theme of this book, we rely on learning a task-invariant embedding space to prevent catastrophic forgetting in this chapter.

Figure 7.1 visualizes this idea. We train a shared encoder across the tasks such that the distributions for sequential tasks are matched in an embedding space. To this end, we learn the current task such that its distribution matches the shared distribution in the embedding space. As a result, since the newly learned knowledge about the current task is accumulated consistently to the past learned tasks, catastrophic forgetting does not occur. This processes is similar to chapters 4 and 5 in that the distributions of the tasks are matched in the embedding space. However, note that the tasks arrive in a sequentially in a continual learning setting and as a result learning the tasks jointly is not feasible. We will develop an algorithm to match the distributions in this setting.

To overcome catastrophic forgetting, we are inspired by complementary learning systems theory [142, 143]. We address the challenges of our problem using *experience replay* by equipping the network with a notion of short and long term memories. We train a generative model that can generate samples from past tasks without requiring to store

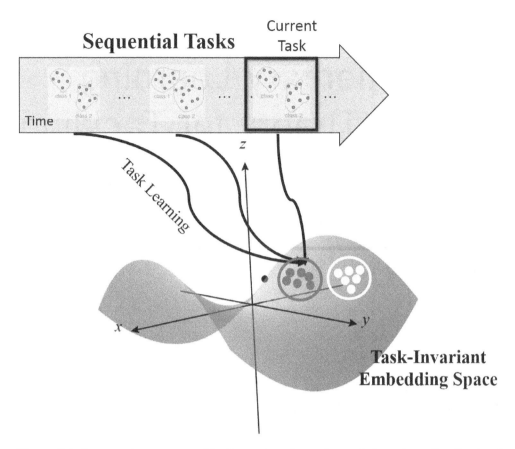

Figure 7.1 Overcoming catastrophic forgetting through a task-invariant distribution in an embedding space: in this figure, the tasks are coupled in the embedding space to share similar distributions. As a result, when a new task is learned, the newly learned knowledge is accumulated to the past learned knowledge consistently, which in turn mitigates catastrophic forgetting.

past task data points in a buffer. These samples are replayed to the network, along with the current task sample to prevent catastrophic forgetting. In order to learn a generative distribution across the tasks, we couple the current task to the past learned tasks through a discriminative embedding space. By doing so, current learned knowledge is always added to the past learned knowledge consistently. We learn an abstract generative distribution in the embedding that allows the generation of data points to represent past experience. The learned distribution captures high-level concepts that are shared across the related tasks. We sample from this distribution and utilize experience replay to avoid forgetting and simultaneously accumulate new knowledge to the abstract distribution in order to couple the current task with past experience. We demonstrate theoretically and empirically that our framework learns a distribution in the embedding which is shared across all tasks and as a result, catastrophic forgetting is prevented. Results of this chapter have been presented in Refs. [201, 203].

7.1 OVERVIEW

The recent breakthrough of deep learning may seem natural as these networks are designed to mimic the human nervous system, and to some extent, they do [152]. However, this success is highly limited to single-task learning, and retaining learned knowledge in a continual learning setting remains a major challenge. That is, when a deep network is trained on multiple sequential tasks with diverse data distributions, the newly obtained knowledge usually interferes with past learned knowledge. As a result, the network is often unable to accumulate the newly learned knowledge in a manner consistent with the past experience and forgets past learned tasks by the time the new task is learned. This phenomenon is called *catastrophic forgetting* catastrophic forgetting in the literature [61]. This phenomenon is in contrast with the continual learning ability of humans over their lifetime. When humans learn a new task, not only they benefit from past experiences to learn the new task more efficiently, but also usually newly learned knowledge does not interfere with past knowledge.

One of the main approaches to mitigate catastrophic forgetting is to replay data points from past tasks that are stored selectively in a memory buffer [181]. This is consistent with the Complementary Learning Systems (CLS) theory [142]. CLS theory hypothesizes that a dual long-term and short-term memory system, involving the neocortex and the hippocampus, is necessary for the continual, lifelong learning ability of humans. In particular, the hippocampus rapidly encodes recent experiences as a short-term memory that is used to consolidate the knowledge in the slower neocortex as long-term memory through experience replay during sleep [52]. Similarly, if we selectively store samples from past tasks in a buffer, like in the neocortex, they can be replayed to the deep network in an interleaved manner with current task samples from recent-memory hippocampal storage to train the deep network jointly on past and current experiences. In other words, the online sequential learning problem is recast as an offline multi-task learning problem that supports performance on all tasks. A major issue with this approach is that the memory size for storing data points grows as more tasks are learned. Building upon recent successes of generative models, we can address this challenge by amending the network structure such that it can generate pseudo-data points for the past learned tasks without storing data points explicitly [225].

In this chapter, our goal is to address catastrophic forgetting via coupling sequential tasks in a latent embedding space. We model this space as the output of a deep encoder, which is between the input and the output layers of a deep classifier. Representations in this embedding space can be thought of as neocortex representations in the brain, which capture learned knowledge. To consolidate knowledge, we minimize the discrepancy between the distributions of all tasks in the embedding space. In order to mimic the offline memory replay process in the sleeping brain [177], we amend the deep encoder with a decoder network to make the classifier network generative. The resulting autoencoding pathways can be thought of as neocortical areas, which encode and remember past experiences. We fit a parametric distribution to the empirical distribution of data representations in the embedding space. This distribution can be used to generate pseudo-data points through sampling, followed by passing the samples into the decoder network. The pseudo-data points can then be used for experience replay of the previous tasks toward the incorporation of new knowledge. This would enforce the embedding to be invariant with respect to the tasks as more tasks are learned; i.e., the network would retain the past learned knowledge as more tasks are learned.

7.2 RELATED WORK

Past works have addressed catastrophic forgetting using two main approaches: model consolidation [100] and experience replay [181]. Both approaches are inspired from the processes that are used by the nervous system implement a notion of memory to enable a network to remember the distributions of past learned tasks.

7.2.1 Model Consolidation

The idea of model consolidation is based upon separating the information pathway for different tasks in the network such that new experiences do not interfere with past learned knowledge. This is inspired from the notion of structural plasticity in the nervous system [115]. This means that the nervous system is able to change the physical structure of connections between the neurons due to learning new concepts. Similarly, during the learning of a task with a deep neural network, important weight parameters for that task can be identified. The weights usually are only a small subset of the total network weights, which suggests that the rest of the weights do not encode important knowledge about that task. These weights are consolidated when future tasks are learned to mitigate catastrophic forgetting. As a result, the new tasks are learned through free pathways in the network; i.e., the weights that are important to retain knowledge about distributions of past tasks mostly remain unchanged. Several methods exist for identifying important weight parameters. Elastic Weight Consolidation (EWC) models the posterior distribution of weights of a given network as a Gaussian distribution that is centered around the weight values from past learned tasks and a precision matrix, defined as the Fisher information matrix of all network weights. The weights are then consolidated according to their importance, the value of Fisher coefficient [100].

In contrast to EWC, Zenke et al. [283] consolidate weights in an online scheme during task learning. If a network weight contributes considerably to changes in the network loss, it is identified as an important weight. More recently, Aljundi et al. [6] use a semi-Hebbian learning procedure to compute the importance of the weight parameters in both an unsupervised and online scheme. The issue with the methods based on structural plasticity is that the network learning capacity is compromised to avoid catastrophic forgetting. As a result, the learning ability of the network decreases as more tasks are learned. In the extreme case, when all the weights are consolidated, no new task can be learned. This may seem natural, but as we will see in our experiments, catastrophic forgetting can be mitigated without compromising the network learning capacity.

7.2.2 Experience Replay

Methods that use experience replay retain the past tasks' distributions via replaying selected representative samples of past tasks continuously. These samples need to be stored in a memory buffer and hence, can grow as most tasks are learned. Prior works have mostly investigated how to identify and store a subset of past experiences to reduce dependence on a memory buffer and meanwhile retain the knowledge about these tasks. These samples can be selected in different ways. Schaul et al. select samples such that the effect of uncommon samples in the experience is maximized [218]. Isele and Cosgun explore four potential strategies to select more helpful samples in a buffer for replay [93]. The downside is that storing samples requires memory, and selection becomes more complex as more tasks are learned.

To reduce dependence on a memory buffer, similar to humans [61], Shin et al. [225] developed a more efficient alternative by considering a generative model that can produce pseudo-data points of past tasks to avoid storing real data points. They use a generative adversarial structure to learn the tasks' distributions to allow for generating pseudo-data points without storing data. However, adversarial learning is known to require deliberate architecture design and selection of hyper-parameters [209], and can suffer from mode collapse [231]. Alternatively, we demonstrate that a simple autoencoder structure can be used as the base generative model. Similar to the rest of the contributions in this book, our contribution is to match the distributions of the tasks in the embedding layer of the autoencoder and learn a shared distribution across the tasks to couple them. The shared distribution is then used to generate samples for experience replay to avoid forgetting. We demonstrate the effectiveness of our approach theoretically and empirically validate our method on benchmark tasks that have been used in the literature.

7.3 GENERATIVE CONTINUAL LEARNING

Similar to the previous chapter, we consider a lifelong learning setting [40], where a learning agent faces multiple, consecutive tasks $\{\mathcal{Z}^{(t)}\}_{t=1}^{T_{\text{Max}}}$ in a sequence $t = 1, \ldots, T_{\text{Max}}$. The agent learns a new task at each time step and proceeds to learn the next task. Each task is learned based upon the experiences gained from learning past tasks. Additionally, the agent may encounter the learned tasks in future and hence must optimize its performance across all tasks; i.e., not to forget learned tasks when future tasks are learned. The agent also does not know *a priori* the total number of tasks, which potentially might not be finite, the distributions of the tasks, and the order of tasks.

Suppose that at time t, the current task $\mathcal{Z}^{(t)}$ with training dataset $\mathcal{Z}^{(t)} = \langle X^{(t)}, Y^{(t)} \rangle$ arrives. In this chapter, we consider classification tasks where the training data points are drawn i.i.d. in pairs from the joint probability distribution, i.e., $(x_i^{(t)}, y_i^{(t)}) \sim p^{(t)}(x, y)$, which has the marginal distribution $q^{(t)}$ over x. We assume that the lifelong learning agent trains a deep neural network $f_\theta : \mathbb{R}^d \to \mathbb{R}^k$ with learnable weight parameters θ to map the data points $X^{(t)} = [x_1^{(t)}, \ldots, x_{n_t}^{(t)}] \in \mathbb{R}^{d \times n_t}$ to the corresponding one-shot labels $Y^{(t)} = [y_1^{(t)}, \ldots, y_n^{(t)}] \in \mathbb{R}^{k \times n_t}$. Learning a single task in isolation is a standard classical learning problem. The agent can solve for the optimal network weight parameters using standard Empirical Risk Minimization (ERM), $\hat{\theta}^{(t)} = \arg\min_\theta \hat{e}_\theta = \arg\min_\theta \sum_i \mathcal{L}_d(f_\theta(x_i^{(t)}), y_i^{(t)})$, where $\mathcal{L}_d(\cdot)$ is a proper loss function, e.g., cross-entropy. Given large enough number of labeled data points n_t, the model trained on a single task $\mathcal{Z}^{(t)}$ will generalize well on the task test samples, as the empirical risk would be a suitable surrogate for the real risk function (Bayes optimal solution), $e = \mathbb{E}_{(x,y) \sim p^{(t)}(x,y)}(\mathcal{L}_d(f_{\theta^{(t)}}(x), y))$ [221]. The agent then can advance to learn the next task, but the challenge is that ERM is unable to tackle catastrophic

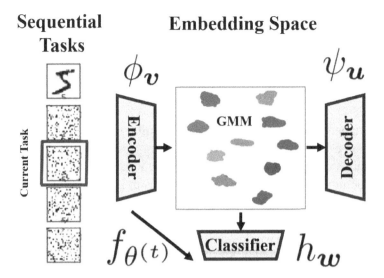

Figure 7.2 The architecture of the proposed framework for learning without forgetting: when a task is learned, pseudo-data points of the past learned tasks are generated and replayed along with the current task data to mitigate catastrophic forgetting.

forgetting as the model parameters are learned using solely the current task data, which can potentially have a very different distribution.

Catastrophic forgetting can be considered as the result of considerable deviations of $\theta^{(T)}$ from past optimal values over $\{\theta^{(t)}\}_{t=1}^{T-1}$ time as a result of drift in tasks' distributions $p^{(t)}(\boldsymbol{x}, \boldsymbol{y})$. As a result, the updated $\theta^{(t)}$ can potentially be highly non-optimal for previous tasks. This means that if the distribution of the same task changes, the network naturally would forget what has been learned. Our idea is to prevent catastrophic forgetting by mapping all tasks' data into an embedding space, where the tasks share a common distribution. This distribution would model the abstract similarities across the tasks and would allow for consistent knowledge transfer across the tasks. We represent this space by the output of a deep network mid-layer, and we condition updating $\theta^{(t)}$ to what has been learned before in this discriminative embedding space. In other words, we want to train the deep network such the tasks are coupled in the embedding space by updating the parameters $\theta^{(T)}$ conditioned on $\{\theta^{(t)}\}_{t=1}^{T-1}$.

The performance of deep networks stems from learning data-driven and task-dependent high-quality features that can be learned in an end-to-end blind data-driven scheme [109]. In other words, a deep network maps data points into a discriminative embedding space, captured by network layers, where classification can be performed easily, e.g., classes become separable in the embedding. Following this intuition, we consider the deep network f_θ to be composed of an encoder $\phi_v(\cdot)$ with learnable parameters $\boldsymbol{v}$, i.e., early layers of the network, and a classifier network $h_w(\cdot)$ with learnable parameters $\boldsymbol{w}$, i.e., higher layers of the network. The encoder sub-network $\phi_v : \mathcal{X} \rightarrow \mathcal{Z}$ maps the data points into the embedding space $\mathcal{Z} \subset \mathbb{R}^f$, which describes the input in terms of abstract discriminative features. Note that after training, as a deterministic function, the encoder network changes the input task data distribution in the embedding. Figure 7.2 presents a high-level block-diagram visualization of our framework.

If the embedding space is discriminative for classification, this distribution can be modeled as a multi-modal distribution for a given task, e.g., using a Gaussian mixture model (GMM). This is because the distribution captures high-level abstract notions of classes in terms of geometric distances in the embedding space, where data points belonging to the same class form a mode for the distribution. Catastrophic forgetting occurs because this distribution is not kept stationary with respect to different tasks. The idea that we want to explore is based on training ϕ_v such that all tasks share a similar high-level distribution in the embedding; i.e., the new tasks are learned such that their distribution in the embedding matches the past experience. By doing so, the embedding space becomes invariant with respect to any learned input task, which in turn mitigates catastrophic forgetting.

The key question is how to adapt the standard supervised learning model $f_\theta(\cdot)$ such that the embedding space, captured in the deep network, becomes task-invariant. Following prior discussion, we use experience replay as the main strategy by making the model generative. We expand the base network $f_\theta(\cdot)$ into a generative model by amending the model with a decoder $\psi_u : \mathcal{Z} \rightarrow \mathcal{X}$, with learnable parameters u. The decoder structure can be similar to the decoder, in reverse order. The decoder maps the data representation back to the input space $\mathcal{X}$ and effectively makes the pair (ϕ_u, ψ_u) an autoencoder. If implemented properly, we would learn a discriminative data distribution in the embedding space, which can be approximated by a GMM. This distribution captures our knowledge about past learned tasks. When a new task arrives, pseudo-data points for past tasks can be generated by sampling from this distribution and feeding the samples to the decoder network. These pseudo-data points can be used for experience replay in order to tackle catastrophic forgetting. Additionally, we need to learn the new task such that its distribution matches the past shared distribution. As a result, future pseudo-data points would represent the current task as well.

7.4 OPTIMIZATION METHOD

Following the above framework, learning the first task ($t = 1$) reduces to minimizing discrimination loss for classification and reconstruction loss for the autoencoder to solve for optimal weight parameters $\hat{v}^{(1)}$, $\hat{w}^{(1)}$, and $\hat{u}^{(1)}$:

$$\min_{v,w,u} \sum_{i=1}^{n_1} \mathcal{L}_d\left(h_w(\phi_v(x_i^{(1)})), y_i^{(1)}\right) + \gamma \mathcal{L}_r\left(\psi_u(\phi_v(x_i^{(1)})), x_i^{(1)}\right) , \tag{7.1}$$

where $\mathcal{L}_r$ is the reconstruction loss, and γ is a trade-off parameter between the two loss terms.

Upon learning the first task and formation of the clusters of classes, we fit a GMM distribution with k components to the empirical distribution represented by data samples $(\phi_v(x_i^{(0)}), y_i^{(0)})_{i=1}^{n_1}$ in the embedding space. The intuition behind this possibility is that as the embedding space is discriminative due to supervised learning, we expect data points of each class to form a cluster in the embedding. Let $\hat{p}_J^{(0)}(z)$ denote this parametric distribution when the first task is learned. When subsequent future tasks are learned, we update this distribution to accumulate what has been learned from the new task into the distribution using the current task samples $(\phi_v(x_i^{(t)}), y_i^{(t)})_{i=1}^{n_t}$. As a result, this distribution captures knowledge about past experiences. Upon learning this distribution, experience replay is also feasible without saving data points. One can generate pseudo-data points in future through random sampling from $\hat{p}_J^{(T-1)}(z)$ at $t = T$ and then passing the samples through the decoder sub-network. These samples are replayed along with the current task samples. It is also crucial to learn the current task such that its distribution in the embedding matches $\hat{p}_J^{(T-1)}(z)$. Doing so ensures suitability of GMM with k components to model the empirical distribution.

Let $\mathcal{Z}_{ER}^{(T)} = \langle X_{ER}^{(T)}, Y_{ER}^{(T)} \rangle$ denote the pseudo-dataset generated at $t = T$. Following our framework, learning subsequent tasks reduces to solving the following problem:

$$
\begin{aligned}
\min_{v,w,u} &\sum_{i=1}^{n_t} \mathcal{L}_d\Big(h_w(\phi_v(x_i^{(T)})), y_i^{(T)}\Big) + \gamma \mathcal{L}_r\Big(\psi_u(\phi_v(x_i^{(T)})), x_i^{(T)}\Big) \\
&+ \sum_{i=1}^{n_{er}} \mathcal{L}_d\Big(h_w(\phi_v(x_{er,i}^{(T)})), y_{er,i}^{(T)}\Big) + \gamma \mathcal{L}_r\Big(\psi_u(\phi_v(x_{er,i}^{(T)})), x_{er,i}^{(T)}\Big) \qquad (7.2) \\
&+ \lambda \sum_{j=1}^{k} D\Big(\phi_v(q^{(T)}(X^{(T)}|C_j)), \hat{p}_J^{(T-1)}(Z_{ER}^{(T)}|C_j)\Big) \ ,
\end{aligned}
$$

where $D(\cdot, \cdot)$ is a discrepancy measure (metric) between two probability distributions, and λ is a trade-off parameter. The first four terms in Eq. (7.2) are empirical classification risk and autoencoder reconstruction loss terms for the current task and the generated pseudo-dataset. The third and fourth terms enforce learning the current task such that the past learned knowledge is not forgotten. The fifth term is added to enforce the learned embedding distribution for the current task to be similar to what has been learned in the past, i.e., task-invariant. Note that we have conditioned the distance between the two distributions on classes to avoid the class matching challenge, i.e., when wrong classes across two tasks are matched in the embedding, as well as to prevent mode collapse from happening. Class-conditional matching is considerably easier compared to chapter 4 because we have labels for both distributions. This term guarantees that we can continually use GMM with k components to fit the shared distribution in the embedding space.

The main remaining question is selecting the metric $D(\cdot, \cdot)$ such that it fits our problem. Similar to chapters 4 and 5 and because the same reasoning is valid here, we rely on Sliced Wasserstein Distance (SWD) [173], which approximates the optimal transport metric, but can be computed efficiently. By utilizing the SWD as the discrepancy measure between the distributions in Eq. (7.2), it can be solved using the first-order optimization techniques that are suitable for deep learning. We tackle catastrophic forgetting using the proposed procedure. Our algorithm, named Continual Learning using Encoded Experience Replay (CLEER), is summarized in Algorithm 8.

7.5 THEORETICAL JUSTIFICATION

We again rely on theoretical results about using optimal transport within domain adaptation [178] to justify why our algorithm can tackle catastrophic forgetting. Note that the hypothesis class in our learning problem is the set of all functions represented by the network $f_\theta(\cdot)$ parameterized by θ. For a given model in this class, let e_t denote the observed risk for

---

Algorithm 8 CLEER (L, λ)

1: **Input:** data $\mathcal{D}^{(t)} = (\boldsymbol{X}^{(t)}, \boldsymbol{Y}^{(t)})_{t=1}^{T_{\text{Max}}}$.

2: **Pre-training**: learning the first task $(t = 1)$

3: $\quad\quad \hat{\theta}^{(1)} \quad\quad = \quad\quad (\boldsymbol{u}^{(1)}, \boldsymbol{v}^{(1)}, \boldsymbol{w}^{(1)}) \quad\quad = \arg\min_\theta \sum_i \mathcal{L}_d(f_\theta(\boldsymbol{x}_i^{(t)}), \boldsymbol{y}_i^{(t)}) \quad +$
   $\quad \gamma \mathcal{L}_r(\psi_{\boldsymbol{u}}(\phi_{\boldsymbol{v}}(\boldsymbol{x}_i^{(1)})), \boldsymbol{x}_i^{(1)})$

4: Estimate $\hat{p}_J^{(0)}(\cdot)$ using $\{\phi_{\boldsymbol{v}}(\boldsymbol{x}_i^{(1)})\}_{i=1}^{n_t}$

5: **for** $t = 2, \ldots, T_{\text{Max}}$ **do**

6: $\quad$ **Generate pseudo-dataset:**

7: $\quad\quad \mathcal{D}_{\text{ER}} = \{(\boldsymbol{x}_{er,i}^{(t)} = \psi(\boldsymbol{z}_{er,i}^{(t)}), \boldsymbol{y}_{er,i}^{(t)}) \sim \hat{p}_J^{(t-1)}(\cdot)\}_{i=1}^{n_{er}}$

8: $\quad$ **Update** learnable parameters using pseudo-dataset: Eq. (7.2)

9: $\quad$ **Estimate:** $\hat{p}_J^{(t)}(\cdot)$

10: $\quad\quad$ use $\{\phi_{\boldsymbol{v}}(\boldsymbol{x}_i^{(t)})), \phi_{\boldsymbol{v}}(\boldsymbol{x}_{er,i}^{(t)})\}_{i=1}^{n_t}$

11: **end for**

---

a particular task $\mathcal{Z}^{(t)}$ and e_t^J denote the observed risk for learning the network on samples of the distribution $\hat{p}_J^{(t-1)}$. For the convenience of the reader, we list the following theorem again [178].

Theorem 7.5.1. *Consider two tasks $\mathcal{Z}^{(t)}$ and $\mathcal{Z}^{(t')}$, and a model $f_{\theta^{(t')}}$ trained for $\mathcal{Z}^{(t')}$, then for any $d' > d$ and $\zeta < \sqrt{2}$, there exists a constant number N_0 depending on d' such that for any $\xi > 0$ and $\min(n_t, n_{t'}) \geq \max(\xi^{-(d'+2)}, 1)$ with probability at least $1 - \xi$ for all $f_{\theta^{(t')}}$, the following holds:*

$$e_t \leq e_{t'} + W(\hat{p}^{(t)}, \hat{p}^{(t')}) + e_C(\theta^*) +$$
$$\sqrt{(2 \log(\frac{1}{\xi})/\zeta)}(\sqrt{\frac{1}{n_t}} + \sqrt{\frac{1}{n_{t'}}}) \ , \tag{7.3}$$

where $W(\cdot)$ denotes the Wasserstein distance between empirical distributions of the two tasks and θ^* denotes the optimal parameter for training the model on tasks jointly, i.e., $\theta^* = \arg\min_\theta e_C(\theta) = \arg\min_\theta \{e_t + e_{t'}\}$.

We observe from Theorem 7.5.1 that performance, i.e., real risk, of a model learned for task $\mathcal{Z}^{(t')}$ on another task $\mathcal{Z}^{(t)}$ is upper-bounded by four terms: (i) model performance on task $\mathcal{Z}^{(t')}$, (ii) the distance between the two distributions, (iii) performance of the jointly learned model f_{θ^*}, and (iv) a constant term that depends on the number of data points for each task. Note that we do not have a notion of time in this Theorem; i.e., the roles of $\mathcal{Z}^{(t)}$ and $\mathcal{Z}^{(t')}$ can be shuffled and the theorem would still hold. In our framework, we consider the task $\mathcal{Z}^{(t')}$ to be the pseudo-task, i.e., the task derived by drawing samples from $\hat{p}_J^{t'}$ and then feeding the samples to the decoder sub-network. We use this result to conclude the following theorem.

Theorem 7.5.2. *Consider CLEER algorithm for lifelong learning after $\mathcal{Z}^{(T)}$ is learned at time $t = T$. Then all tasks $t < T$ and under the conditions of Theorem 1, we can conclude* *the following inequality:*

$$
\begin{aligned}
e_t \leq & e_{T-1}^J + W(\hat{q}^{(t)}, \psi(\hat{p}_J^{(t)})) + \sum_{s=t}^{T-2} W(\psi(\hat{p}_J^{(s)}), \psi(\hat{p}_J^{(s+1)})) \\
& + e_{\mathcal{C}}(\theta^*) + \sqrt{(2\log(\frac{1}{\xi})/\zeta)}\left(\sqrt{\frac{1}{n_t}} + \sqrt{\frac{1}{n_{er,t-1}}}\right) ,
\end{aligned}
\tag{7.4}
$$

Proof: We consider $\mathcal{Z}^{(t)}$ with empirical distribution $\hat{q}^{(t)}$ and the pseudo-task with the distribution $\psi(\hat{p}_J^{(T-1)})$ in the network input space, in Theorem 1. Using the triangular inequality on the term $W(\hat{q}^{(t)}, \psi(\hat{p}_J^{(T-1)}))$ recursively, i.e., $W(\hat{q}^{(t)}, \psi(\hat{p}_J^{(s)})) \leq W(\hat{p}^{(t)}, \psi(\hat{p}_J^{(s-1)})) + W(\psi(\hat{p}_J^{(s)}), \psi(\hat{p}_J^{(s-1)}))$ for all $t \leq s < T$, Theorem 7.5.2 can be derived ■

Theorem 7.5.2 explains why our algorithm can tackle catastrophic forgetting. When future tasks are learned, our algorithms updates the model parameters conditioned on minimizing the upper-bound of e_t in Eq. 7.4. Given a suitable network structure and in the presence of enough labeled data points, the terms e_{t-1}^J and $e_{\mathcal{C}}(\theta^*)$ are minimized using ERM, and the last constant term would be small. The term $W(\hat{q}^{(t)}, \psi(\hat{p}_J^{(t)}))$ is minimal because we deliberately fit the distribution $\hat{p}_J^{(t)}$ to the distribution $\phi(\hat{q}^{(t)})$ in the embedding space and ideally learn ϕ and ψ such that we have $\psi \approx \phi^{-1}$. This term demonstrates that minimizing the discrimination loss is critical as only then can we fit a GMM distribution on $\phi(\hat{p}^{(t)})$ with high accuracy. Similarly, the sum terms in Eq. 7.4 are minimized because at $t = s$, we draw samples from $\hat{p}_J^{(s-1)}$ and enforce $\hat{p}_J^{(s-1)} \approx \phi(\psi(\hat{p}_J^{(s-1)}))$ indirectly. Since the upper-bound of e_t in Eq. 7.4 is minimized and conditioned on its tightness, the task $\mathcal{Z}^{(t)}$ will not be forgotten.

7.6 EXPERIMENTAL VALIDATION

We validate our method on learning two sets of sequential tasks: independent permuted MNIST tasks and related digit classification tasks.

7.6.1 Learning Sequential Independent Tasks

Following the literature, we use permuted MNIST tasks to validate our framework. The sequential tasks involve classification of handwritten images of MNIST ($\mathcal{M}$) dataset [118], where pixel values for each data point are shuffled randomly by a fixed permutation order for each task. As a result, the tasks are independent and quite different from each other. Since knowledge transfer across tasks is less likely to happen, these tasks are a suitable benchmark to investigate the effect of an algorithm on mitigating catastrophic forgetting as past learned tasks are not similar to the current task. We compare our method against: (a) normal backpropagation (BP) as a lower bound, (b) full experience replay (FR) of data for all the previous tasks as an upper-bound, and (c) EWC as a competing model consolidation framework.

We learn permuted MNIST tasks using a simple multi-layer perceptron (MLP) network trained via standard stochastic gradient descent and compute the performance of the network

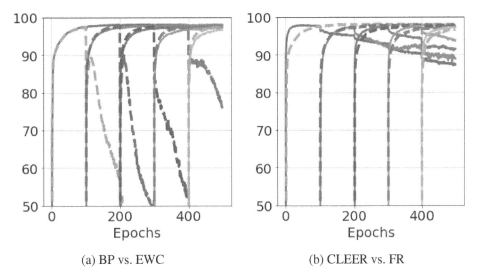

(a) BP vs. EWC (b) CLEER vs. FR

Figure 7.3 Performance results for permuted MNIST tasks: (a) the dashed curves denote results for back-propagation (BP) and the solid curves denote the results for EWC; (b) the dashed curves denote results for full replay (FR) and the solid curves denote the results for our algorithm (CLEER). (best viewed in color).

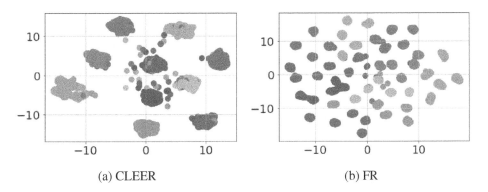

(a) CLEER (b) FR

Figure 7.4 UMAP visualization of CLEER versus FR for permuted MNIST tasks. (best viewed in color.)

on the testing split of each task data at each iteration. Figure 7.3 presents results on five permuted MNIST tasks. Figure 7.3a presents learning curves for BP (dotted curves) and EWC (solid curves) [1].

We observe that EWC is able to address catastrophic forgetting quite well. However, a close inspection reveals that as more tasks are learned, the asymptotic performance on subsequent tasks is less than the single task learning performance (roughly 4% less for the fifth task). This can be understood as a side effect of model consolidation, which limits the learning capacity of the network. This is an inherent limitation for techniques that regularize network parameters to prevent catastrophic forgetting. Figure 7.3b presents

---

[1]We have used PyTorch implementation of EWC [81].

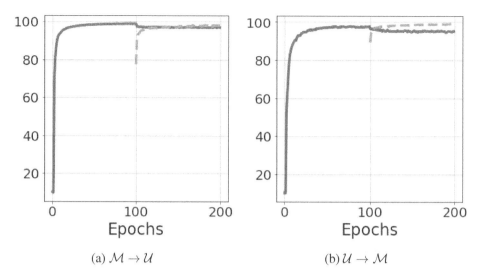

(a) $\mathcal{M} \rightarrow \mathcal{U}$ (b) $\mathcal{U} \rightarrow \mathcal{M}$

Figure 7.5 Performance results on MNIST and USPS digit recognition tasks versus learning iterations: the solid curve denotes performance of the network on the first task and the dashed curve denotes the performance on the second task. (best viewed in color.)

learning curves for our method (solid curves) versus FR (dotted curves). As expected, FR can prevent catastrophic forgetting perfectly, but as we discussed the downside is the memory growth challenge. FR result in Figure 7.3b demonstrates that the network learning capacity is sufficient for learning these tasks and that if we have a perfect generative model, we can prevent catastrophic forgetting without compromising the network learning capacity. Despite more forgetting in our approach compared to EWC, the asymptotic performance after learning each task, just before advancing to learn the next task, has been improved. We also observe that our algorithm suffers an initial drop in performance of previous tasks when we proceed to learn a new task. Every time that a new task is learned, performance on all the prior learned tasks suffers from this initial drop. Forgetting beyond this initial forgetting is negligible. This can be understood as the existing distance between $\hat{p}_J^{(T-1)}$ and $\phi(q^{(t)})$ at $t = T$. In other words, our method can be improved, if better autoencoder structures are used. This will require a search on the structure of the autoencoder, e.g., number of layers, number of filters in the convolutional layer, etc., which we leave for the future. These results suggest that catastrophic forgetting may be tackled better if both model consolidation and experience replay are combined.

To provide a better intuitive understating, we have also included the representations of the testing data for all tasks in the embedding space of the MLP in Figures 7.4. We have used UMAP [146] to reduce the dimensions for visualization purpose. In these figures, each color corresponds to a specific class of digits. We can see that although FR is able to learn all tasks and form distinct clusters for each digit class for each task, five different clusters are formed for each class in the embedding space. This suggests that FR is unable to learn the concept of the same class across different tasks in the embedding space. In comparison, we observe that CLEER is able to match the same class across different tasks; i.e., we have exactly ten clusters for the ten digits. This empirical observation demonstrates that we can

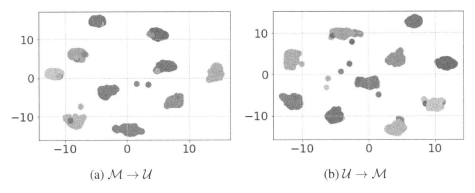

(a) $\mathcal{M} \to \mathcal{U}$　　　　　(b) $\mathcal{U} \to \mathcal{M}$

Figure 7.6 UMAP visualization for $\mathcal{M} \to \mathcal{U}$ and $\mathcal{U} \to \mathcal{M}$ tasks. (best viewed in color.)

model the data distribution in the embedding using a multi-modal distribution such as a GMM [84].

7.6.2　Learning Sequential Tasks in Related Domains

We performed a second set of experiments on related tasks to investigate the ability of the algorithm to learn new domains. We consider two digit classification datasets for this purpose: MNIST ($\mathcal{M}$) and USPS ($\mathcal{U}$) datasets. Despite being similar, USPS dataset is a more challenging task as the size of the training set is smaller (20,000 compared to 60,000 images). We consider the two possible sequential learning scenarios: $\mathcal{M} \to \mathcal{U}$ and $\mathcal{U} \to \mathcal{M}$. We resized the USPS images to 28×28 pixels to be able to use the same encoder network for both tasks. The experiments can be considered as a special case of domain adaptation as both tasks are digit recognition tasks but in different domains. To capture relations between the tasks, we use a CNN for these experiments.

Figure 7.5 presents learning curves for these two tasks. We observe that the network retains the knowledge about the first domain, after learning the second domain. We also see that forgetting is negligible compared to unrelated tasks, and there is a jump-start in performance. These observations suggest relations between the tasks help to avoid forgetting. As a result of task similarities, the empirical distribution can capture the task distribution more accurately. As expected from the theoretical justification, this empirical result suggests the performance of our algorithm depends on the closeness of the distribution $\psi(\hat{p}_J^{(t)})$ to the distributions of previous tasks. Moreover, improving probability estimation will increase the performance of our approach. We have also presented UMAP visualization of all tasks' data in the embedding space in Figure 7.6. We can see that as expected, the distributions are matched in the embedding space. We also see a number of stray dots. These are data points that the network has not been able to classify well.

7.7　CONCLUSIONS

Inspired from CLS theory, we addressed the challenge of catastrophic forgetting for sequential learning of multiple tasks using experience replay. We amend a base learning model with a generative pathway that encodes experiences meaningfully as a parametric distribution in an embedding space. This idea makes experience replay feasible without requiring a memory buffer to store task data. The algorithm is able to accumulate new knowledge in a manner consistent with past learned knowledge, as the parametric distribution in the embedding space is enforced to be shared across all tasks. Compared to model-based approaches that regularize the network to consolidate the important weights for past tasks, our approach is able to address catastrophic forgetting without limiting the learning capacity of the network. Future works for our approach may extend to learning new tasks and/or classes with limited labeled data points and to investigating how to select the suitable network layer and its dimensionality for the embedding. Additionally, in our approach, the GMM only captures the classes. Using hierarchical GMM models that allow for a hierarchical embedding spaces that separates the data points not only based on their class but also based on the corresponding tasks, can help to capture data distributions in a more descriptive way.

One important observation in this chapter is the CLEER algorithm helps to learn a concept across several related tasks. Building upon this observation, we develop an algorithm for continual concept learning in the next chapter. The goal would be similar to this chapter in the sense that when a network learns new forms of a concept, it should remember the old learned forms as well. The difference would be that the goal is to generalize a concept to the new domains using a minimal number of labeled data points.

CHAPTER 8

Continual Concept Learning

In this chapter, we study an extension of the learning setting that we studied in the previous chapter. We assume that upon learning the initial task in a sequential learning setting, only a few labeled data is accessible for the subsequent tasks. In terms of mathematical formulation, the difference between this chapter and the previous chapter might seem minor, but the question that we try to answer is different. In chapter 7, the focus was solely tackling catastrophic forgetting in a sequential learning setting. In contrast, our goal in this chapter is to generalize a learned concept to new domains using a few labeled samples. For this reason, the goal is to match the concepts across the tasks, rather merely remembering the past tasks. Although we formulate the problem in a sequential learning setting of tasks, this setting can be considered as learning a single task when the underlying distribution changes over time. In this context, this setting can be considered a concept learning setting, where the goal is to generalize the concepts that have been learned to new domains using the minimal number of labeled data. After learning a concept, humans are able to continually generalize their learned concepts to new domains by observing only a few labeled instances, without any interference with the past learned knowledge. Note that this is different from ZSL for the unseen classes, where a new concept is learned using knowledge transfer from another domain. In contrast, learning concepts efficiently in a continual learning setting remains an open challenge for current ML algorithms, as persistent model retraining is necessary.

In the previous chapter, we addressed catastrophic forgetting for a deep network that is being trained in a sequential learning setting. One of the observations was that when we trained a deep network on a related set of classification tasks, each class was encoded as a cluster in the embedding space across the tasks. This suggested that the network was able to identify each class as a concept across the tasks. Inspired by the observations in the previous chapter, we develop a computational model in this chapter that is able to expand its previously learned concepts efficiently to new domains using a few labeled samples. We couple the new form of a concept to its past learned forms in an embedding space for effective continual learning. To this end, we benefit from the idea that we used in chapter 5, where we demonstrated that one could learn a domain-invariant and discriminative embedding space for a source domain with labeled data and a target domain with few labeled data points. In other words, we address the problem of domain adaption in a continual learning setting, where the goal is not only to learn the new domain using few-labeled data points but also to remember old domains. We demonstrate that our idea in the previous chapter can be used to address the challenges of this learning setting. Results of this chapter have been presented in Refs. [204, 202].

8.1 OVERVIEW

An important ability of humans is to build and update abstract concepts continually. Humans develop and learn abstract concepts to characterize and communicate their perception and ideas [112]. These concepts often are evolved and expanded efficiently as more experience about new domains is gained. Consider, for example, the concept of the printed character "4". This concept is often taught to represent the "natural number four" in the mother language of elementary school students. Upon learning this concept, humans can efficiently expand it by observing only a few samples from other related domains, e.g., a variety of hand-written digits or different fonts.

Despite remarkable progress in machine learning, learning concepts efficiently in a way similar to humans, remains an unsolved challenge for AI, including methods based on deep neural networks. Even simple changes such as minor rotations of input images can degrade the performance of deep neural networks. Since deep networks are trained in an end-to-end supervised learning setting, access to labeled data is necessary for learning any new distribution or variations of a learned concept. For this reason and despite the emergence of behaviors similar to the nervous system in deep nets, adapting a deep neural network to learn a concept in a new domain usually requires model retraining from scratch which is conditioned on the availability of a large number of labeled samples in the new domain. Moreover, as we discussed in the previous chapter, training deep networks in a continual learning setting, is challenging due to the phenomenon of catastrophic forgetting [61]. When a network is trained on multiple sequential tasks, the newly learned knowledge can interfere with past learned knowledge, causing the network to forget what has been learned before.

In this chapter, we develop a computational model that is able to expand and generalize learned concepts efficiently to new domains using a few labeled data from the new domains. We rely on Parallel Distributed Processing (PDP) paradigm [144] for this purpose. Work on semantic cognition within the parallel distributed processing hypothesizes that abstract semantic concepts are formed in higher-level layers of the nervous system [143, 216]. Hereafter we call this the PDP hypothesis. We can model this hypothesis by assuming that the data points are mapped into an embedding space, which captures existing concepts. From the previous chapter, we know that this is the case with deep networks.

To prevent catastrophic forgetting, we again rely on the Complementary Learning Systems (CLS) theory [142], discussed in the previous chapter. CLS theory hypothesizes that continual lifelong learning ability of the nervous system is a result of a dual long- and short-term memory system. The hippocampus acts as short-term memory and encodes recent experiences that are used to consolidate the knowledge in the neocortex as long-term memory through offline experience replay during sleep [52]. This suggests that if we store suitable samples from past domains in a memory buffer, like in the neocortex, these samples can be replayed along with current task samples from recent-memory hippocampal storage to train the base model jointly on the past and the current experiences to tackle catastrophic forgetting.

More specifically, we model the latent embedding space via responses of a hidden layer in a deep neural network. Our idea is to stabilize and consolidate the data distribution in this space, where domain-independent abstract concepts are encoded. By doing so, new forms of concepts can be learned efficiently by coupling them to their past learned forms in the embedding space. Data representations in this embedding space can be considered as neocortical representations in the brain, where the learned abstract concepts are captured. We model concept learning in a sequential task learning framework, where learning concepts in each new domain is considered to be a task.

Similar to the previous chapter, we use an autoencoder as the base network to benefit from the efficient coding ability of deep autoencoders to generalize the learned concepts without forgetting. We model the embedding space as the middle layer of the autoencoder. This will also make our model generative, which can be used to implement the offline memory replay process in the sleeping brain [177]. To this end, we fit a parametric multi-modal distribution to the training data representations in the embedding space. The drawn points from this distribution can be used to generate pseudo-data points through the decoder network for experience replay to prevent catastrophic forgetting. While in the previous chapter, the data points for all the tasks were labeled, we demonstrate that this learning procedure enables the base model to generalize its learned concepts to new domains using a few labeled samples.

8.2 RELATED WORK

Lake et al. [112] modeled human concept learning within a *Bayesian probabilistic learning* Bayesian probabilistic learning (BPL) paradigm. They present BPL as an alternative for deep learning to mimic the learning ability of humans. While deep networks require a data greedy learning scheme, BPL models require considerably less amount of training data. The concepts are represented as probabilistic programs that can generate additional instances of a concept given a few samples of that concept. However, the proposed algorithm in Lake et al. [112], requires human supervision and domain knowledge to tell the algorithm how the real-world concepts are generated. This approach seems feasible for the recognition task that they have designed to test their idea, but it does not scale to other, more challenging concept learning problems.

Our framework similarly relies on a generative model that can produce pseudo-samples of the learned concepts, but we follow an end-to-end deep learning scheme that automatically encodes concepts in the hidden layer of the network with a minimal human supervision requirement. Our approach can be applied to a broader range of problems. The price is that we rely on data to train the model, but only a few data points are labeled. This is similar to humans with respect to how they too need the practice to generate samples of a concept when they do not have domain knowledge [130]. This generative strategy has been used in the Machine Learning (ML) literature to address *few-shot learning* few-shot learning (FSL) [229, 154]. As we saw in chapter 5, the goal of FSL is to adapt a model that is trained on a source domain with sufficient labeled data to generalize well on a *related* target domain with a few labeled data points. In our work, the domains are different but also are related in that similar concepts are shared across the domains.

Most FSL algorithms consider only one source and one target domain, which are learned jointly. Moreover, the main goal is to learn the target task. In contrast, we consider a continual learning setting in which the domain-specific tasks arrive sequentially.

Hence, catastrophic forgetting becomes a major challenge. An effective approach to tackle catastrophic forgetting is to use experience replay [145, 181]. Experience replay addresses catastrophic forgetting via storing and replaying data points of past learned tasks continually. Consequently, the model retains the probability distributions of the past learned tasks. To avoid requiring a memory buffer to store past task samples, we can use generative models to produce pseudo-data points for past tasks. To this end, generative adversarial learning can be used to match the cumulative distribution of the past tasks with the current task distribution to allow for generating pseudo-data points for experience replay [225]. Similarly, the autoencoder structure can also be used to generate pseudo-data points [168]. We develop a new method for generative experience replay to tackle catastrophic forgetting. Although prior works require access to labeled data for all the sequential tasks for experience replay, we demonstrate that experience replay is feasible even in the setting where only the initial task has labeled data. Our contribution is to combine ideas of few-shot learningwith generative experience replay to develop a framework that can continually update and generalize learned concepts when new domains are encountered in a lifelong learning setting. We couple the distributions of the tasks in the middle layer of an autoencoder and use the shared distribution to expand concepts using a few labeled data points without forgetting the past.

8.3 PROBLEM STATEMENT AND THE PROPOSED SOLUTION

In our framework, learning concepts in each domain is considered to be a classification task, e.g., a different type of digit character. We consider a continual learning setting [211], where an agent receives consecutive tasks $\{\mathcal{Z}^{(t)}\}_{t=1}^{T_{\text{Max}}}$ in a sequence $t = 1, \ldots, T_{\text{Max}}$ over its lifetime. The total number of tasks, distributions of the tasks, and the order of tasks is not known a priori. Each task denotes a particular domain, e.g., different types of digit characters. Analogously, we may consider the same task when the task distribution changes over time. Since the agent is a lifelong learner, the current task is learned at each time step, and the agent then proceeds to learn the next task. The knowledge that is gained from experiences is used to learn the current task efficiently, using a minimal quantity of labeled data. The newly learned knowledge from the current task also would be accumulated to the past experiences to ease learning in future potentially. Additionally, this accumulation must be done consistently to generalize the learned concepts as the agent must perform well on all learned task and not to forget the concepts in the previous domains. This ability is necessary because the learned tasks may be encountered at any time in the future. Figure 8.1 presents a high-level block-diagram visualization of this framework.

We model an abstract concept as a class within a domain-dependent classification task. Data points for each task are drawn i.i.d. from the joint probability distribution, i.e., $(\boldsymbol{x}_i^{(t)}, \boldsymbol{y}_i^{(t)}) \sim p^{(t)}(\boldsymbol{x}, \boldsymbol{y})$ which has the marginal distribution $q^{(t)(\boldsymbol{x})}$ over $\boldsymbol{x}$. We consider a deep neural network $f_\theta : \mathbb{R}^d \to \mathbb{R}^k$ as the base learning model, where θ denote the learnable weight parameters. A deep network is able to solve classification tasks through extracting task-dependent high-quality features in a data-driven end-to-end learning setting [109]. Within the PDP paradigm [144, 143, 216], this means that the data points are mapped into a discriminative embedding space, modeled by the network hidden layers, where the classes become separable, data points belonging to a class are grouped as an abstract concept. On this basis, the deep network f_θ is a functional composition of an encoder $\phi_{\boldsymbol{v}}(\cdot) : \mathbb{R}^d \to \mathcal{Z} \subset \mathbb{R}^f$

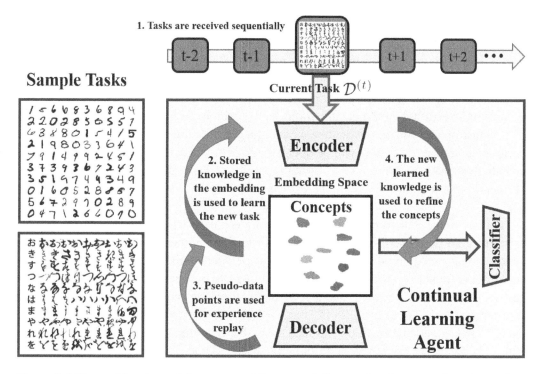

Figure 8.1 The architecture of the proposed framework for continual concept learning: when a task is learned, pseudo-data points of the past learned tasks are generated and replayed along with the current task data for both avoiding catastrophic forgetting and generalizing the past concept to the new related domain.

with learnable parameter v, that encode the input data into the embedding space $\mathcal{Z}$ and a classifier sub-network $h_w(\cdot) : \mathbb{R}^f \to \mathbb{R}^k$ with learnable parameters w, that maps encoded information into the label space. In other words, the encoder network changes the input data distribution as a deterministic function. Because the embedding space is discriminative, the data distribution in the embedding space would be a multi-modal distribution that can be modeled as a (GMM). Figure 8.1 visualizes this intuition based on experimental data, used in the experimental validation section.

Following the classic ML formalism, the agent can solve the task $\mathcal{Z}^{(1)}$ using standard Empirical Risk Minimization (ERM). Given the labeled training dataset $\mathcal{D}^{(1)} = \langle X^{(1)}, Y^{(1)} \rangle$, where $X^{(1)} = [x_1^{(1)}, \ldots, x_{n_1}^{(1)}] \in \mathbb{R}^{d \times n_1}$ and $Y^{(1)} = [y_1^{(1)}, \ldots, y_n^{(1)}] \in \mathbb{R}^{k \times n_t}$, we can solve for the network optimal weight parameters: $\hat{\theta}^{(t)} = \arg\min_\theta \hat{e}_\theta = \arg\min_\theta 1/n_t \sum_i \mathcal{L}_d(f_\theta(x_i^{(t)}), y_i^{(t)})$. Here, $\mathcal{L}_d(\cdot)$ is a suitable loss function such as cross-entropy. If a large enough number of labeled data points n_1 is available, the empirical risk would be a suitable function to estimate the real risk function, $e = \mathbb{E}_{(x,y) \sim p^{(t)}(x,y)}(\mathcal{L}_d(f_{\theta^{(t)}}(x), y))$ [221] as the Bayes optimal objective. Hence, the trained model will generalize well on test data points for the task $\mathcal{Z}^{(1)}$.

Good generalization performance means that each class would be learned as a concept which is encoded in the hidden layers. Our goal is to consolidate these learned concepts and generalize them when the next tasks with a minimal number of labeled data points arrive.

That is, for tasks $\mathcal{Z}^{(t)}, t > 1$, we have access to the dataset $\mathcal{D}^{(t)} = \langle \{\boldsymbol{X}^{('t)}, \boldsymbol{Y}^{(t)}\}, \boldsymbol{X}^{(t)} \rangle$, where $\boldsymbol{X}^{('t)} \in \mathbb{R}^{d \times n_t}$ denotes the labeled data points and $\boldsymbol{X}^{(t)} \in \mathbb{R}^{d \times n_t}$ denotes unlabeled data points. This learning setting means that the learned concepts must be generalized in the subsequent domains with minimal supervision. Standard ERM cannot be used to learn the subsequent tasks because the number of labeled data points is not sufficient, and as a result, overfitting would occur. Additionally, even in the presence of enough labeled data, catastrophic forgetting would be a consequence of using ERM. This consequence is because the model parameters will be updated using solely the current task data, which can potentially deviate the values of $\theta^{(T)}$ from the previously learned values in the past time step. Hence, the agent would not retain its learned knowledge when drifts in data distributions occur.

Following the PDP hypothesis and ability of deep networks to implement this hypothesis, our goal is to use the encoded distribution in the embedding space to expand the concepts that are captured in the embedding space. Meanwhile, we would like to prevent catastrophic forgetting. The gist of our idea is to update the encoder sub-network such that each subsequent task is learned such that its distribution in the embedding space matches the distribution that is shared by $\{\mathcal{Z}^{(t)}\}_{t=1}^{T-1}$ at $t = T$. Since this distribution is initially learned via $\mathcal{Z}^{(1)}$ and subsequent tasks are enforced to share this distribution in the embedding space with $\mathcal{Z}^{(1)}$, we do not need to learn it from scratch as the concepts are shared across the tasks. As a result, since the embedding space becomes invariant with respect to any learned input task, catastrophic forgetting would not occur as the newly learned knowledge does interfere with what has been learned before.

The key challenge is to adapt the standard ERM such that the tasks share the same distribution in the embedding space that is shared across the tasks. To this end, we modify the base network $f_\theta(\cdot)$ to form a generative autoencoder by amending the model with a decoder $\psi_{\boldsymbol{u}} : \mathcal{Z} \rightarrow \mathcal{X}$ with learnable parameters $\boldsymbol{u}$. We train the model such the pair $(\phi_{\boldsymbol{u}}, \psi_{\boldsymbol{u}})$ to form an autoencoder. Doing so, we enhance the ability of the model to encode the concepts as separable clusters in the embedding. We use the knowledge about data distribution form in the embedding to match the distributions of all tasks in the embedding. This leads to a consistent generalization of the learned concepts. Additionally, since the model is generative and knowledge about past experiences is encoded in the network, we can use the CLS process [142] to prevent catastrophic forgetting. In other words, we extend the CLS process to generative CLS process. When learning a new task, pseudo-data points for the past learned tasks can be generated by sampling from the shared distribution in the embedding and feeding the samples to the decoder sub-network. These pseudo-data points are used along with new task data to learn each task. Since the new task is learned such that its distribution matches the past shared distribution, pseudo-data points generated for learning future tasks would also represent the current task as well upon the time it is learned.

8.4 PROPOSED ALGORITHM

Following the above framework, learning the first task ($t = 1$) reduces to minimizing the discrimination loss for classification and the autoencoder reconstruction loss to solve for optimal parameters:

$$\min_{v,w,u} \mathcal{L}_c(\boldsymbol{X}^{(1)}, \boldsymbol{Y}^{(1)}) = \min_{v,w,u} \frac{1}{n_1} \sum_{i=1}^{n_1} \mathcal{L}_d\Big(h_w(\phi_v(\boldsymbol{x}_i^{(1)})), \boldsymbol{y}_i^{(1)}\Big) + \gamma \mathcal{L}_r\Big(\psi_u(\phi_v(\boldsymbol{x}_i^{(1)})), \boldsymbol{x}_i^{(1)}\Big) \ , \quad (8.1)$$

where $\mathcal{L}_r$ is the reconstruction point-wise loss, $\mathcal{L}_c$ is the combined loss, and γ is a trade-off parameter between the two loss terms.

If the base learning model is complex enough, the concepts would be formed in the embedding space as separable clusters upon learning the first task. This means that the data distribution can be modeled as a GMM distribution in the embedding. We can use standard methods such as expectation maximization to fit a GMM distribution with k components to the multimodal empirical distribution formed by the drawn samples $\{(\phi_v(\boldsymbol{x}_i^{(1)}), \boldsymbol{y}_i^{(1)})_{i=1}^{n_1}\}_{i=1}^{n_1} \sim p_J^{(0)}$ in the embedding space. Let $\hat{p}_{J,k}^{(0)}(\boldsymbol{z})$ denote the estimated parametric GMM distribution. The goal is to retain this initial estimation that captures concepts when future domains are encountered. Following the PDP framework, we learn the subsequent tasks such that the current task shares the same GMM distribution with the previously learned tasks in the embedding space. We also update the estimate of the shared distribution after learning each subsequent task. Updating this distribution means generalizing the concepts to the new domains without forgetting the past domains. As a result, the distribution $\hat{p}_{J,k}^{(t-1)}(\boldsymbol{z})$ captures knowledge about past domains when $\mathcal{Z}^{(t)}$ is being learned. Moreover, we can perform experience replay by generating pseudo-data points by first drawing samples from $\hat{p}_{J,k}^{(t-1)}(\boldsymbol{z})$ and then passing the samples through the decoder sub-network. The remaining challenge is to update the model such that each subsequent task is learned such that its corresponding empirical distribution matches $\hat{p}_{J,k}^{(t-1)}(\boldsymbol{z})$ in the embedding space. Doing so, ensures the suitability of GMM to model the empirical distribution and as a result, a learned concept can continually be encoded as one of the modes in this distribution.

To match the distributions, consider $\mathcal{Z}_{ER}^{(T)} = \langle \psi(\boldsymbol{Z}_{ER}^{(T)}), \boldsymbol{Y}_{ER}^{(T)} \rangle$ denotes the pseudo-dataset for tasks $\{\mathcal{Z}^{(t)}\}_{t=1}^{T-1}$, generated for experience replay when $\mathcal{Z}^{(T)}$ is being learned. Following the described framework, we form the following optimization problem to learn $\mathcal{Z}^{(t)}$ and generalized concepts:

$$\min_{v,w,u} \mathcal{L}_{SL}(\boldsymbol{X}^{('t)}, \boldsymbol{Y}^{(t)}) + \mathcal{L}_{SL}(\boldsymbol{X}_{(ER)}^T, \boldsymbol{Y}_{(ER)}^T) + \eta D\Big(\phi_v(q^{(t)}(\boldsymbol{X}^{(t)})), \hat{p}_{J,k}^{(t)}(\boldsymbol{Z}_{ER}^{(T)})\Big)$$

$$\lambda \sum_{j=1}^{k} D\Big(\phi_v(q^{(t)}(\boldsymbol{X}^{('t)})|C_j), \hat{p}_{J,k}^{(t)}(\boldsymbol{Z}_{ER}^{(T)}|C_j)\Big) \quad \forall t \geq 2 \ , \qquad (8.2)$$

where $D(\cdot,\cdot)$ is a suitable metric function to measure the discrepancy between two probability distributions, and λ and η are trade-off parameters. The first two terms in Eq. (8.2) denote the combined loss terms for each of the current task few labeled data points and the generated pseudo-dataset, defined similarly to Eq. (8.1). The third and fourth terms implement our idea and enforce the distribution for the current task to be close to the distribution shared by the past learned task. The third term is added to minimize the distance between the distribution of the current tasks and $\hat{p}_{J,k}^{(t-1)}(\boldsymbol{z})$ in the embedding space. Data labels are not needed to compute this term. The fourth term may look similar to the third term, but note that we have conditioned the distance between the two distribution on the

---

Algorithm 9 ECLA (L, λ, η)

1: **Input:** data $\mathcal{D}^{(1)} = (\boldsymbol{X}^{(1)}, \boldsymbol{Y}^{(t)})$.
2: $\quad \mathcal{D}^{(t)} = (\{\boldsymbol{X}^{('t)}, \boldsymbol{Y}^{(t)}\}, \boldsymbol{X}^{(t)})_{t=2}^{T_{\text{Max}}}$
3: **Concept Learning:** learn the first task $(t = 1)$ by solving (8.1)
4: **Fitting GMM:**
5: Estimate $\hat{p}_{J,k}^{(0)}(\cdot)$ using $\{\phi_{\boldsymbol{v}}(\boldsymbol{x}_i^{(1)}))\}_{i=1}^{n_t}$
6: **for** $t \geq 2$ **do**
7: $\quad$ **Generate the pseudo dataset:**
8: $\quad$ Set $\mathcal{D}_{\text{ER}} = \{(\boldsymbol{x}_{er,i}^{(t)} = \psi(\boldsymbol{z}_{er,i}^{(t)}), \boldsymbol{y}_{er,i}^{(t)})\}$
9: $\quad$ Draw $(\boldsymbol{z}_{er,i}^{(t)}, \boldsymbol{y}_{er,i}^{(t)})) \sim \hat{p}_{J,k}^{(t-1)}(\cdot)$
10: $\quad$ **Update:**
11: $\quad$ Solve Eq. (8.2) and update the learnable parameters are updated
12: $\quad$ **Concept Generalization:**
13: $\quad$ Update $\hat{p}_{J,k}^{(t)}(\cdot)$ using the combined samples $\{\phi_{\boldsymbol{v}}(\boldsymbol{x}_i^{(t)})), \phi_{\boldsymbol{v}}(\boldsymbol{x}_{er,i}^{(t)}))\}_{i=1}^{n_t}$
14: **end for**

---

concepts to avoid the matching challenge, which occurs when wrong concepts (or classes) across two tasks are matched in the embedding space [66]. We use the few labeled data that are accessible for the current task to compute this term. These terms guarantees that we can continually use GMM to model the shared distribution in the embedding.

The main remaining question is the selection of a suitable probability distance metric $D(\cdot, \cdot)$. Following our discussion in chapter 4 on conditions for selecting the distance metric, we again use Sliced Wasserstein Distance (SWD) for this purpose. Our concept learning algorithm, Efficient Concept Learning Algorithm (ECLA), is summarized in Algorithm 9.

8.5 THEORETICAL ANALYSIS

We again use the result from classic domain adaptation [178] to demonstrate the effectiveness of our algorithm. We perform the analysis in the embedding space $\mathcal{Z}$, where the hypothesis class is the set of all the classifiers $h_{\boldsymbol{w}}(\cdot)$ parameterized by $\boldsymbol{w}$. For any given model h in this class, let $e_t(h)$ denotes the observed risk for the domain that contains the task $\mathcal{Z}^{(t)}$, $e_{t'}(h)$ denotes the observed risk for the same model on another secondary domain, and $\boldsymbol{w}^*$ denotes the optimal parameter for training the model on these two tasks jointly, i.e., $\boldsymbol{w}^* = \arg\min_{\boldsymbol{w}} e_{\mathcal{C}}(\boldsymbol{w}) = \arg\min_{\boldsymbol{w}}\{e_t(h) + e_{t'}(h)\}$. We also denote the Wasserstein distance between two given distributions as $W(\cdot, \cdot)$. We reiterate the following theorem [178], which relates the performance of a model trained on a particular domain to another secondary domain.

Theorem 8.5.1. *Consider two tasks $\mathcal{Z}^{(t)}$ and $\mathcal{Z}^{(t')}$, and a model $h_{\mathbf{w}^{(t')}}$ trained for $\mathcal{Z}^{(t')}$, then for any $d' > d$ and $\zeta < \sqrt{2}$, there exists a constant number N_0 depending on d' such that for any $\xi > 0$ and $\min(n_t, n_{t'}) \geq \max(\xi^{-(d'+2),1})$ with probability at least $1 - \xi$ for all $f_{\theta^{(t')}}$, the following holds:*

$$e_t(h) - e_{t'}(h) \leq W(\hat{p}^{(t)}, \hat{p}^{(t')}) e_{\mathcal{C}}(\boldsymbol{w}^*) + \sqrt{(2\log(\tfrac{1}{\xi})/\zeta)} \left(\sqrt{\frac{1}{n_t}} + \sqrt{\frac{1}{n_{t'}}}\right), \qquad (8.3)$$

where $\hat{p}^{(t)}$ and $\hat{p}^{(t')}$ are empirical distributions formed by the drawn samples from $p^{(t)}$ and $p^{(t')}$.

Theorem 8.5.1 is a broad result that provides an upper-bound on performance degradation of a trained model when used in another domain. It suggests that if the model performs well on $\mathcal{Z}^{(t')}$ and if the upper-bound is small, then the model performs well on $\mathcal{Z}^{(t')}$. The last term is a constant term which depends on the number of available samples. This term is negligible when $n_t, n_{t'} \gg 1$. The two important terms are the first and second terms. The first term is the Wasserstein distance between the two distributions. It may seem that according to this term, if we minimize the WD between two distributions, then the model should perform well on $\mathcal{Z}^{(t)}$. But it is crucial to note that the upper-bound depends on the second term as well. Despite being the third term suggests that the base model should be able to learn both tasks jointly. However, in the presence of "XOR classification problem", the tasks cannot be learned by a single model [137]. This means that not only the WD between two distributions should be small, but the distributions should be aligned class-conditionally. Building upon Theorem 8.5.1, we provide the following theorem for our framework.

Theorem 8.5.2. *Consider ECLA algorithm at learning time step $t = T$. Then all tasks $t < T$ and under the conditions of Theorem 8.5.1, we can conclude:*

$$
\begin{aligned}
e_t \leq & e_{T-1}^J + W(\phi(\hat{q}^{(t)}), \hat{p}_{J,k}^{(t)}) + \sum_{s=t}^{T-2} W(\hat{p}_{J,k}^{(s)}, \hat{p}_{J,k}^{(s+1)}) \\
& + e_{\mathcal{C}}(\boldsymbol{w}^*) + \sqrt{(2\log(\frac{1}{\xi})/\zeta)}\left(\sqrt{\frac{1}{n_t}} + \sqrt{\frac{1}{n_{er,t-1}}}\right),
\end{aligned}
\tag{8.4}
$$

where e_{T-1}^J denotes the risk for the pseudo-task with the distribution $\psi(\hat{p}_{J,k}^{(T-1)})$.

Proof: In Theorem 8.5.1, consider the task $\mathcal{Z}^{(t)}$ with the distribution $\phi(q^{(t)})$ and the pseudo-task with the distribution $p_{J,k}^{(T-1)}$ in the embedding space. We can use the triangular inequality recursively on the term $W(\phi(\hat{q}^{(t)}), \hat{p}_{J,k}^{(T-1)})$ in Eq. (8.3), i.e., $W(\phi(\hat{q}^{(t)}), \hat{p}_{J,k}^{(s)}) \leq W(\phi(\hat{q}^{(t)}), \hat{p}_{J,k}^{(s-1)}) + W(\hat{p}_{J,k}^{(s)}, \hat{p}_{J,k}^{(s-1)})$ for all time steps $t \leq s < T$. Adding up all the terms, concludes Eq. (8.4) ▪

Similar to the previous chapter, we can rely on Theorem 8.5.2 to demonstrate why our algorithm can generalize concepts without forgetting the past learned knowledge. The first term in Eq. (8.4) is small because experience replay minimizes this term using the labeled pseudo-data set via ERM. The fourth term is small since we use the few labeled data points to align the distributions class conditionally in Eq. (8.2). The last term is a negligible constant for $n_t, n_{er,t-1} \gg 1$. The second term denotes the distance between the task distribution and the fitted GMM. When the PDP hypothesis holds, and the model learns a task well, this term is small as we can approximate $\phi(\hat{q}^{(t)})$ with $\hat{p}_{J,k}^{(s-1)}$ (see Ashtiani et al. [10] for a rigorous analysis of estimating a distribution with GMM). In other words, this term is small if the classes are learned as concepts. Finally, the terms in the sum term in Eq 8.4 are minimized because at $t = s$ we draw samples from $p_{J,k}^{(s-1)}$ and by learning $\psi^{-1} = \psi$ enforce that $\hat{p}_{J,k}^{(s-1)} \approx \phi(\psi(\hat{p}_{J,k}^{(s-1)}))$. The sum term in Eq 8.4, models the effect of past experiences. After learning a task and moving forward, this term potentially grows as more tasks are learned. This means that forgetting effects would increase as more subsequent tasks are learned, which is intuitive. To sum up, ECLA minimizes the upper-bound of e_t in Eq 8.4. This means that the model can learn and remember $\mathcal{Z}^{(t)}$ which in turn means that the concepts have been generalized without being forgotten on the old domains.

8.6 EXPERIMENTAL VALIDATION

We validate our method on learning two sets of sequential learning tasks that we used in the previous chapter: permuted MNIST tasks and digit recognition tasks. These are standard benchmark classification tasks for sequential task learning. We adjust them for our learning setting. Each class in these tasks is considered to be a concept, and each task of the sequence is considered to be learning the concepts in a new domain.

8.6.1 Learning Permuted MNIST Tasks

Permuted MNIST tasks is a standard benchmark that is designed for testing the abilities of AI algorithms to overcome catastrophic forgetting [225, 100]. The sequential tasks are generated using the MNIST ($\mathcal{M}$) digit recognition dataset [118]. Each task in the sequence is generated by applying a fixed random shuffling to the pixel values of digit images across the MNIST dataset [100]. As a result, generated tasks are homogeneous in terms of difficulty for a base model and are suitable to perform controlled experiments to study the effects of knowledge transfer . Our learning setting is different compared to prior works as we considered the case where only the data for the initial MNIST task is fully labeled. In the subsequent tasks, only a few data points are labeled.

To the best of our knowledge, no precedent method addresses this learning scenario for direct comparison, so we only compared against: (a) classic backpropagation (BP) single task learning, (b) full experience replay (FR) using full stored data for all the previous tasks, and (c) learning using fully labeled data which is analogous to using CLEER algorithm from the previous chapter. We use the same base network structure for all the methods for fair comparison. BP is used to demonstrate that our method can address catastrophic forgetting. FR is used as a lower-bound to demonstrate that our method is able to learn cross-task concepts without using fully labeled data. CLEER is an instance of ECLA where fully labeled data is used to learn the subsequent tasks. We used CLEER to compare our method against an upper-bound.

We used standard stochastic gradient descent to learn the tasks and created learning curves by computing the performance of the model on the standard testing split of the current and the past learned tasks at each learning iteration. Figure 8.2 presents learning curves for four permuted MNIST tasks. Figure 8.2a presents learning curves for BP (dashed curves) and CLEER (solid curves). As can be seen, CLEER (i.e., ECLA with fully labeled data) is able to address catastrophic forgetting. This figure demonstrates that our method can be used as a new algorithm on its own to address catastrophic forgetting using experience replay [225]. Figure 8.2b presents learning curves for FR (dashed curves) and ECLA (solid curve) when five labeled data points per class are used respectively. We observe that FR can tackle catastrophic forgetting perfectly, but the challenge is the memory buffer requirement,

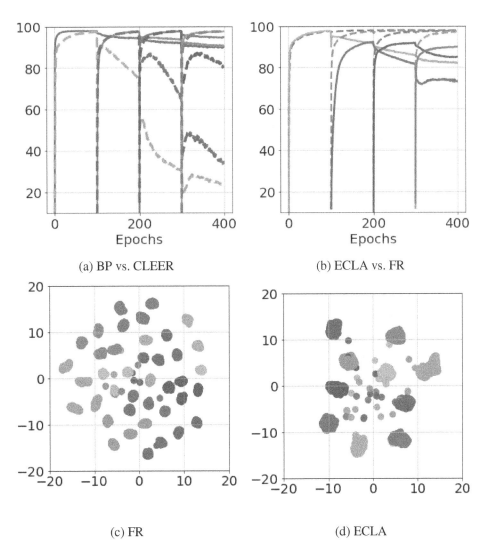

(a) BP vs. CLEER

(b) ECLA vs. FR

(c) FR

(d) ECLA

Figure 8.2 Learning curves for four permuted MNIST tasks((a) and (b)), where the blue curve denotes performance on the first task and the orange curve denotes performance on the second task; UMAP visualization of ECLA and FR in the embedding ((c) and (d)). (Best viewed in color.)

which grows linearly with the number of learned tasks, making this method only suitable for comparison as an upper-bound. FR result also demonstrates that if we can generate high-quality pseudo-data points, catastrophic forgetting can be prevented completely. Deviation of the pseudo-data from the real data is the major reason for the initial performance degradation of ECLA on all the past learned tasks when a new task arrives, and its learning starts. This degradation can be ascribed to the existing distance between $\hat{p}_{J,k}^{(T-1)}$ and $\phi(q^{(s)})$ at $t = T$ for $s < T$. Note also as our theoretical analysis predicts, the performance on a past learned task degrades more as more tasks are learned subsequently. This is compatible with the nervous

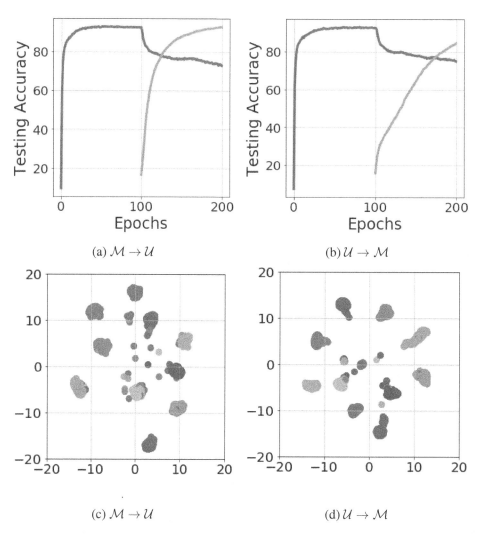

(a) $\mathcal{M} \rightarrow \mathcal{U}$ (b) $\mathcal{U} \rightarrow \mathcal{M}$

(c) $\mathcal{M} \rightarrow \mathcal{U}$ (d) $\mathcal{U} \rightarrow \mathcal{M}$

Figure 8.3 Performance results on MNIST and USPS digit recognition tasks ((a) and (b)). UMAP visualization for $\mathcal{M} \rightarrow \mathcal{U}$ and $\mathcal{U} \rightarrow \mathcal{M}$ tasks ((c) and (d)). (Best viewed in color.)

system as memories fade out as time passes unless enhanced by continually experiencing a task or a concept.

In addition to requiring fully labeled data, we demonstrate that FR does not identify concepts across the tasks. To this end, we have visualized the testing data for all the tasks in the embedding space $\mathcal{Z}$ in Figures 8.2 for FR and ECLA after learning the fourth task. For visualization purpose, we have used UMAP [146], which reduces the dimensionality of the embedding space to two. In Figures 8.2c and 8.2d, each color denotes the data points of one of the digits $\{0, 1, \dots, 9\}$ (each circular shape indeed is a cluster of data points). We can see that the digits form separable clusters for both methods. This result is consistent with the PDP hypothesis and is the reason behind the good performance of both methods. It also demonstrates why GMM is a suitable selection to model the data distribution in the embedding space. However, we can see that when FR is used, four distinct clusters for each digit are formed (i.e., one cluster per domain for each digit class). In other words, FR is unable to identify and generalize abstract concepts across the domains, and each class is learned as an independent concept in each domain. In contrast, we have exactly ten clusters for the ten digits when ECLA is used, and hence, the concepts are identified across the domains. This is the reason that we can generalize the learned concepts to new domains, despite using a few labeled data.

8.6.2   Learning Sequential Digit Recognition Tasks

We performed a second set of experiments on a more realistic scenario. We consider two handwritten digit recognition datasets for this purpose: MNIST ($\mathcal{M}$) and USPS ($\mathcal{U}$) datasets. USPS dataset is a more challenging classification task as the size of the training set is smaller (20,000 compared to 60,000 images). We performed experiments on the two possible sequential learning scenarios $\mathcal{M} \rightarrow \mathcal{U}$ and $\mathcal{M} \rightarrow \mathcal{U}$. We resized the USPS images to 28×28 pixels to be able to use the same encoder network for both tasks. The experiments can be considered as concept learning for numeral digits as both tasks are digit recognition tasks but in different domains, i.e., written by different people.

Figures 8.3a and 8.3b present learning curves for these two tasks when ten labeled data points per class are used for the training of the second task. First, note that the network mostly retains the knowledge about the first task following the learning of the second task. Also note that the generalization to the second domain, i.e., the second task learning is faster in Figure 8.3a. Because MNIST dataset has more training data points, the empirical distribution $\hat{p}_{J,k}^{(1)}$ can capture the task distribution more accurately and hence the concepts would be learned better which in turn makes learning the second task easier. As expected from the theoretical justification, this empirical result suggests the performance of our algorithm depends on the closeness of the distribution $\psi(\hat{p}_{J,k}^{(t)})$ to the distributions of previous tasks, and improving probability estimation will boost the performance of our approach. We have also presented UMAP visualization of the data points for the tasks in the embedding space in Figures 8.3c and 8.3d. We observe that the distributions are matched in the embedding space, and cross-domain concepts are learned by the network. These results demonstrate that our algorithm, inspired by PDP and CLS theories, can generalize concepts to new domains using few labeled data points.

8.7   CONCLUSIONS

Inspired by the CLS theory and the PDP paradigm, we developed an algorithm that enables a deep network to update and generalize its learned concepts in a continual learning setting by observing few data points in a new domain. Our generative framework is able to encode abstract concepts in a hidden layer of the deep network in the form of a parametric GMM distribution which remains stable when new domains are learned. This distribution can be used to generalize concepts to new domains, where only a few labeled samples are accessible. The proposed algorithm is able to address the learning challenges by accumulating the newly learned knowledge consistently to the past learned knowledge. Additionally, the model is able to generate pseudo-data points for past tasks, which can be used for experience replay to tackle catastrophic forgetting.

In the next part of this book, we consider a multi-agent learning setting, where the goal is to improve the learning performance of several agents that collaborate by sharing their learned knowledge. In both Part I and Part II, a major assumption was that centralized access to data across the tasks and domains is possible. In a multi-agent learning setting, this assumption is not valid anymore, and transmitting data to a central server can be expensive. As a result, new challenges need to be addressed. We demonstrate how our ideas from chapters 3 and 6 can be extended to be to address this learning setting by transferring knowledge across the agents.

III

Cross-Agent Knowledge Transfer

In the first two parts of this book, we considered that we have centralized access to the data for all problems. This means that only a single learning agent exists that learns all the problems. However, in a growing class of applications, the data is distributed across different agents. Sometimes the agents are virtual, despite being associated to the same location. For various reasons, including data privacy, distributed computational resources, and limited communication bandwidth, transmitting all data to a central server may not be a feasible solution. As a result, the single-agent learning algorithms may underperform because the amount of data for every single agent may not be sufficient. Cross-agents' knowledge transfer can help several collaborating agents to improve their performance by sharing knowledge and benefiting from the wisdom of the crowd. In this part, we develop an algorithm that enables a network of lifelong machine learning agent to collaborate and share their high-level knowledge to improve their learning speed and performance, without sharing their local data. Similar to the previous parts of the book, the core idea is to enable the agents to share knowledge through an embedding space that captures what has been learned locally by each agent. This embedding space is shared by the agents indirectly by learning agent-specific mappings that can be used to map data to this shared embedding space.

CHAPTER 9

Collective Lifelong Learning for Multi-Agent Networks

In a classic machine learning stetting, usually, a single learning agent has centralized access to all data. However, centralized access to data can be challenging in a multi-agent learning setting. In this chapter, we investigate the possibility of cross-agent knowledge transfer, when the data is distributed across several learning agents. Each agent in our formulation is a lifelong learner that acquires knowledge over a series of consecutive tasks, continually building upon its experience. Meanwhile, the agents can communicate and share locally learned knowledge to improve their collective performance. We extend the idea of lifelong learning from a single agent to a network of multiple agents. The key goal is to share the knowledge that is learned from local, agent-specific tasks with other agents that are trying to learn different (but related) tasks. Building upon our prior works, our idea is to enforce the agents to share their knowledge through an embedding space that captures similarities across the distributed tasks. Extending the ELLA framework, introduced in chapter 6, we model the embedding space using a dictionary that sparsifies the optimal task parameters. These agents learn this dictionary collectively, and as a result, their experiences are shared through the dictionary. Our Collective Lifelong Learning Algorithm (CoLLA) provides an efficient way for a network of agents to share their learned knowledge in a distributed and decentralized manner through the shared dictionary while eliminating the need to share locally observed data. Note that a decentralized scheme is a subclass of distributed algorithms where a central server does not exist and in addition to data, computations are also distributed among the agents. We provide theoretical guarantees for robust performance of the algorithm and empirically demonstrate that CoLLA outperforms existing approaches for distributed multi-task learning on a variety of standard datasets. Results of this chapter have been presented in Refs [186, 199, 198, 190]. We have provided a coherent version within the scope of this book.

9.1 OVERVIEW

Collective knowledge acquisition is common throughout different societies, from the collaborative advancement of human knowledge to the emergent behavior of ant colonies [98]. It is the product of individual agents, each with their own interests and constraints, sharing and accumulating learned knowledge over time in uncertain and often dangerous real-world environments. Our work explores this scenario within machine learning. In particular, we consider learning in a network of lifelong machine learning agents.

Recent work in lifelong machine learning [243, 211, 39] has explored the notion of a single agent accumulating knowledge over its lifetime. Such an individual lifelong learning agent reuses knowledge from previous tasks to improve its learning on new tasks, accumulating an internal repository of knowledge over time. This lifelong learning process improves performance over all tasks and permits the design of adaptive agents that are capable of learning in dynamic environments. Although current work in lifelong learning focuses on a single learning agent that incrementally perceives all task data, many real-world applications involve scenarios in which multiple agents must collectively learn a series of tasks that are distributed among them. Consider the following cases:

- Multi-modal task data could only be partially accessible by each learning agent. For example, financial decision support agents may have access only to a single data view of tasks or a portion of the non-stationary data distribution [82].

- Local data processing can be inevitable in some applications, such as when health care regulations prevent personal medical data from being shared between learning systems [284].

- Data communication may be costly or time-consuming [189]. For instance, home service robots must process perceptions locally due to the volume of perceptual data, or wearable devices may have limited communication bandwidth [97].

- As a result of data size or the geographical distribution of data centers, parallel processing can be essential. Modern big data systems often necessitate parallel processing in the cloud across multiple virtual agents, i.e., CPUs or GPUs [285].

Inspired by the above scenarios, we explore the idea of *multi-agent lifelong learning*. We consider multiple collaborating lifelong learning agents, each facing their own series of tasks, that transfer knowledge to collectively improve task performance and increase learning speed. Existing methods in the literature have mostly investigated special cases of this setting for distributed multi-task learning (MTL) [33, 166, 97].

To develop multi-agent distributed lifelong learning, we follow a parametric approach and formulate the learning problem as an online MTL optimization over a network of agents. Each agent seeks to learn parametric models for its own series of (potentially unique) tasks. The network topology imposes communication constraints among the agents. For each agent, the corresponding task model parameters are represented as a task-specific sparse combination of atoms of its local knowledge base [110, 211, 141]. The local knowledge bases allow for knowledge transfer from learned tasks to the future tasks for each individual agent. The agents share their knowledge bases with their neighbors, update them to incorporate the learned knowledge representations of their neighboring agents, and come to a local consensus to improve learning quality and speed. We use the Alternating Direction Method of Multipliers (ADMM) algorithm [25, 80] to solve this global optimization problem in an online distributed setting; our approach decouples this problem into local optimization problems that are individually solved by the agents. ADMM allows for transferring the learned local knowledge bases without sharing the specific learned model parameters among neighboring agents. We propose an algorithm with nested loops to allow for keeping the procedure both online and distributed. Although our approach eliminates the need for the agents to share local models and data, note that we do not address the privacy considerations that may arise from transferring knowledge between agents. Also, despite potential extensions to parallel processing systems, our focus here is on collaborative agents that receive consecutive tasks.

We call our approach the *Collective Lifelong Learning Algorithm* (CoLLA). We provide a theoretical analysis of CoLLA's convergence and empirically validate the practicality of the proposed algorithm on a variety of standard MTL benchmark datasets.

Distributed Machine Learning: There has been a growing interest in developing scalable learning algorithms using distributed optimization [289], motivated by the emergence of big data, security, and privacy constraints [273], and the notion of cooperative and collaborative learning agents [34]. Distributed machine learning allows multiple agents to collaboratively mine information from large-scale data. The majority of these settings are graph-based, where each node in the graph represents a portion of data or an agent. Communication channels between the agents, then, can be modeled via edges in the graph. Some approaches assume there is a central server (or a group of server nodes) in the network, and the worker agents transmit locally learned information to the server(s), which then perform knowledge fusion [268]. Other approaches assume that processing power is distributed among the agents, which exchange information with their neighbors during the learning process [33]. We formulate our problem in the latter setting, as it is less restrictive. Following the dominant paradigm of distributed optimization, we also assume that the agents are synchronized.

These methods formulate learning as an optimization problem over the network and use distributed optimization techniques to acquire the global solution. Various techniques have been explored, including stochastic gradient descent [268], proximal gradients [122], and ADMM [268]. Within the ADMM framework, it is assumed that the objective function over the network can be decoupled into a sum of independent local functions for each node (usually risk functions) [134], constrained by the network topology. Through a number of iterations on primal and dual variables of the Lagrangian function, each node solves a local optimization, and then through information exchange, constraints imposed by the network are realized by updating the dual variable. In scenarios where maximizing a cost for some agents translates to minimizing the cost for others (e.g., adversarial games), game-theoretical notions are used to define a global optimal state for the agents [124].

Distributed Multi-task Learning: Although it seems natural to consider MTL agents that collaborate on related tasks, most prior distributed learning work focuses on the setting where all agents try to learn a single task. Only recently have MTL scenarios been investigated where the tasks are distributed [97, 140, 255, 14, 267, 126]. In such a setting, data must not be transferred to a central node because of communication and privacy/security constraints. Only the learned models or high-level information can be exchanged by neighboring agents. These distributed MTL methods are mostly limited to off-line (batch) settings where each agent handles only one task [140, 255]. Jin et al. [97] consider an online setting but require the existence of a central server node, which is restrictive. In contrast, our work considers decentralized and distributed multi-agent MTL in a lifelong learning setting, without the need for a central server. Moreover, our approach employs homogeneous agents that collaborate to improve their collective performance over consecutive distributed tasks. This can be considered as a special case of concurrent learning, where learning a task concurrently by multiple agents can accelerate learning [96].

Similar to prior works [140, 255], we use distributed optimization to tackle the collective lifelong learning problem. These existing approaches can only handle an off-line setting where all the task data is available in batch for each agent. In contrast, we propose an online learning procedure which can address consecutive tasks. In each iteration, the agents receive and learn their local task models. Since the agents are synchronous, once the tasks are learned, a message-passing scheme is then used to transfer and update knowledge between the neighboring agents in each iteration. In this manner, knowledge will disseminate among all agents over time, improving collective performance. Similar to most distributed learning settings, we assume there is a latent knowledge base that underlies all tasks, and that each agent is trying to learn a local version of that knowledge base based on its own (local) observations and knowledge exchange with neighboring agents, modeled by edges (links) of the representing network graph.

9.2 LIFELONG MACHINE LEARNING

Following chapter 6, we consider a set of T related (but different) supervised regression or classification tasks. For each task, we have access to a labeled training dataset, i.e., $\left\{\mathcal{Z}^{(t)} = \left(\boldsymbol{X}^{(t)}, \boldsymbol{y}^{(t)}\right)\right\}_{t=1}^{T}$, where $\boldsymbol{X}^{(t)} = [\boldsymbol{x}_1, \ldots, \boldsymbol{x}_M] \in \mathbb{R}^{d \times M}$. The vectore $\boldsymbol{X}^{(t)}$ represents M data instances that are characterized by d features. The corresponding labels are given by $\boldsymbol{y}^{(t)} = [y_1, \ldots, y_m]^{\top} \in \mathcal{Y}^M$. Typically, $\mathcal{Y} = \{\pm 1\}$ for binary classification tasks and $\mathcal{Y} = \mathbb{R}$ for regression tasks. We assume that for each task t, the mapping $f : \mathbb{R}^d \to \mathcal{Y}$ from each data point $\boldsymbol{x}_m$ to its target y_m can be modeled as $y_m = f(\boldsymbol{x}_m; \boldsymbol{\theta}^{(t)})$, where $\boldsymbol{\theta}^{(t)} \in \mathbb{R}^d$. In particular, we consider a linear mapping $f(\boldsymbol{x}_m; \boldsymbol{\theta}^{(t)}) = \langle \boldsymbol{\theta}^{(t)}, \boldsymbol{x}_m \rangle$ where $\boldsymbol{\theta}^{(t)} \in \mathbb{R}^d$, but our framework is readily generalizable to nonlinear parametric mappings (e.g., via generalized dictionaries [253]). After receiving a task $\mathcal{Z}^{(t)}$, the agent models the mapping $f(\boldsymbol{x}_m; \boldsymbol{\theta}^{(t)})$ by estimating the corresponding optimal task parameters $\boldsymbol{\theta}^{(t)}$ using the training data such that it well-generalizes on testing data points from that task. An agent can learn the task models by solving for the optimal parameters $\boldsymbol{\Theta}^* = [\boldsymbol{\theta}^{(1)}, \ldots, \boldsymbol{\theta}^{(T)}]$ in the following Empirical Risk Minimization (ERM) problem:

$$\min_{\boldsymbol{\Theta}} \frac{1}{T} \sum_{t=1}^{T} \mathbb{E}_{\boldsymbol{X}^{(t)} \sim \mathcal{D}^{(t)}} \left(\mathcal{L}\left(\boldsymbol{X}^{(t)}, \boldsymbol{y}^{(t)}; \boldsymbol{\theta}^{(t)}\right) \right) + \Omega(\boldsymbol{\Theta}) \ , \tag{9.1}$$

where $\mathcal{L}(\cdot)$ is a loss function for measuring data fidelity, $\mathbb{E}(\cdot)$ denotes the expectation on the task's data distribution $\mathcal{D}^{(t)}$, and $\Omega(\cdot)$ is a regularization function that models task relations by coupling model parameters to transfer knowledge among the tasks. Almost all parametric MTL, online, and lifelong learning algorithms solve instances of Eq. (9.1) given a particular form of $\Omega(\cdot)$ to impose a specific coupling scheme and an optimization mode, i.e., online or batch offline.

To model task relations, the GO-MTL algorithm [110] uses classic ERM to estimate the expected loss and solve the objective (9.1). It assumes that the task parameters can be decomposed into a shared dictionary knowledge base $\boldsymbol{L} \in \mathbb{R}^{d \times u}$ to facilitate knowledge transfer and task-specific sparse coefficients $\boldsymbol{s}^{(t)} \in \mathbb{R}^u$, such that $\boldsymbol{\theta}^{(t)} = \boldsymbol{L}\boldsymbol{s}^{(t)}$. In this factorization, the hidden structure of the tasks is represented in the dictionary knowledge base, and similar tasks are grouped by imposing sparsity on the $\boldsymbol{s}^{(t)}$'s. Tasks that use the same columns of the dictionary are clustered to be similar, while tasks that do not share any column can be considered as belonging to different groups. In other words, more overlap in the sparsity patterns of two tasks implies more similarity between those two task models. This factorization has been shown to enable knowledge transfer when dealing with related tasks by grouping similar tasks [110, 141]. Following this assumption and employing ERM, the objective (9.1) can be expressed as:

$$\min_{\boldsymbol{L},\boldsymbol{S}} \frac{1}{T} \sum_{t=1}^{T} \left[\hat{\mathcal{L}} \left(\boldsymbol{X}^{(t)}, \boldsymbol{y}^{(t)}, \boldsymbol{L}\boldsymbol{s}^{(t)} \right) + \mu \|\boldsymbol{s}^{(t)}\|_1 \right] + \lambda \|\boldsymbol{L}\|_{\mathsf{F}}^2 , \tag{9.2}$$

where $\boldsymbol{S} = [\boldsymbol{s}^{(1)} \cdots \boldsymbol{s}^{(T)}]$ is the matrix of sparse vectors, $\hat{\mathcal{L}}(\cdot)$ is the empirical loss function on task training data, $\| \cdot \|_{\mathsf{F}}$ is the Frobenius norm to regularize complexity and impose uniqueness, $\| \cdot \|_1$ denotes the L_1 norm to impose sparsity on each $\boldsymbol{s}^{(t)}$, and μ and λ are regularization parameters. Eq. (9.2) is not a convex problem in its general form, but with a convex loss function, it is convex in each individual optimization variable $\boldsymbol{L}$ and $\boldsymbol{S}$. Given all tasks' data in batch, Eq. (9.2) can be solved offline by an alternating optimization scheme [110]. In each alternation step, Eq. (9.2) is solved to update a single variable by treating the other variable to be constant. This scheme leads to an MTL algorithm that shares information selectively among the task models.

Solving Eq. (9.2) offline is not suitable for lifelong learning. A lifelong learning agent [243, 211] faces tasks sequentially, where each task should be learned using knowledge transfer red from past experience. In other words, for each task $\mathcal{Z}^{(t)}$, the corresponding parameter $\boldsymbol{\theta}^{(t)}$ is learned using knowledge obtained from tasks $\{\mathcal{Z}^{(1)}, \ldots, \mathcal{Z}^{(t-1)}\}$. Upon learning $\mathcal{Z}^{(t)}$, the learned or updated knowledge is stored to benefit future learning. The agent does not know the total number of tasks, nor the task order *a priori*. To solve Eq. (9.2) in an online setting, Ruvolo and Eaton [211] first approximate the loss function $\mathcal{L}(\boldsymbol{X}^{(t)}, \boldsymbol{y}^{(t)}, \boldsymbol{L}\boldsymbol{s}^{(t)})$ using a second-order Taylor expansion of the loss function around the single-task ridge-optimal parameters. This technique reduces the objective (9.2) to the problem of online dictionary learning [134]:

$$\min_{\boldsymbol{L}} \frac{1}{T} \sum_{t=1}^{T} F^{(t)}(\boldsymbol{L}) + \lambda \|\boldsymbol{L}\|_{\mathsf{F}}^2 , \tag{9.3}$$

$$F^{(t)}(\boldsymbol{L}) = \min_{\boldsymbol{s}^{(t)}} \left[\left\| \boldsymbol{\alpha}^{(t)} - \boldsymbol{L}\boldsymbol{s}^{(t)} \right\|_{\boldsymbol{\Gamma}^{(t)}}^2 + \mu \left\| \boldsymbol{s}^{(t)} \right\|_1 \right] , \tag{9.4}$$

where $\|\boldsymbol{x}\|_A^2 = \boldsymbol{x}^\top \boldsymbol{A}\boldsymbol{x}$, $\boldsymbol{\alpha}^{(t)} \in \mathbb{R}^d$ is the ridge estimator for task $\mathcal{Z}^{(t)}$:

$$\boldsymbol{\alpha}^{(t)} = \arg\min_{\boldsymbol{\theta}^{(t)}} \left[\hat{\mathcal{L}} \left(\boldsymbol{\theta}^{(t)} \right) + \gamma \left\| \boldsymbol{\theta}^{(t)} \right\|_2^2 \right] \tag{9.5}$$

with ridge regularization parameter $\gamma \in \mathbb{R}^d$, and $\boldsymbol{\Gamma}^{(t)}$ is the Hessian of the loss $\hat{\mathcal{L}}(\cdot)$ at $\boldsymbol{\alpha}^{(t)}$, which is assumed to be strictly positive definite. When a new task arrives, only the corresponding sparse vector $\boldsymbol{s}^{(t)}$ is computed using $\boldsymbol{L}$ to update $\sum_t F(\boldsymbol{L})$. To solve Eq. (9.3) in an online setting, still, an alternation scheme is used, but when a new task arrives, only the corresponding sparse vector $\boldsymbol{s}^{(t)}$ for that tasks is computed using $\boldsymbol{L}$ to update the sum $\sum_{t=1}^{T} F(\boldsymbol{L})$. In this setting, Eq. (9.3) is a task-specific online operation that leverages knowledge transfer. Finally, the shared basis $\boldsymbol{L}$ is updated via Eq. (9.3) to store the learned knowledge from $\mathcal{Z}^{(t)}$ for future use. Despite using Eq. (9.3) as an approximation to solve for $\boldsymbol{s}^{(t)}$, Ruvolo and Eaton[211] proved that the learned knowledge base $\boldsymbol{L}$ stabilizes as more tasks are learned and would eventually converge to the offline solution of Kumand and Daume [110]. Moreover, the solution of Eq. (9.1) converges almost surely to the solution of Eq. (9.2) as $T \rightarrow \infty$. While this technique leads to an efficient algorithm for lifelong learning, it requires centralized access to all tasks' data by a single agent. The approach we explore, CoLLA, benefits from the idea of the second-order Taylor approximation and online optimization scheme proposed by Ruvolo and Eaton [211], but eliminates the need for centralized data access. CoLLA achieves a distributed and decentralized knowledge update by formulating a multi-agent lifelong learning optimization problem over a network of collaborating agents. The resulting optimization can be solved in a distributed setting, enabling collective learning, as we describe next.

9.3   MULTI-AGENT LIFELONG LEARNING

Consider a network of N collaborating lifelong learning agents. Each agent receives a (potentially unique) task at each time step. We assume there is some true underlying hidden knowledge base for all tasks; each agent learns a local view of this knowledge base based on its own task distribution. To accomplish this, each agent i solves a local version of the objective (9.3) to estimate its own local knowledge base $\boldsymbol{L}_i$. We also assume that the agents are synchronous (at each time step, they simultaneously receive and learn one task), and there is an arbitrary order over the agents. We represent the communication among these agents by an undirected graph $\mathcal{G} = (\mathcal{V}, \mathcal{E})$, where the set of static nodes $\mathcal{V} = \{1, \ldots, N\}$ denotes the agents and the set of edges $\mathcal{E} \subset \mathcal{V} \times \mathcal{V}$, with $|\mathcal{E}| = e$, specifies the possibility of communication between pairs of agents. For each edge $(i, j) \in \mathcal{E}$, the nodes i and j are connected and so can communicate information, with $j > i$ for uniqueness and set orderability. The neighborhood $\mathcal{N}(i)$ of node i is the set of all nodes that are connected to it. To allow knowledge to flow between all agents, we further assume that the network graph is connected. Note that there is no central server to guide collaboration among the agents.

We use the graph structure to formulate a lifelong machine learning problem on this network. Although each agent learns its own individual dictionary, we encourage local dictionaries of neighboring nodes (agents) to be similar by adding a set of soft equality constraints on neighboring dictionaries: $\boldsymbol{L}_i = \boldsymbol{L}_j, \forall (i, j) \in \mathcal{E}$. We can represent all these constraints as a single linear operation on the local dictionaries. It is easy to show these e equality constraints can be written compactly as $(\boldsymbol{H} \otimes \boldsymbol{I}_{d \times d}) \tilde{\boldsymbol{L}} = \boldsymbol{0}_{ed \times u}$, where $\boldsymbol{H} \in \mathbb{R}^{e \times N}$ is the node arc-incident matrix[1] of $\mathcal{G}$, $\boldsymbol{I}_{d \times d}$ is the identity matrix, $\boldsymbol{0}$ is the zero matrix,

---

[1]For a given row $1 \leq l \leq e$, corresponding to the lth edge (i, j), $H_{lq} = 0$ except for $H_{li} = 1$, and $H_{lj} = -1$.

$\tilde{\boldsymbol{L}} = [\boldsymbol{L}_1^\top, \ldots, \boldsymbol{L}_N^\top]^\top$, and $\otimes$ denotes the Kronecker product. Let $\boldsymbol{E}_i \in \mathbb{R}^{ed \times d}$ be a column partition of $\boldsymbol{E} = (\boldsymbol{H} \otimes \boldsymbol{I}_d) = [\boldsymbol{E}_1, \ldots, \boldsymbol{E}_N]$. We can compactly write the e equality constraints as $\sum_i \boldsymbol{E}_i \boldsymbol{L}_i = \boldsymbol{0}_{ed \times u}$.

Each of the $\boldsymbol{E}_i \in \mathbb{R}^{de \times d}$ matrices is a tall block matrix consisting of $d \times d$ blocks, $\{[\boldsymbol{E}_i]_j\}_{j=1}^e$, that are either the zero matrix ($\forall j \notin \mathcal{N}(i)$), $\boldsymbol{I}_d$ ($\forall j \in \mathcal{N}(i), j > i$), or $-\boldsymbol{I}_d$ ($\forall j \in \mathcal{N}(i), j < i$). Note that $\boldsymbol{E}_i^\top \boldsymbol{E}_j = \boldsymbol{0}_d$ if $j \notin \mathcal{N}(i)$, where $\boldsymbol{0}_d$ is the $d \times d$ zero matrix. Following this notation, we can reformulate the MTL objective (9.3) for multiple agents as the following linearly constrained optimization problem over the network graph $\mathcal{G}$:

$$\min_{\boldsymbol{L}_1, \ldots \boldsymbol{L}_N} \frac{1}{T} \sum_{t=1}^T \sum_{i=1}^N F_i^{(t)}(\boldsymbol{L}_i) + \lambda \|\boldsymbol{L}_i\|_{\mathsf{F}}^2$$

$$\text{s.t.} \sum_{i=1}^N \boldsymbol{E}_i \boldsymbol{L}_i = \boldsymbol{0}_{ed \times u} \ . \tag{9.6}$$

Note that in Eq. (9.6), the optimization variables are not coupled by a global variable and hence in addition to being a distributed problem, Eq. (9.6) is also a decentralized problem. In order to deal with the dynamic nature and time-dependency of the objective (9.6), we assume that at each time step t, each agent receives a task and computes $F_i^{(t)}(\boldsymbol{L}_i)$ locally via Eq. (9.3) based on this local task. Then, through K information exchanges during that time step, the local dictionaries are updated such that the agents reach a local consensus, sharing knowledge between tasks and hence benefit from all the tasks that are received by the network in that time step.

To split the constrained objective (9.6) into a sequence of local unconstrained agent-level problems, we use the extended ADMM algorithm [134, 153]. This algorithm generalizes ADMM [25] to account for linearly constrained convex problems with a sum of N separable objective functions. Similar to ADMM, we first need to form the augmented Lagrangian $\mathcal{J}_T(\boldsymbol{L}_1, \ldots, \boldsymbol{L}_N, \boldsymbol{Z})$ for problem (9.6) at time t in order to replace the constrained problem by an unconstrained objective function which has an added penalty term:

$$\mathcal{J}_T(\boldsymbol{L}_1, \ldots, \boldsymbol{L}_N, \boldsymbol{Z}) = \frac{1}{T} \sum_{t=1}^T \sum_{i=1}^N F_i^{(t)}(\boldsymbol{L}_i) +$$

$$\lambda \|\boldsymbol{L}_i\|_{\mathsf{F}}^2 + \left\langle \boldsymbol{Z}, \sum_{i=1}^N \boldsymbol{E}_i \boldsymbol{L}_i \right\rangle + \frac{\rho}{2} \left\| \sum_{i=1}^N \boldsymbol{E}_i \boldsymbol{L}_i \right\|_{\mathsf{F}}^2, \tag{9.7}$$

where $\langle \boldsymbol{Z}, \sum_{i=1}^N \boldsymbol{E}_i \boldsymbol{L}_i \rangle = \text{tr}\left(\boldsymbol{Z}^\top \sum_{i=1}^N \boldsymbol{E}_i \boldsymbol{L}_i \right)$ denotes the matrix trace inner product, $\rho \in \mathbb{R}^+$ is a regularization penalty term parameter for violation of the constraint, and the block matrix $\boldsymbol{Z} = [\boldsymbol{Z}_1^\top, \ldots, \boldsymbol{Z}_e^\top]^\top \in \mathbb{R}^{ed \times u}$ is the ADMM dual variable. The extended ADMM algorithm solves Eq. (9.6) by iteratively updating the dual and primal variables using the following local split iterations:

$$L_1^{k+1} = \operatorname{argmin}_{L_1} \mathcal{J}_T \left(L_1, L_2^k \dots, L_N^k, Z^k \right) \ ,$$

$$L_2^{k+1} = \operatorname{argmin}_{L_2} \mathcal{J}_T \left(L_1^{k+1}, L_2, \dots, L_N^k, Z^k \right) \ ,$$

$$\vdots \tag{9.8}$$

$$L_N^{k+1} = \operatorname{argmin}_{L_N} \mathcal{J}_T \left(L_1^{k+1}, L_2^{k+1}, \dots, L_N, Z^k \right) \ ,$$

$$Z^{k+1} = Z^k + \rho \left(\sum_{i=1}^N E_i L_i^{k+1} \right) \ . \tag{9.9}$$

The first N problems (9.8) are primal agent-specific problems to update each local dictionary, and the last problem (9.9) updates the dual variable. These iterations split the objective (9.7) into local primal optimization problems to update each of the L_i's, and then synchronize the agents to share information through updating the dual variable. Note that the j'th column of E_i is only non-zero when $j \in \mathcal{N}(i)$ $[E_i]_j = 0_d, \forall j \notin \mathcal{N}(i)$, hence the update rule for the dual variable is indeed e local block updates by adjacent agents:

$$Z_l^{k+1} = Z_l^k + \rho \left(L_i^{k+1} - L_j^{k+1} \right) \ , \tag{9.10}$$

for the lth edge (i,j). This means that to update the dual variable, agent i solely needs to keep track of copies of those blocks Z_l that are shared with neighboring agents, reducing (9.9) to a set of distributed local operations. Note that iterations in (9.8) and (9.10) are performed K times at each time step t for each agent to allow for agents to converge to a stable solution. At each time step t, the stable solution from the previous time step $t-1$ is used to initialize dictionaries and the dual variable in (9.8). Due to convergence guarantees of extended ADMM [134], this simply means that at each iteration all tasks that are received by the agents are considered to update the knowledge bases.

9.3.1 Dictionary Update Rule

Splitting an optimization using ADMM is particularly helpful if the optimization on primal variables can be solved efficiently, e.g., it has a closed-form solution. We show that the local primal updates in Eq. (9.8) can be solved in closed form. We simply compute and then null the gradients of the primal problems, which leads to systems of linear problems for each local dictionary L_i:

$$0 = \frac{\partial \mathcal{J}_T}{\partial L_i} = \frac{2}{T} \sum_{t=1}^T \Gamma_i^{(t)} \left(L_i s_i^{(t)} - \alpha_i^{(t)} \right) s_i^{(t)\top} +$$

$$E_i^\top \left(E_i L_i + \sum_{j,j>i} E_j L_j^k + \sum_{j,j<i} E_j L_j^{k+1} + \frac{1}{\rho} Z \right) + 2\lambda L_i \ . \tag{9.11}$$

Note that despite our compact representation, primal iterations in (9.8) involve only dictionaries from neighboring agents ($\forall j \notin \mathcal{N}(i)$ because $E_i E_j = 0$ and $[E_i]_j = 0_d, \forall j \notin \mathcal{N}(i)$). Moreover, only blocks of the dual variable Z that correspond to neighboring agents are

---

Algorithm 10 CoLLA $(k, d, \lambda, \mu, \rho)$

1: $T \leftarrow 0, \ \boldsymbol{A} \leftarrow \boldsymbol{zeros}_{kd,kd}$,

2: $\boldsymbol{b} \leftarrow \mathbf{zeros}_{k,1}, \ \boldsymbol{L}_i \leftarrow \mathbf{zeros}_{d,k}$

3: **while** MoreTrainingDataAvailable() **do**

4:      $T \leftarrow T + 1$

5:      **while** $i \leq N$ **do**

6:          $\left(\mathbf{X}_i^{(t)}, \mathbf{y}_i^{(t)}, t \right) \leftarrow$ getTrainingData()

7:          $\left(\boldsymbol{\alpha}_i^{(t)}, \boldsymbol{\Gamma}_i^{(t)} \right) \leftarrow$ singleTaskLearner$(X^{(t)}, y^{(t)})$

8:          $\boldsymbol{s}_i^{(t)} \leftarrow$ Equation 9.3

9:          **while** $k \leq K$ **do**

10:              $\boldsymbol{A}_i \leftarrow \boldsymbol{A}_i + \left(\boldsymbol{s}_i^{(t)} \boldsymbol{s}_i^{(t)\top} \right) \otimes \boldsymbol{\Gamma}_i^{(t)}$

11:              $\boldsymbol{b}_i \leftarrow \boldsymbol{b}_i + \mathrm{vec}\left(\boldsymbol{s}_i^{(t)\top} \otimes \left(\boldsymbol{\alpha}_i^{(t)\top} \boldsymbol{\Gamma}_i^{(t)} \right) \right)$

12:              $\boldsymbol{L}_i \leftarrow$ reinitializeAllZero$(\boldsymbol{L}_i)$

13:              $\boldsymbol{b}_i \leftarrow \dfrac{1}{T}\boldsymbol{b}_i + \mathrm{vec}\left(-\dfrac{1}{2}\displaystyle\sum_{j\in\mathcal{N}(i)} \boldsymbol{E}_i^\top \boldsymbol{Z}_j - \dfrac{\rho}{2}\left(\displaystyle\sum_{j<i,j\in\mathcal{N}(i)} \boldsymbol{E}_i^\top \boldsymbol{E}_j \boldsymbol{L}_j^{k+1} + \displaystyle\sum_{j>i,j\in\mathcal{N}(i)} \boldsymbol{E}_i^\top \boldsymbol{E}_j \boldsymbol{L}_j^{k} \right) \right)$

14:              $\boldsymbol{L}_i^k \leftarrow \mathrm{mat}\left(\left(\dfrac{1}{T}\boldsymbol{A}_i + \left(\dfrac{\rho}{2}|\mathcal{N}(i)| + \lambda \right)\boldsymbol{I}_{kd} \right)^{-1} \boldsymbol{b}_i \right)$

15:              $\boldsymbol{Z}^{k+1} = \boldsymbol{Z}^k + \rho\left(\sum_i \boldsymbol{E}_i \boldsymbol{L}_i^{k+1} \right)$ //distributed

16:          **end while**

17:      **end while**

18: **end while**

---

needed to update each knowledge base. This means that iterations in (9.11) are also fully distributed and decentralized local operations.

To solve for $\boldsymbol{L}_i$, we vectorize both sides of Eq. (9.11), and then after applying a property of Kronecker $((\boldsymbol{B}^\top \otimes \boldsymbol{A})\mathrm{vec}(\boldsymbol{X}) = \mathrm{vec}(\boldsymbol{A}\boldsymbol{X}\boldsymbol{B}))$, Eq. (9.11) simplifies to the following linear update rules for the local knowledge base dictionaries:

$$\boldsymbol{A}_i = \left(\frac{\rho}{2}|\mathcal{N}(i)| + \lambda \right)\boldsymbol{I}_{dk} + \frac{1}{T}\sum_{t=1}^{T}\left(\boldsymbol{s}_i^{(t)}\boldsymbol{s}_i^{(t)\top} \right) \otimes \boldsymbol{\Gamma}_i^{(t)} \ ,$$

$$\boldsymbol{b}_i = \mathrm{vec}\left(\frac{1}{T}\sum_{t=1}^{T}\boldsymbol{s}_i^{(t)\top} \otimes \left(\boldsymbol{\alpha}_i^{(t)\top}\boldsymbol{\Gamma}_i^{(t)} \right) - \frac{1}{2}\sum_{j\in\mathcal{N}(i)}\boldsymbol{E}_i^\top \boldsymbol{Z}_j - \frac{\rho}{2}\left(\sum_{j<i,j\in\mathcal{N}(i)}\boldsymbol{E}_i^\top \boldsymbol{E}_j \boldsymbol{L}_j^{k+1} + \sum_{j>i,j\in\mathcal{N}(i)}\boldsymbol{E}_i^\top \boldsymbol{E}_j \boldsymbol{L}_j^{k} \right) \right) ,$$

$$\boldsymbol{L} \leftarrow \mathrm{mat}_{d,k}\left(\boldsymbol{A}_i^{-1}\boldsymbol{b}_i \right) \ , \tag{9.12}$$

where $\mathrm{vec}(\cdot)$ denotes the matrix to vector (via column stacking), and $\mathrm{mat}(\cdot)$ denotes the vector to matrix operations. To avoid the sums over all tasks $1 \leq t \leq T$ and the need to store all previous tasks' data, we construct both $\boldsymbol{A}_i$ and $\boldsymbol{b}_i$ incrementally as tasks are learned. Our method, the Collective lifelong learning Algorithm (CoLLA), is summarized in Algorithm 10.

9.4 THEORETICAL GUARANTEES

An important question about Algorithm 10 is whether it is a converging algorithm. We use techniques from Ref. [211], adapted originally from Ref. [134] to demonstrate that Algorithm 10 converges to a stationary point of the risk function. We make the following assumptions:

i) The data distribution has a compact support. This assumption enforces boundedness on $\boldsymbol{\alpha}^{(t)}$ and $\boldsymbol{\Gamma}^{(t)}$, and subsequently on $\boldsymbol{L}_i$ and $\boldsymbol{s}^{(t)}$ (see Ref. [134] for details).

ii) The LASSO problem in Eq. (9.3) admits a unique solution according to one of the uniqueness conditions for LASSO [244]. As a result, the functions $F_i^{(t)}$ are well-defined.

iii) The matrices $\boldsymbol{L}_i^\top \boldsymbol{\Gamma}^{(t)} \boldsymbol{L}_i$ are strictly positive definite. As a result, the functions $F_i^{(t)}$ are all strongly convex.

Our proof involves two steps. First, we show that the inner loop with variable k in Algorithm 10 converges to a consensus solution for all i and all t. Next, we prove that the outer loop on t is also convergent, showing that the collectively learned dictionary stabilizes as more tasks are learned. For the first step, we outline the following theorem on the convergence of the extended ADMM algorithm:

Theorem 9.4.1. *(Theorem 4.1 in [79])*
Suppose we have an optimization problem in the form of Eq. (9.6), where the functions $g_i(\boldsymbol{L}_i) := \sum_i F_i^{(t)}(\boldsymbol{L}_i)$ are strongly convex with modulus η_i. Then, for any $0 < \rho < min_i \left\{ \frac{2\eta_i}{3(N-1)\|\boldsymbol{E}_i\|^2} \right\}$, iterations in Eqs. (9.8) and (9.9) converge to a solution of Eq. (9.6).

Note that in Algorithm 10, $F_i^{(t)}(\boldsymbol{L}_i)$ is a quadratic function of $\boldsymbol{L}_i$ with a symmetric positive definite Hessian and thus $g_i(\boldsymbol{L}_i)$, as an average of strongly convex functions, is also strongly convex. So the required condition for Theorem 9.4.1 is satisfied, and at each time step, the inner loop on k would converge. We represent the consensus dictionary of the agents after ADMM convergence at time $t = T$ with $\boldsymbol{L}_T = \boldsymbol{L}_i|_{t=T}, \forall i$ (the solution obtained via Eqs. (9.9) and (9.6) at $t = T$) and demonstrate that this matrix becomes stable as t grows (the outer loop converges), proving overall convergence of the algorithm. More precisely, $\boldsymbol{L}_T$ is the minimizer of the augmented Lagrangian $\mathcal{J}_T(\boldsymbol{L}_1, \ldots, \boldsymbol{L}_N, \boldsymbol{Z})$ at $t = T$ and $\boldsymbol{L}_1 = \ldots = \boldsymbol{L}_N$. Also note that upon convergence of ADMM, $\sum_i \boldsymbol{E}_i \boldsymbol{L}_i = \boldsymbol{O}$. Hence, $\boldsymbol{L}_T$ is the minimizer of the following risk function, derived from Eq. (9.7):

$$\hat{\mathcal{R}}_T(\boldsymbol{L}) = \frac{1}{T} \sum_{t=1}^T \sum_{i=1}^N F_i^{(t)}(\boldsymbol{L}) + \lambda \|\boldsymbol{L}\|_{\mathsf{F}}^2 . \qquad (9.13)$$

We also use the following lemma in our proof [211]:

Lemma 1. *The function $\hat{\mathcal{Q}}_T(\boldsymbol{L}) = \hat{\mathcal{R}}_T(\boldsymbol{L}) - \hat{\mathcal{R}}_{T+1}(\boldsymbol{L})$ is a Lipschitz function:* $\forall \ \boldsymbol{L}, \boldsymbol{L}'$, $\left| \hat{\mathcal{Q}}_T(\boldsymbol{L}') - \hat{\mathcal{Q}}_T(\boldsymbol{L}) \right| \leq O\left(\frac{1}{T+1}\right) \|\boldsymbol{L}' - \boldsymbol{L}\|.$

Proof. After algebraic simplifications, we can conclude that $\hat{\mathcal{Q}}_T(\boldsymbol{L}) = \left(\frac{1}{T(T+1)} \sum_{t=1}^T \sum_{i=1}^N F_i^{(t)}(\boldsymbol{L}) \right) - \frac{1}{T+1} F_i^{(T+1)}$. The functions $F_i^{(t)}(\boldsymbol{L})$ are quadratic forms with positive definite Hessian matrices and hence are Lipschitz functions, all with Lipschitz parameters upper-bounded by the largest eigenvalue of all Hessian matrices. Using the definition for a Lipschitz function, it is easy to demonstrate that $\hat{\mathcal{R}}_T(\cdot)$ is also Lipschitz with Lipschitz parameter $O\left(\frac{1}{T+1}\right)$, because of averaged quadratic terms in Eq. (9.13). □

Now we can prove the convergence of Algorithm 10:

Lemma 2. $L_{T+1} - L_T = O\left(\frac{1}{T+1}\right)$, *showing that Algorithm 1 converges to a stable dictionary as T grows large.*

Proof. First, note that $\hat{\mathcal{R}}_T(\cdot)$ is a strongly convex function for all T. Let η_T be the strong convexity modulus. From the definition, for two points L_{T+1} and L_T, we have: $\hat{\mathcal{R}}_T(L_{T+1}) \geq \hat{\mathcal{R}}_T(L_T) + \nabla\hat{\mathcal{R}}_T^\top(L_T)(L_T - L_{T+1}) + \frac{\eta_T}{2}\|L_{T+1} - L_T\|_F^2$. Since L_T is minimizer of $\hat{\mathcal{R}}_T(\cdot)$:

$$\hat{\mathcal{R}}_T(L_{T+1}) - \hat{\mathcal{R}}_T(L_T) \geq \frac{\eta_T}{2}\|L_{T+1} - L_T\|_F^2 . \tag{9.14}$$

On the other hand, from Lemma 1:

$$\hat{\mathcal{R}}_T(L_{T+1}) - \hat{\mathcal{R}}_T(L_T) = \hat{\mathcal{R}}_T(L_{T+1}) - \hat{\mathcal{R}}_{T+1}(L_{T+1}) +$$
$$\hat{\mathcal{R}}_{T+1}(L_{T+1}) - \hat{\mathcal{R}}_{T+1}(L_T) + \hat{\mathcal{R}}_{T+1}(L_T) - \hat{\mathcal{R}}_T(L_T) \tag{9.15}$$
$$\leq \hat{\mathcal{Q}}_T(L_{T+1}) - \hat{\mathcal{Q}}_T(L_T) \leq O\left(\frac{1}{T+1}\right)\|L_{T+1} - L_T\| .$$

Note that the first two terms on the second line in the above as a whole is negative since L_{T+1} is the minimizer of $\hat{\mathcal{R}}_{T+1}$. Now combining (9.14) and (9.15), it is easy to show that :

$$\|L_{T+1} - L_T\|_F^2 \leq O\left(\frac{1}{T+1}\right) , \tag{9.16}$$

thereby proving the lemma ■ □

Thus, Algorithm 10 converges as the number of tasks T increases. We also show that the distance between L_T and the set of stationary points of the agents' true expected costs $\mathcal{R}_T = \mathbb{E}_{X^{(t)}\sim\mathcal{D}^{(t)}}\left(\hat{\mathcal{R}}_T\right)$ converges almost surely to 0 as $T \to \infty$. We use two theorems [134] for this purpose:

Theorem 9.4.2. *(From [134])* *Consider the empirical risk function* $\hat{q}_T(L) = \frac{1}{T}\sum_{t=1}^T F^{(t)}(L) + \lambda\|L\|_F^2$ *with $F^{(t)}$ as defined in Eq. (9.3) and the true risk function* $q_T(L) = \mathbb{E}_{X^{(t)}\sim\mathcal{D}^{(t)}}(\hat{g}(L))$, *and make assumptions (A)–(C). Then both risk functions converge almost surely as* $\lim_{T\to\infty}\hat{q}_T(L) - q_T(L) = 0$.

Note that we can apply this theorem on $\mathcal{R}_T$ and $\hat{\mathcal{R}}_T$ because the inner sum in Eq. (9.13) does not violate the assumptions of Theorem 9.4.2. This is because the functions $g_i(\cdot)$ are all well-defined and are strongly convex with strictly positive definite Hessians (the sum of positive definite matrices is positive definite). Thus, $\lim_{T\to\infty}\hat{\mathcal{R}}_T - \mathcal{R}_T = 0$ almost surely.

Theorem 9.4.3. *(From Ref. [134])* *Under assumptions (A)–(C), the distance between the minimizer of $\hat{q}_T(L)$ and the stationary points of $q_T(L)$ converges almost surely to zero.*

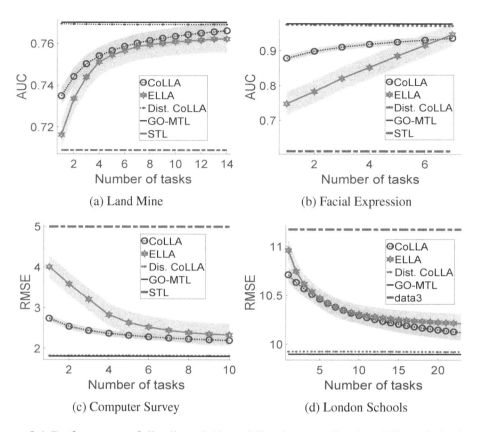

Figure 9.1 Performance of distributed (dotted lines), centralized (solid), and single-task learning (dashed) algorithms on benchmark datasets. The shaded region shows standard error. (Best viewed in color.)

Again, this theorem is applicable on $\mathcal{R}_T$ and $\hat{\mathcal{R}}_T$, and thus Algorithm 10 converges to a stationary point of the true risk.

Computational Complexity At each time-step, each agent computes the optimal ridge parameter $\boldsymbol{\alpha}^{(t)}$ and the Hessian matrix $\boldsymbol{\Gamma}^{(t)}$ for the received task. This has a cost of $O(\xi(d, M))$, where $\xi()$ depends on the base learner. The cost of updating $\boldsymbol{L}_i$ and $\boldsymbol{s}_i^{(t)}$ alone is $O(u^2 d^3)$ [211], and so the cost of updating all local dictionaries by the agents is $O(Nu^2 d^3)$. Note that this step is performed K times in each time-step. Finally, updating the dual variable requires a cost of eud. This leads to the overall cost of $O(N\xi(d, M) + K(Nu^2 d^3 + eud))$, which is independent of T but accumulates as more tasks are learned. We can think of the factor K in the second term as communication cost because, in a centralized scheme, we would not need these repetitions, which requires sharing the local bases with the neighbors. Also, note that if the number of data points per task is big enough, it certainly is more costly to send data to a single server and learn the tasks in a centralized optimization scheme.

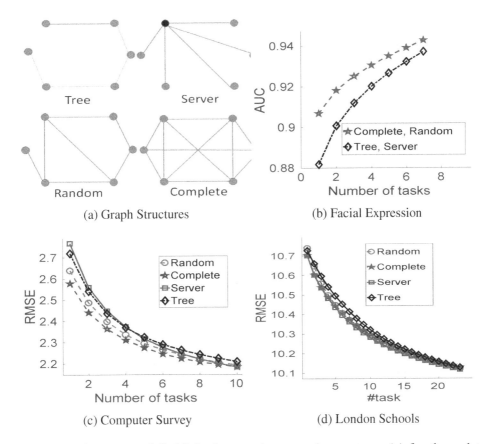

(a) Graph Structures   (b) Facial Expression

(c) Computer Survey   (d) London Schools

Figure 9.2 Performance of CoLLA given various graph structures (a) for three datasets (b–d).

9.5 EXPERIMENTAL RESULTS

To assess the performance of CoLLA from different perspectives, we compare it against: (*a*) single-task learning (STL), a lower-bound to measure the effect of positive transfer among the tasks, (*b*) ELLA [211], to demonstrate that collaboration between the agents improves overall performance in comparison, (*c*) offline CoLLA, as an upper-bound to our online distributed algorithm, and finally (*d*) GO-MTL [110], as an absolute upper-bound (since GO-MTL is a batch MTL method). Throughout all experiments, we present and compare the average performance of all agents.

9.5.1 Datasets

We used four benchmark MTL datasets in our experiments, including two classifications and two regression datasets: (1) land mine detection in radar images [272], (2) facial expression identification from photographs of a subject's face [249], (3) predicting London students' scores using school-specific and student-specific features [9], and (4) predicting ratings of customers for different computer models [121]. Below we describe each dataset.

Land Mine Detection: This dataset consists of binary classification tasks to detect whether an area contains land mines from radar images [272]. There are 29 tasks, each corresponding to a different geographical region, with a total 14,820 data points. Each data point consists of nine features, including four moment-based features, three correlation-based features, one energy ratio feature, and one spatial variance feature, all extracted from radar images. We added a bias term as a 10th feature. The dataset has a natural dichotomy between foliated and dessert regions. We assumed there are two collaborating agents, each dealing solely with one region type.

Facial Expression Recognition: This dataset consists of binary facial expression recognition tasks [249]. We followed Ruvolo and Eaton [211] and chose tasks detecting three facial action units (upper lid raiser, upper lip raiser, and lip corner pull) for seven different subjects, resulting in 21 total tasks, each with 450–999 data points. A Gabor pyramid scheme is used to extract a total of 2,880 Gabor features from images of each subject's face (see Ref. [211] for details). Each data point consists of the first 100 PCA components of these Gabor features. We used three agents, each of which learns seven randomly selected tasks. Given that facial expression recognition is a core task for personal assistant robots, each agent can be considered a personal service robot that interacts with few people in a specific environment.

London Schools: This dataset [9] was provided by the Inner London Education Authority. It consists of examination scores of 15,362 students (each assumed to be a data point) in 139 secondary schools (each assumed to be a single task) during three academic years. The goal is to predict the score of students of each school using provided features as a regression problem. We used the same 27 categorical features as described by Kumar et al. [110], consisting of eight school-specific features and 19 student-specific features, all encoded as binary features. We also added a feature to account for the bias term. For this dataset, we considered six agents and allocated 23 tasks randomly to each agent.

Computer Survey: The goal in this dataset [121] is to predict the likelihood of purchasing one of 20 different computers by 190 subjects; each subject is assumed to be a different task. Each data point consists of 13 binary features, e.g., guarantee, telephone hot line, etc. (see Ref [121] for details). We added a feature to account for the bias term. The output is a rating on a scale 0–10 collected in a survey from the subjects. We considered 19 agents and randomly allocated ten tasks to each.

9.5.2 Evaluation Methodology

For each dataset, we assume that the tasks are distributed equally among the agents. We used different numbers of agents across the datasets, as described in the previous section, to explore various sizes of the multi-agent system.

For each experiment, we randomly split the data for each task evenly into training and testing sets. We performed 100 learning trials on the training sets and reported the average performance on the testing sets for these trials as well as the performance variance. For the online settings (CoLLA and ELLA), we randomized the task order in each trial. For the offline settings (GO-MTL, Dist. CoLLA, STL), we reported the average asymptotic performance on all task because all tasks are presented and learned simultaneously. We used brute force search to cross-validate the parameters u, λ, μ, and ρ for each dataset; these parameters were selected to maximize the performance on a validation set for each algorithm independently. Parameters λ, μ, and ρ are selected from the set $\{10^n \mid -6 \leq n \leq 6\}$ and u from $\left\{1, \ldots, \max\left(10, \frac{T}{4}\right)\right\}$ (note that $u \ll T$).

For the two regression problems, we used root-mean-squared error (RMSE) on the testing set to measure the performance of the algorithms. For the two classification problems, we used the area under the ROC curve (AUC) to measure performance, since both datasets have skewed class distributions, making RMSE and other error measures less informative. Unlike AUC, RMSE is agnostic to the trade-off between false-positives and false-negatives, which can vary in terms of importance in different applications.

Quality of Agreement Among the Agents: The inner loop in Algorithm 10 implements information exchange between the agents. For effective collective learning, agents need to come to an agreement at each time step, which is guaranteed by ADMM if K is chosen large enough. During our experiments, we noticed that initially K needs to be fairly large but as more tasks are learned, it can be decreased over time $K \propto K_1 + K_2/t$ without considerable change in performance ($K_1 \in \mathbb{N}$ is generally small and $K_2 \in \mathbb{N}$ is large). This is expected because the tasks learned by all agents are related, and hence, as more tasks are learned, knowledge transfer from previous tasks makes local dictionaries closer.

9.5.3 Results

For the first experiment on CoLLA, we assumed a minimal linearly connected (path graph) tree, which allows for information flow among the agents $\mathcal{E} = \{(i, i+1) \mid 1 \leq i \leq N\}$. Figure 9.1 compares CoLLA against ELLA (which does not use collective learning), GO-MTL, and single-task learning. The number of learned tasks is equal for both COLLA and ELLA. ELLA can be considered as a special case of COLLA with an edgeless graph topology (no communication). Moreover, we also performed an offline distributed batch MTL optimization of Eq. (9.6), i.e., offline CoLLA, and plot the learning curves for the online settings and the average performance on all tasks for offline settings.

At each time step t, the vertical axis shows the average performance of the online algorithms on all tasks learned so far (up to that time step). The horizontal axis denotes the number of tasks learned by each individual agent. The shaded plot regions denote the standard error. This would allow us to assess whether a positive/ transfer has occurred consistently. A progressive increase in the average performance on the learned tasks demonstrates that positive transfer has occurred and allows plotting learning curves. Moreover, we also performed an offline distributed batch MTL optimization of Eq. (9.6), i.e., offline CoLLA. For comparison, we plot the learning curves for the online settings and the average asymptotic performance on all tasks for offline settings in the same plot. The shaded regions on the plots denote the standard error for 100 trials.

Figure 9.1 shows that collaboration among agents improves lifelong learning, both in terms of learning speed and asymptotic performance, to a level that is not feasible for a single lifelong learning agent. The performance of offline CoLLA is comparable with GO-MTL, demonstrating that our algorithm can also be used effectively as a distributed MTL

Method \ Dataset	Land Mine	London Schools	Computer Survey	Facial Expression
CoLLA	6.87	29.62	51.44	40.87
ELLA	6.21	29.30	37.99	38.69
Dist. CoLLA	32.21	37.30	61.71	59.89
GO-MTL	8.63	32.40	61.81	60.17

Table 9.1 Jumpstart comparison (improvement in percentage) on the Land Mine (LM), London Schools (LS), Computer Survey (CS), and Facial Expression (FE) datasets.

algorithm. As expected, both CoLLA and ELLA lead to the same asymptotic performance because they solve the same optimization problem as the number of tasks grows large. These results demonstrate the effectiveness of our algorithm for both offline and online optimization settings. We also measured the improvement in the initial performance on a new task due to transfer (the *jumpstart* [240]) in Table 9.1, highlighting COLLA's effectiveness in collaboratively learning knowledge bases suitable for transfer.

We conducted a second set of experiments to study the effect of the communication mode (i.e., the graph structure) on distributed lifelong learning. We performed experiments on four graph structures visualized in Figure 9.2a: tree, server (star graph), complete, and random. The server graph structure connects all client agents through a central server (a master agent, depicted in black in the figure), and the random graph was formed by randomly selected half of the edges of a complete graph while still ensuring that the resulting graph was connected. Note that some of these structures coincide when the network is small (for this reason, results on the land mine dataset, which only uses two agents, are not presented for this second experiment). Performance results for these structures on the London schools, computer survey, and facial expression recognition datasets are presented in Figures 9.2b–9.2d. Note that for the facial recognition dataset, results for the only two possible structures are presented. From these figures, we can roughly conclude that for network structures with more edges, learning is faster. Intuitively, this empirical result suggests that more communication and collaboration between the agents can accelerate learning.

9.6 CONCLUSIONS

In this chapter, we proposed a distributed optimization algorithm for enabling collective multi-agent lifelong learning. Collaboration among the agents not only improves the asymptotic performance on the learned tasks but allows the agent to learn faster (i.e., using fewer data to reach a specific performance threshold). Our experiments demonstrated that the proposed algorithm outperforms other alternatives on a variety of MTL regression and classification problems. Extending the proposed framework to a network of asynchronous agents with dynamic links is a potential future direction to improve the applicability of the algorithm on real-world problems. This chapter is our last contribution in this book. In the next chapter, we list potential research directions for the future.

CHAPTER 10

Concluding Remarks and Potential Future Research Directions

In this concluding chapter of the book, we summarize our contributions. We also discuss the limitations of the developed algorithms and potential improvements that can be pursued. Finally, we list potential research directions for the future.

10.1   SUMMARY AND DISCUSSIONS

Data-driven Machine Learning (ML) has led to a dramatic improvement of ML algorithms over the past decade. This success, however, is still far away from the goal to develop algorithms with human-level performance in many application areas. There are many areas that further improvement of current ML methods and techniques is necessary. In particular, the current algorithms usually use deep networks as the base learning model. Since deep networks require a large labeled training dataset, data labeling has become a major expensive task for ML. Crowdsourcing data labeling platforms such as Amazon Mechanical Turk may be sufficient to label datasets for research purpose, but many practical ML tasks require high-quality annotated data which requires training the annotators.

For this reason, there are companies that are founded solely for the propose of labeling and annotating data by training and employing a pool of human workers to generate labeled datasets for costumers. On the other hand, theoretical ML usually considers that the data distribution is stationary, and upon training a model, it should generalize only on data samples that are drawn from the same distribution. This assumption is also too restrictive, as data distribution can change dramatically in many applications. From a practical point of view, these assumptions are too simplistic and restrictive. As a result, many current ML algorithms underperform in practice. For these reasons, improving learning speed, learning efficiency, and generalizability of the existing algorithms had been a significant research focus recently. Transfer learning is a broad area of research that addresses these challenges by transferring knowledge from related learned problems. In this book, we investigated the possibility of knowledge transfer in ML to address challenges of labeled data scarcity and drifts in the data distribution. We studied the possibility of transferring knowledge through an intermediate embedding space that captures meta-information about a group of ML problems. This idea can be considered similar to the neurological functioning of the brain, where hierarchical knowledge sensory system input is encoded according to the abstractness of concepts. More specifically, *parallel distributed processing* and *complementary learning systems theory* are two paradigms within the connectionist model in neuroscience that hypothesize this learning scheme. Throughout this book, we demonstrated that this broad idea could be used to develop algorithms for various learning settings that may seem too different at the surface. The main contribution of this book is to group and address the challenges of all these learning setting using a similar strategy.

In the first part of the book, we focused on transferring knowledge across different learning domains. In chapter 3, we demonstrated that transferring knowledge across heterogeneous domains can help to learn classes with no labeled data in the visual domain, through descriptive information from the textual domain in a multiclass classification problem, i.e., zero-shot learning. Zero-shot learning ability seems to be necessary nowadays as many classes emerge each day, and retraining a trained model does not seem to be a feasible solution. We concluded that using two dictionaries that couple the visual and the textual domains, can address challenges of domain shift and hubness problem in zero-shot learning. We also provided theoretical results on PAC-learnability of our algorithm to justify why our algorithm is effective. We then investigated knowledge transfer across homogeneous visual domains in chapters 4 and 5, where the goal is to address the challenge of labeled data scarcity in a domain, by transferring knowledge from a secondary homogeneous domain with labeled data. We demonstrated that our ideas could address both unsupervised and semi-supervised domain adaptation scenarios in chapters 4 and 5, respectively. Our method for unsupervised domain adaptation is developed for similar domains, where domain gap is not significant. For this reason, the same features can be used for both domains. As a result, a shared deep network model can be trained to generalize well on both domains by matching the data distribution in mid-layers of the network as the intermediate embedding space. In contrast, we developed a semi-supervised domain adaptation algorithm to transfer knowledge across two domains with a considerable gap, e.g., EO-to-SAR knowledge transfer , where only a portion of the network higher-level layers are shared. The early layers were set to be domain-specific to reduce the domain gap in their output as the embedding space. We also provided theoretical results to demonstrate that our approach is effective due to minimizing an upper-bound of the target risk.

The algorithms that we developed in the first part have their own limitations. Our ZSL algorithm is designed for the situation that only unseen classes are observed during testing time. Despite being the common assumption in ZSL, this assumption is not practical. For this reason, recently, a new learning setting has been suggested to generalize ZSL, call generalized zero-shot learning (GZSL) [264, 111]. In this setting, both the seen and unseen classes are observed during testing. A potential improvement for our algorithm is to address challenges of GZLS, where domain shift problem is going to be more challenging to overcome. Another area of further investigation is low-shot learning over knowledge graphs [150] that has gained interest recently. The domain adaptation algorithms that we developed are designed for quite simple classification tasks, e.g., hand-written digit recognition or binary ship image classification. Applying these algorithms to more challenging problems such as face recognition person re-identification as well as problems with many classes is an area that needs further investigation. Finally, since we aligned marginal distributions of the two domains, we assumed that both domains share the same classes. However, a more realistic scenario would be considering that only a subset of classes to be shared across the two domains. Our framework can potentially be adapted to consider this assumption but it certainly requires further investigation.

In the second part of the book, we considered knowledge transfer across different tasks that are defined in a single domain. In chapter 6, we first extended our idea in chapter 3, to develop a zero-shot learning algorithm in a lifelong multi-task learning setting, where the goal is to enable learning ML tasks using their high-level descriptors. Lifelong machine learning is designed to model the learning mechanisms of humans, where the goal is to make the learning algorithm adaptive concerning changes in the data distribution. We demonstrated that using our method; we can learn a task using its high-level descriptors without using any data. Our algorithm is a general algorithm that can be used in classification, regression, and reinforcement learning tasks. We then developed an algorithm to mitigate catastrophic forgetting in chapter 7, where multiple tasks are learned sequentially. Most of the current ML models face this challenge as the learned knowledge for different tasks usually interferes with each other, causing performance degradation on previously learned task. For this reason, overcoming catastrophic forgetting can be considered as addressing a particular case of negative knowledge transfer [73]. Our idea is to use a generative model that can generate pseudo-data points for old tasks to tackle catastrophic forgetting using experience replay [225]. To this end, we couple the tasks in an embedding space that is modeled by middle-layer of an autoencoder. The idea is to enforce all tasks to share the same distribution in the embedding space such that this distribution encodes abstract concepts. As a result, this distributing can be used to generate pseudo-data points for experience replay and learning future tasks such that the newly learned knowledge does not interfere with past learned knowledge. In chapter 8, we then extended our idea in chapter 7, to develop a method for generalizing the learned concepts by a deep network to new domains by observing only a few labeled data points in the new domain. This idea can be considered as domain adaptation in a lifelong learning setting, where the goal is to continually adapt a model to incorporate newly learned knowledge without forgetting the past. We also provided theoretical results to demonstrate why our algorithms are able to mitigate catastrophic forgetting.

Our algorithms in Part II are more limited compared to the algorithms in Part I. In chapter 6, we assumed that the task descriptors are given but determining meaningful descriptions can be quite challenging in practice. A practical improvement for our algorithm would be learning meaningful descriptions from data to broaden the applications that our algorithm can address. In chapters 7 and 8, we considered quite simple tasks, i.e., digit recognition tasks. Our algorithms in these chapters require further improvement to be applicable to realistic problems. Another limitation is that we considered that the tasks share the same classes. In practice, new classes are going to be learned at different times. Hence, it is more realistic to consider that new classes can be introduced in future tasks, and only a subset of the classes are shared with the past learned tasks [234].

Finally, we focused on transferring knowledge across multiple various learning agents in the third part of the book. In many applications, the data is inevitably distributed among multiple agents, and collaboration among the agents can increase learning performance.

In particular, smart-phones and available sensors on them are an important application area for distributed learning setting. We considered lifelong machine learning agents that learn tasks synchronously. Similar to chapter 6, we assumed that the optimal parameters for the tasks could be represented sparsely in a dictionary domain in chapter 9. To transfer knowledge across the agents, we assumed that all agents learn homogeneous tasks, and for this reason, all learn the same underlying dictionary. We demonstrated that the agents could share their high-level learned knowledge through a global embedding space that is modeled by this dictionary without sharing private data. We tested our algorithm on four different datasets and different topological arrangement of the graph that models communication mode between the agents. We also provided theoretical results for convergence of our iterative algorithm to a stable solution across the agents.

Synchronicity is a major restriction for our algorithm in chapter 9. In practice, it is unlikely that the agents learn the tasks at the same time. We can always wait for the agents to become synchronous, but this will make the slowest agent a bottleneck, which seems undesirable. Extending our algorithm to asynchronous agents is an important challenge from the practical point of view. Another restriction is that we assumed that all the agents learn the same shared model. However, the agents may learn heterogeneous tasks that enforces discrepancy among the agent-specific models. Using the same global model across the agents may lead to negative transfer among the agents. To tackle this challenge, we need to extend our algorithm by considering different models among the agents and meanwhile model the relations among the agents to allow for knowledge transfer .

10.2 FUTURE RESEARCH DIRECTIONS

There are important unexplored ideas that we leave for future investigation. We foresee four major areas that deserve attention from the ML community.

Throughout the book, our selection procedure for the embedding space has been mostly arbitrary. We have not developed a systematic method to select parameters such as the dimension of the embedding space or the suitable depth for the embedding space in a deep neural network. Some of our experiments in chapters 3, 5, and 6 demonstrate that these parameters can have a huge effect on learning performance. In order to transfer knowledge through an embedding space, it is essential to study the effects of these parameters and then provide a systematic method for selecting the embedding space. Additionally, we simply related two problems through a single embedding space. In contrast, it seems that the nervous system uses a set of hierarchical embedding spaces which encode concepts according to different levels of abstractness. Hierarchical representation of data through deep nets is known in the ML community, but using these representations to transfer knowledge through different tasks according to their relatedness requires further investigations.

We mainly focused on classification tasks in this book (with the exception of chapter 6). Deep Reinforcement Learning (DRL) has gained considerable attention because through the power of deep nets; it is possible to learn quite complicated tasks to the human-level performance blindly [151]. However, DRL algorithms are highly time-consuming and require huge training datasets, considerably more compared to what is necessary for supervised learning algorithms. For this reason, transfer learning is an important tool that can be used to make DRL more practical. We did not explore DRL in this book, but as evident from chapter 6, our ideas may be applicable to this area. In RL context, an embedding space may encode skills that can be helpful to perform different sets of tasks. Recently, latent and embedding spaces have been found helpful in this area [76, 210], where similar to chapter 8 of this book, the goal is to enforce state-space of several RL tasks to share similar distributions in a latent space.

An important application area that we did not touch is machine translation and natural language processing. Some of the most popular ML algorithms that benefit from embedding spaces have been developed in this area, e.g., word2vec. The idea of using an embedding space to relate several languages and transfer knowledge across different languages seems to be very feasible. In particular, according to "triangle of reference" linguistic model, there is a hierarchical relationship between symbols of language and meaning, i.e., meaning transcends linguistic symbols [160, 41]. This seems to be the reasons behind the ability of humans to learn and communicate through different languages. Similarly, recent works in this area demonstrate that learning an embedding space that can capture meanings irrespective of languages can help to improve the current machine translation algorithms [72]. We foresee a considerable potential in this area for future research.

Finally, the ultimate goal of AI is to develop machines that behave and learn similar to human. This goal is far beyond this book, but it seems that the integration of the three parts of this book is essential to reach this goal. Transferring knowledge through embedding spaces might not be the best solution, but we demonstrated that it is a helpful and broad strategy. However, we addressed problems in each part of this book independently, and the integration of the abilities of these algorithms is not trivial. A long term goal for machine learning is to develop learning agents that are able to benefit from knowledge transfer across different domains and tasks and are able to collaborate and benefit from other agents. This challenging goal can serve to fuel research in ML and AI community for at least another few decades.

Bibliography

[1] NASDAQ Companies. `https://www.nasdaq.com/screening/companies-by-industry.aspx?sortname=marketcap&sorttype=1&exchange=NASDAQ`, 2019. [Online; accessed 11-June-2019].

[2] Statistics of acceptance rate for the main AI conferences. `https://github.com/lixin4ever/Conference-Acceptance-Rate`, 2019. [Online; accessed 11-June-2019].

[3] M. Aharon, M. Elad, and A. Bruckstein. K-SVD: An algorithm for designing overcomplete dictionaries for sparse representation. *IEEE Transactions on Signal Processing*, 54(11):4311–4322, 2006.

[4] Z. Akata, F. Perronnin, Z. Harchaoui, and C. Schmid. Label-embedding for attribute-based classification. In *Proceedings of the IEEE International Conference Computer Vision and Pattern Recognition*, pages 819–826, 2013.

[5] Z. Akata, S. Reed, D. Walter, H. Lee, and B. Schiele. Evaluation of output embeddings for fine-grained image classification. In *Proceedings of the IEEE Conference on Computer Vision and Pattern Recognition (CVPR)*, pages 2927–2936, 2015.

[6] R. Aljundi, F. Babiloni, M. Elhoseiny, M. Rohrbach, and T. Tuytelaars. Memory aware synapses: Learning what (not) to forget. In *Proceedings of the European Conference on Computer Vision (ECCV)*, pages 139–154, 2018.

[7] H. B. Ammar, E. Eaton, P. Ruvolo, and M. Taylor. Online multi-task learning for policy gradient methods. In *Proceedings of the International Conference on Machine Learning*, pages 1206–1214, 2014.

[8] R. K. Ando and T. Zhang. A framework for learning predictive structures from multiple tasks and unlabeled data. *The Journal of Machine Learning Research*, 6:1817–1853, 2005.

[9] A. Argyriou, T. Evgeniou, and M. Pontil. Convex multi-task feature learning. *Machine learning*, 73(3):243–272, 2008.

[10] H. Ashtiani, S. Ben-David, N. Harvey, C. Liaw, A. Mehrabian, and Y. Plan. Nearly tight sample complexity bounds for learning mixtures of Gaussians via sample compression schemes. In *Advances in Neural Information Processing Systems*, pages 3412–3421, 2018.

[11] B. Bakker and T. Heskes. Task clustering and gating for Bayesian multitask learning. *The Journal of Machine Learning Research*, 4:83–99, 2003.

[12] M. Baktashmotlagh, M. T. Harandi, B. C. Lovell, and M. Salzmann. Unsupervised domain adaptation by domain invariant projection. In *Proceedings of the IEEE International Conference on Computer Vision*, pages 769–776, 2013.

[13] J. Baxter. A model of inductive bias learning. *The Journal of Artificial Intelligence Research*, 12:149–198, 2000.

[14] I. M. Baytas, M. Yan, A. K. Jain, and J. Zhou. Asynchronous multi-task learning. In *Proceedings of the IEEE 16th International Conference on Data Mining (ICDM)*, pages 11–20, 2016.

[15] A. Beck and M. Teboulle. A fast iterative shrinkage-thresholding algorithm for linear inverse problems. *SIAM Journal on Imaging Sciences*, 2(1):183–202, 2009.

[16] M. Belkin, I. Matveeva, and P. Niyogi. Regularization and semi-supervised learning on large graphs. In *Proceedings of the Conference on Learning Theory*, pages 624–638. Springer, 2004.

[17] S. Ben-David, J. Blitzer, K. Crammer, and F. Pereira. Analysis of representations for domain adaptation. *Advances in Neural Information Processing Systems*, 19:137–144, 2007.

[18] B. Bhushan Damodaran, B. Kellenberger, R. Flamary, D. Tuia, and N. Courty. Deep-JDOT: Deep joint distribution optimal transport for unsupervised domain adaptation. In *Proceedings of the European Conference on Computer Vision (ECCV)*, pages 447–463, 2018.

[19] S. Bickel, C. Sawade, and T. Scheffer. Transfer learning by distribution matching for targeted advertising. In *Advances in Neural Information Processing Systems*, volume 8, pages 105–112, 2008.

[20] F. Bolley, A. Guillin, and C. Villani. Quantitative concentration inequalities for empirical measures on non-compact spaces. *Probability Theory and Related Fields*, 137(3-4):541–593, 2007.

[21] E. V. Bonilla, F. V. Agakov, and C. K. Williams. Kernel multi-task learning using task-specific features. In *Artificial Intelligence and Statistics*, pages 43–50. PMLR, 2007.

[22] N. Bonnotte. *Unidimensional and evolution methods for optimal transportation*. PhD thesis, Paris 11, 2013.

[23] S. Bouabdallah and R. Siegwart. Backstepping and sliding-mode techniques applied to an indoor micro quadrotor. In *Proceedings of the 2005 IEEE international conference on robotics and automation*, pages 2247–2252. IEEE, 2005.

[24] K. Bousmalis, N. Silberman, D. Dohan, D. Erhan, and D. Krishnan. Unsupervised pixel-level domain adaptation with generative adversarial networks. In *Proceedings of the IEEE Conference on Computer Vision and Pattern Recognition*, pages 3722–3731, 2017.

[25] S. Boyd, N. Parikh, E. Chu, B. Peleato, and J. Eckstein. Distributed optimization and statistical learning via the alternating direction method of multipliers. *Foundations and Trends® in Machine Learning*, 3(1):1–122, 2011.

[26] M. Bucher, S. Herbin, and F. Jurie. Improving semantic embedding consistency by metric learning for zero-shot classification. In *Proceedings of European Conference on Computer Vision (ECCV)*, pages 730–746. Springer, 2016.

[27] M. Bucher, S. Herbin, and F. Jurie. Generating visual representations for zero-shot classification. In *Proceedings of International Conference on Computer Vision (ICCV) Workshops: TASK-CV: Transferring and Adapting Source Knowledge in Computer Vision*, 2017.

[28] L. Busoniu, R. Babuska, B. De Schutter, and D. Ernst. *Reinforcement Learning and Dynamic Programming Using Function Approximators*. CRC Press, 2010.

[29] R. Caruana. Multitask learning. *Machine learning*, 28(1):41–75, 1997.

[30] G. Cavallanti, N. Cesa-Bianchi, and C. Gentile. Linear algorithms for online multitask classification. *The Journal of Machine Learning Research*, 11:2901–2934, 2010.

[31] S. Changpinyo, W. Chao, B. Gong, and F. Sha. Synthesized classifiers for zero-shot learning. In *Proceedings of the IEEE Conference on Computer Vision and Pattern Recognition*, pages 5327–5336, 2016.

[32] C. Chen, W. Xie, W. Huang, Y. Rong, X. Ding, Y. Huang, T. Xu, and J. Huang. Progressive feature alignment for unsupervised domain adaptation. In *Proceedings of the IEEE Conference on Computer Vision and Pattern Recognition*, pages 627–636, 2019.

[33] J. Chen, C. Richard, and A. H. Sayed. Multitask diffusion adaptation over networks. *IEEE Transactions on Signal Processing*, 62(16):4129–4144, 2014.

[34] J. Chen and A. H. Sayed. Diffusion adaptation strategies for distributed optimization and learning over networks. *IEEE Transactions on Signal Processing*, 60(8):4289–4305, 2012.

[35] L.-C. Chen, G. Papandreou, F. Schroff, and H. Adam. Rethinking atrous convolution for semantic image segmentation, 2017.

[36] S. Chen, H. Wang, F. Xu, and Y. Jin. Target classification using the deep convolutional networks for SAR images. *IEEE Transactions on Geoscience and Remote Sensing*, 54(8):4806–4817, 2016.

[37] Y. Chen, W. Li, X. Chen, and L. V. Gool. Learning semantic segmentation from synthetic data: A geometrically guided input-output adaptation approach, 2018.

[38] Y.-H. Chen, W.-Y. Chen, Y.-T. Chen, B.-C. Tsai, Y.-C. F. Wang, and M. Sun. No more discrimination: Cross city adaptation of road scene segmenters, 2017.

[39] Z. Chen and B. Liu. Topic modeling using topics from many domains, lifelong learning and big data. In *Proceedings of the International Conference on Machine Learning*, pages 703–711, 2014.

[40] Z. Chen and B. Liu. Lifelong machine learning. *Synthesis Lectures on Artificial Intelligence and Machine Learning*, 10(3):1–145, 2016.

[41] C. Cherry. On human communication; a review, a survey, and a criticism., 1957.

[42] J. Choi, T. Kim, and C. Kim. Self-ensembling with GAN-based data augmentation for domain adaptation in semantic segmentation, 2019.

[43] P. Ciaccia and M. Patella. PAC nearest neighbor queries: Approximate and controlled search in high-dimensional and metric spaces. In *Proceedings of 16th International Conference on Data Engineering*, pages 244–255, 2000.

[44] A. Coates and A. Y. Ng. The importance of encoding versus training with sparse coding and vector quantization. In *Proceedings of the 28th International Conference on International Conference on Machine Learning*, pages 921–928, 2011.

[45] P. Comon and C. Jutten. *Handbook of Blind Source Separation: Independent Component Analysis and Applications*. Academic Press, 2010.

[46] M. Cordts, M. Omran, S. Ramos, T. Rehfeld, M. Enzweiler, R. Benenson, U. Franke, S. Roth, and B. Schiele. The cityscapes dataset for semantic urban scene understanding. In *Proceedings of the IEEE Conference on Computer Vision and Pattern Recognition*, pages 3213–3223, 2016.

[47] P. I. Corke. Autonomous cross-domain knowledge transfer in lifelong policy gradient reinforcement learning. In *Robotics, Vision & Control: Fundamental Algorithms in MATLAB*. Springer, 2011.

[48] N. Courty, R. Flamary, D. Tuia, and A. Rakotomamonjy. Optimal transport for domain adaptation. *IEEE Transactions on Pattern Analysis and Machine Intelligence*, 39(9):1853–1865, 2017.

[49] O. Dekel, P. M. Long, and Y. Singer. Online multitask learning. In *Proceedings of the International Conference on Computational Learning Theory*, pages 453–467. Springer, 2006.

[50] J. Deng, W. Dong, R. Socher, L.-J. Li, K. Li, and L. Fei-Fei. ImageNet: A large-scale hierarchical image database. In *Proceedings of the 2009 IEEE Conference on Computer Vision and Pattern Recognition (CVPR)*, pages 248–255, IEEE 2009.

[51] S. Dhouib, I. Redko, and C. Lartizien. Margin-aware adversarial domain adaptation with optimal transport. In *Thirty-seventh International Conference on Machine Learning*, 2020.

[52] S. Diekelmann and J. Born. The memory function of sleep. *Nature Review Neuroscience*, 11(114), 2010.

[53] Z. Ding, M. S., and Y. Fu. Low-rank embedded ensemble semantic dictionary for zero-shot learning. In *Proceedings of the IEEE Conference on Computer Vision and Pattern Recognition*, pages 2050–2058, 2017.

[54] G. Dinu, A. Lazaridou, and M. Baroni. Improving zero-shot learning by mitigating the hubness problem. In *International Conference on Learning Representations Workshops*, 2015.

[55] W. Dong, C. Moses, and K. Li. Efficient k-nearest neighbor graph construction for generic similarity measures. In *Proceedings of the 20th International Conference on World Wide Web*, pages 577–586. ACM, 2011.

[56] D. L. Donoho. For most large underdetermined systems of linear equations the minimal 1-norm solution is also the sparsest solution. *Communications on Pure and Applied Mathematics*, 59(6):797–829, 2006.

[57] D. L. Donoho, M. Elad, and V. N. Temlyakov. Stable recovery of sparse overcomplete representations in the presence of noise. *IEEE Transactions on Information Theory*, 52(1):6–18, 2006.

[58] M. Dredze and K. Crammer. Online methods for multi-domain learning and adaptation. In *Proceedings of the Conference on Empirical Methods in Natural Language Processing*, pages 689–697. Association for Computational Linguistics, 2008.

[59] T. Evgeniou and M. Pontil. Regularized multi–task learning. In *Proceedings of the International Conference on Knowledge Discovery and Data Mining*, pages 109–117. ACM, 2004.

[60] B. Fernando, A. Habrard, M. Sebban, and T. Tuytelaars. Unsupervised visual domain adaptation using subspace alignment. In *Proceedings of the IEEE International Conference on Computer Vision*, pages 2960–2967, 2013.

[61] R. M. French. Catastrophic forgetting in connectionist networks. *Trends in Cognitive Sciences*, 3(4):128–135, 1999.

[62] Y. Fujiwara and G. Irie. Efficient label propagation. In *Proceedings of the 31st International Conference on Machine Learning*, pages 784–792, 2014.

[63] A. J. Gabourie, M. Rostami, S. Kolouri, and K. Kim. System and method for unsupervised domain adaptation via Sliced-Wasserstein distance, Apr. 23 2020. US Patent App. 16/719,668.

[64] A. J. Gabourie, M. Rostami, P. E. Pope, S. Kolouri, and K. Kim. Learning a domain-invariant embedding for unsupervised domain adaptation using class-conditioned distribution alignment. In *2019 57th Annual Allerton Conference on Communication, Control, and Computing (Allerton)*, pages 352–359, 2019.

[65] Y. Ganin and V. Lempitsky. Unsupervised domain adaptation by backpropagation. In *Proceedings of the International Conference on Machine Learning (ICML)*, 2014.

[66] A. Globerson and S. T. Roweis. Metric learning by collapsing classes. In *Advances in Neural Information Processing Systems*, pages 451–458, 2006.

[67] B. Gong, Y. Shi, F. Sha, and K. Grauman. Geodesic flow kernel for unsupervised domain adaptation. In *Computer Vision and Pattern Recognition (CVPR), 2012 IEEE Conference on*, pages 2066–2073. IEEE, 2012.

[68] I. Goodfellow, J. Pouget-Abadie, M. Mirza, B. Xu, D. Warde-Farley, S. Ozair, A. Courville, and Y. Bengio. Generative adversarial nets. In *Advances in Neural Information Processing Systems*, pages 2672–2680, 2014.

[69] Y. Grandvalet and Y. Bengio. Semi-supervised learning by entropy minimization. In *Advances in Neural Information Processing Systems*, volume 17, pages 529–536, 2004.

[70] A. Gretton, A. Smola, J. Huang, M. Schmittfull, K. Borgwardt, and B. Schölkopf. Covariate shift by kernel mean matching. *Dataset Shift in Machine Learning*, 3(4):5, 2009.

[71] R. Gribonval, R. Jenatton, F. Bach, M. Kleinsteuber, and M. Seibert. Sample complexity of dictionary learning and other matrix factorizations. *IEEE Transactions on Information Theory*, 61(6):3469–3486, 2015.

[72] J. Gu, H. Hassan, J. Devlin, and V. O. Li. Universal neural machine translation for extremely low resource languages. In *The Annual Conference of the North American Chapter of the Association for Computational Linguistics*, pages 344–354, 2018.

[73] L. Gui, R. Xu, Q. Lu, J. Du, and Y. Zhou. Negative transfer detection in transductive transfer learning. *International Journal of Machine Learning and Cybernetics*, 9(2):185–197, 2018.

[74] M. Guo, H. Zhang, J. Li, L. Zhang, and H. Shen. An online coupled dictionary learning approach for remote sensing image fusion. *IEEE Journal of Selected Topics in Applied Earth Observations and Remote Sensing*, 7(4):1284–1294, 2014.

[75] A. Gupta, C. Devin, Y. Liu, P. Abbeel, and S. Levine. Learning invariant feature spaces to transfer skills with reinforcement learning. In *Proceedings of the International Conference on Learning Representation (ICLR)*, pages 1–122, 2017.

[76] T. Haarnoja, K. Hartikainen, P. Abbeel, and S. Levine. Latent space policies for hierarchical reinforcement learning. In *Proceedings of the International Conference on Machine Learning (ICML)*, 2018.

[77] J. Ham, D. D. Lee, and L. K. Saul. Semisupervised alignment of manifolds. In *Proceedings of International Conference on Artificial Intelligence and Statistics*, pages 120–127, 2005.

[78] R. Hammell. Ships in satellite imagery, 2017. data retrieved from Kaggle, `https://www.kaggle.com/rhammell/ships-in-satellite-imagery`.

[79] D. Han and X. Yuan. A note on the alternating direction method of multipliers. *Journal of Optimization Theory and Applications*, 155(1):227–238, 2012.

[80] N. Hao, A. Oghbaee, M. Rostami, N. Derbinsky, and J. Bento. Testing fine-grained parallelism for the ADMM on a factor-graph. In *Proceedings of the 2016 IEEE International Parallel and Distributed Processing Symposium Workshops (IPDPSW)*, pages 835–844. IEEE, 2016.

[81] R. Hataya. EWC PyTorch. `https://github.com/moskomule/ewc.pytorch`, 2018.

[82] J. He and R. Lawrence. A graph-based framework for multi-task multi-view learning. In *Proceedings of the 28th International Conference on Machine Learning*, pages 25–32, 2011.

[83] K. He, X. Zhang, S. Ren, and J. Sun. Deep residual learning for image recognition. In *Proceedings of the International Conference on Computer Vision and Pattern Recognition (CVPR)*, pages 770–778, 2016.

[84] M. R. Heinen, P. M. Engel, and R. C. Pinto. Using a Gaussian mixture neural network for incremental learning and robotics. In *Proceedings of the 2012 International Joint Conference on Neural Networks (IJCNN)*, pages 1–8. IEEE, 2012.

[85] J. Hoffman, E. Tzeng, T. Park, J.-Y. Zhu, P. Isola, K. Saenko, A. Efros, and T. Darrell. CyCADA: Cycle-consistent adversarial domain adaptation. In *International conference on machine learning*, pages 1989–1998. PMLR, 2018.

[86] J. Hoffman, D. Wang, F. Yu, and T. Darrell. FCNs in the wild: Pixel-level adversarial and constraint-based adaptation, 2016.

[87] D.-A. Huang and Y.-C. F. Wang. Coupled dictionary and feature space learning with applications to cross-domain image synthesis and recognition. In *Proceedings of the IEEE international conference on computer vision*, pages 2496–2503, 2013.

[88] E. H. Huang, R. Socher, C. D. Manning, and A. Y. Ng. Improving word representations via global context and multiple word prototypes. In *Proceedings of the 50th Annual Meeting of the Association for Computational Linguistics (Volume 1: Long Papers)*, pages 873–882, 2012.

[89] G. Huang, Z. Liu, K. Q. Weinberger, and L. van der Maaten. Densely connected convolutional networks. In *Proceedings of the IEEE International Conference on Computer Vision*, pages 4700–4708, 2017.

[90] J.-T. Huang, J. Li, D. Yu, L. Deng, and Y. Gong. Cross-language knowledge transfer using multilingual deep neural network with shared hidden layers. In *Proceedings of the IEEE International Conference on Acoustics, Speech and Signal Processing*, pages 7304–7308. IEEE, 2013.

[91] S. Huang, D. N. Tran, and T. D. Tran. Sparse signal recovery based on nonconvex entropy minimization. In *Proceedings of the IEEE International Conference on Image Processing*, pages 3867–3871. IEEE, 2016.

[92] Z. Huang, Z. Pan, and B. Lei. Transfer learning with deep convolutional neural network for SAR target classification with limited labeled data. *Remote Sensing*, 9(9):907, 2017.

[93] D. Isele and A. Cosgun. Selective experience replay for lifelong learning. In *Proceedings of the Thirty-Second AAAI Conference on Artificial Intelligence*, 2018.

[94] D. Isele, M. Rostami, and E. Eaton. Using task features for zero-shot knowledge transfer in lifelong learning. In *Proceedings of International Joint Conference on Artificial Intelligence*, pages 1620–1626, 2016.

[95] V. Jain and E. Learned-Miller. Online domain adaptation of a pre-trained cascade of classifiers. In *Proceedings of the 2011 IEEE Conference on Computer Vision and Pattern Recognition*, pages 577–584, 2011.

[96] T. Jansen and R. P. Wiegand. Exploring the explorative advantage of the cooperative coevolutionary (1+1) ea. In *Proceedings of Genetic and Evolutionary Computation Conference*, pages 310–321. Springer, 2003.

[97] X. Jin, P. Luo, F. Zhuang, J. He, and Q. He. Collaborating between local and global learning for distributed online multiple tasks. In *Proceedings of the 24th ACM International on Conference on Information and Knowledge Management*, pages 113–122. ACM, 2015.

[98] A. B. Kao, N. Miller, C. Torney, A. Hartnett, and I. D. Couzin. Collective learning and optimal consensus decisions in social animal groups. *PLoS Computational Biology*, 10(8):e1003762, 2014.

[99] D. P. Kingma and J. Ba. Adam: A method for stochastic optimization. *arXiv preprint arXiv:1412.6980*, 2014.

[100] J. Kirkpatrick, R. Pascanu, N. Rabinowitz, J. Veness, G. Desjardins, A. A. Rusu, K. Milan, J. Quan, T. Ramalho, A. Grabska-Barwinska, et al. Overcoming catastrophic forgetting in neural networks. *Proceedings of the National Academy of Sciences*, 114(13):3521–3526, 2017.

[101] J. Kober and J. Peters. Policy search for motor primitives in robotics. *Machine learning*, 84(1-2):171–203, 2011.

[102] E. Kodirov, T. Xiang, Z. Fu, and S. Gong. Unsupervised domain adaptation for zero-shot learning. In *Proceedings of the IEEE International Conference on Computer Vision*, pages 2452–2460, 2015.

[103] E. Kodirov, T. Xiang, and S. Gong. Semantic autoencoder for zero-shot learning. In *Proceedings of the IEEE International Conference on Computer Vision*, pages 3174–3183, 2017.

[104] S. Kolouri, G. K. Rohde, and H. Hoffmann. Sliced Wasserstein distance for learning Gaussian mixture models. In *Proceedings of the IEEE Conference on Computer Vision and Pattern Recognition*, pages 3427–3436, 2018.

[105] S. Kolouri, M. Rostami, and K. Kim. Systems and methods for few-shot transfer learning, Apr. 30 2020. US Patent App. 16/532,321.

[106] S. Kolouri, M. Rostami, K. Kim, and Y. Owechko. Attribute aware zero shot machine vision system via joint sparse representations, Jan. 24 2019. US Patent App. 16/033,638.

[107] S. Kolouri, M. Rostami, Y. Owechko, and K. Kim. Joint dictionaries for zero-shot learning. In *Proceedings of the AAAI Conference on Artificial Intelligence*, volume 32, 2018.

[108] V. Koo, Y. Chan, G. Vetharatnam, M. Y. Chua, C. Lim, C. Lim, C. Thum, T. Lim, Z. bin Ahmad, K. Mahmood, et al. A new unmanned aerial vehicle synthetic aperture radar for environmental monitoring. *Progress in Electromagnetics Research*, 122:245–268, 2012.

[109] A. Krizhevsky, I. Sutskever, and G. E. Hinton. ImageNet classification with deep convolutional neural networks. In *Advances in Neural Information Processing Systems*, pages 1097–1105, 2012.

[110] A. Kumar and H. Daume III. Learning task grouping and overlap in multi-task learning. In *Proceedings of the 29th International Conference on Machine Learning*, pages 1383–1390, 2012.

[111] V. Kumar Verma, G. Arora, A. Mishra, and P. Rai. Generalized zero-shot learning via synthesized examples. In *Proceedings of the IEEE Conference on Computer Vision and Pattern Recognition (CVPR)*, pages 4281–4289, 2018.

[112] B. M. Lake, R. Salakhutdinov, and J. B. Tenenbaum. Human-level concept learning through probabilistic program induction. *Science*, 350(6266):1332–1338, 2015.

[113] C. H. Lampert, H. Nickisch, and S. Harmeling. Learning to detect unseen object classes by between-class attribute transfer. In *2009 IEEE Conference on Computer Vision and Pattern Recognition*, pages 951–958. IEEE, 2009.

[114] C. H. Lampert, H. Nickisch, and S. Harmeling. Attribute-based classification for zero-shot visual object categorization. *IEEE Transactions on Pattern Analysis and Machine Intelligence*, 36(3):453–465, 2014.

[115] R. Lamprecht and J. LeDoux. Structural plasticity and memory. *Nature Reviews Neuroscience*, 5(1):45, 2004.

[116] H. Lang, S. Wu, and Y. Xu. Ship classification in SAR images improved by AIS knowledge transfer. *IEEE Geoscience and Remote Sensing Letters*, 15(3):439–443, 2018.

[117] A. Lazaric and M. Ghavamzadeh. Bayesian multi-task reinforcement learning. In *Proceedings of International Conference on Machine Learning*, pages 599–606. Omnipress, 2010.

[118] Y. LeCun, B. E. Boser, J. S. Denker, D. Henderson, R. E. Howard, W. E. Hubbard, and L. D. Jackel. Handwritten digit recognition with a back-propagation network. In *Advances in Neural Information Processing Systems*, pages 396–404, 1990.

[119] C.-Y. Lee, T. Batra, M. H. Baig, and D. Ulbricht. Sliced Wasserstein discrepancy for unsupervised domain adaptation. In *Proceedings of the IEEE Conference on Computer Vision and Pattern Recognition*, pages 10285–10295, 2019.

[120] J. Lei Ba, K. Swersky, S. Fidler, et al. Predicting deep zero-shot convolutional neural networks using textual descriptions. In *Proceedings of the International Conference on Computer Vision and Pattern Recognition (CVPR)*, pages 4247–4255, 2015.

[121] P. J. Lenk, W. S. DeSarbo, P. E. Green, and M. R. Young. Hierarchical Bayes conjoint analysis: Recovery of partworth heterogeneity from reduced experimental designs. *Marketing Science*, 15(2):173–191, 1996.

[122] M. Li, D. G. Andersen, A. J. Smola, and K. Yu. Communication efficient distributed machine learning with the parameter server. In *Advances in Neural Information Processing Systems*, pages 19–27, 2014.

[123] M. Li, Y.-M. Zhai, Y.-W. Luo, P.-F. Ge, and C.-X. Ren. Enhanced transport distance for unsupervised domain adaptation. In *Proceedings of the IEEE/CVF Conference on Computer Vision and Pattern Recognition*, pages 13936–13944, 2020.

[124] N. Li and J. R. Marden. Designing games for distributed optimization. *IEEE Journal of Selected Topics in Signal Processing*, 7(2):230–242, 2013.

[125] Y. Li, D. Wang, H. Hu, Y. Lin, and Y. Zhuang. Zero-shot recognition using dual visual-semantic mapping paths. In *Proceedings of the IEEE International Conference on Computer Vision*, pages 3279–3287, 2017.

[126] S. Liu, S. J. Pan, and Q. Ho. Distributed multi-task relationship learning. In *Proceedings of the 23rd ACM SIGKDD International Conference on Knowledge Discovery and Data Mining*, pages 937–946. ACM, 2017.

[127] J. Long, E. Shelhamer, and T. Darrell. Fully convolutional networks for semantic segmentation. In *Proceedings of the IEEE Conference on Computer Vision and Pattern Recognition*, pages 3431–3440, 2015.

[128] M. Long, Y. Cao, J. Wang, and M. Jordan. Learning transferable features with deep adaptation networks. In *Proceedings of International Conference on Machine Learning*, pages 97–105, 2015.

[129] M. Long, J. Wang, G. Ding, J. Sun, and P. S. Yu. Transfer joint matching for unsupervised domain adaptation. In *Proceedings of the IEEE Conference on Computer Vision and Pattern Recognition*, pages 1410–1417, 2014.

[130] M. Longcamp, M.-T. Zerbato-Poudou, and J.-L. Velay. The influence of writing practice on letter recognition in preschool children: A comparison between handwriting and typing. *Acta Psychologica*, 119(1):67–79, 2005.

[131] P. Luc, C. Couprie, S. Chintala, and J. Verbeek. Semantic segmentation using adversarial networks. In *NIPS Workshop on Adversarial Training*, 2016.

[132] Y. Luo, L. Zheng, T. Guan, J. Yu, and Y. Yang. Taking a closer look at domain shift: Category-level adversaries for semantics consistent domain adaptation. In *Proceedings of the IEEE Conference on Computer Vision and Pattern Recognition*, pages 2507–2516, 2019.

[133] L. v. d. Maaten and G. Hinton. Visualizing data using t-SNE. *Journal of Machine Learning Research*, 9(Nov):2579–2605, 2008.

[134] J. Mairal, F. Bach, J. Ponce, and G. Sapiro. Online learning for matrix factorization and sparse coding. *Journal of Machine Learning Research*, 11:19–60, 2010.

[135] H. Maitre. *Processing of Synthetic Aperture Radar (SAR) Images*. Wiley, 2010.

[136] D. Malmgren-Hansen, A. Kusk, J. Dall, A. Nielsen, R. Engholm, and H. Skriver. Improving SAR automatic target recognition models with transfer learning from simulated data. *IEEE Geoscience and Remote Sensing Letters*, 14(9):1484–1488, 2017.

[137] M. Mangal and M. P. Singh. Analysis of multidimensional XOR classification problem with evolutionary feedforward neural networks. *International Journal on Artificial Intelligence Tools*, 16(01):111–120, 2007.

[138] J. Manyika, S. Lund, M. Chui, J. Bughin, J. Woetzel, P. Batra, R. Ko, and S. Sanghvi. Jobs lost, jobs gained: Workforce transitions in a time of automation. *McKinsey Global Institute*, 2017.

[139] F. Markatopoulou, V. Mezaris, and I. Patras. Deep multi-task learning with label correlation constraint for video concept detection. In *Proceedings of the 24th ACM international conference on Multimedia*, pages 501–505. ACM, 2016.

[140] D. Mateos-Núñez, J. Cortés, and J. Cortes. Distributed optimization for multi-task learning via nuclear-norm approximation. *IFAC-PapersOnLine*, 48(22):64–69, 2015.

[141] A. Maurer, M. Pontil, and B. Romera-Paredes. Sparse coding for multitask and transfer learning. In *International conference on machine learning*, pages 343–351. PMLR, 2013.

[142] J. L. McClelland, B. L. McNaughton, and R. C. O'Reilly. Why there are complementary learning systems in the hippocampus and neocortex: insights from the successes and failures of connectionist models of learning and memory. *Psychological Review*, 102(3):419, 1995.

[143] J. L. McClelland and T. T. Rogers. The parallel distributed processing approach to semantic cognition. *Nature Reviews Neuroscience*, 4(4):310, 2003.

[144] J. L. McClelland, D. E. Rumelhart, P. R. Group, et al. Parallel distributed processing. *Explorations in the Microstructure of Cognition*, 2:216–271, 1986.

[145] M. McCloskey and N. J. Cohen. Catastrophic interference in connectionist networks: The sequential learning problem. In *Psychology of Learning and Motivation*, volume 24, pages 109–165. Elsevier, 1989.

[146] L. McInnes, J. Healy, and J. Melville. UMAP: Uniform manifold approximation and projection for dimension reduction. *arXiv preprint arXiv:1802.03426*, 2018.

[147] T. Mensink, E. Gavves, and C. G. M. Snoek. Costa: Co-occurrence statistics for zero-shot classification. In *Proceedings of the IEEE Conference on Computer Vision and Pattern Recognition*, pages 2441–2448, 2014.

[148] T. Mikolov, I. Sutskever, K. Chen, G. S. Corrado, and J. Dean. Distributed representations of words and phrases and their compositionality. In *Advances in Neural Information Processing Systems*, pages 3111–3119, 2013.

[149] M. Minsky. Semantic information processing, 1982.

[150] M. Mirtaheri, M. Rostami, X. Ren, F. Morstatter, and A. Galstyan. One-shot learning for temporal knowledge graphs. *arXiv preprint arXiv:2010.12144*, 2020.

[151] V. Mnih, K. Kavukcuoglu, D. Silver, A. A. Rusu, J. Veness, M. G. Bellemare, A. Graves, M. Riedmiller, A. K. Fidjeland, G. Ostrovski, et al. Human-level control through deep reinforcement learning. *Nature*, 518(7540):529, 2015.

[152] Y. Morgenstern, M. Rostami, and D. Purves. Properties of artificial networks evolved to contend with natural spectra. *Proceedings of the National Academy of Sciences*, 111(Supplement 3):10868–10872, 2014.

[153] J. F. C. Mota, J. M. F. Xavier, P. M. Q. Aguiar, and M. Puschel. D-ADMM: A communication-efficient distributed algorithm for separable optimization. *IEEE Transactions on Signal Processing*, 61(10):2718–2723, 2013.

[154] S. Motiian, Q. Jones, S. Iranmanesh, and G. Doretto. Few-shot adversarial domain adaptation. In *Advances in Neural Information Processing Systems*, pages 6670–6680, 2017.

[155] Z. Murez, S. Kolouri, D. Kriegman, R. Ramamoorthi, and K. Kim. Image to image translation for domain adaptation. In *Proceedings of the IEEE Conference on Computer Vision and Pattern Recognition (CVPR)*, pages 4500–4509, 2018.

[156] G. L. Murphy and H. H. Brownell. Category differentiation in object recognition: typicality constraints on the basic category advantage. *Journal of Experimental Psychology: Learning, Memory, and Cognition*, 11(1):70, 1985.

[157] S. Negahban, B. Yu, M. Wainwright, and P. Ravikumar. A unified framework for high-dimensional analysis of m-estimators with decomposable regularizers. In *Advances in Neural Information Processing Systems*, pages 1348–1356, 2009.

[158] A. Ng. Nuts and bolts of building AI applications using deep learning. In *Advances in Neural Information Processing Systems*. Advances in Neural Information Processing Systems (NIPS), 2016.

[159] M. Norouzi, T. Mikolov, S. Bengio, Y. Singer, J. Shlens, A. Frome, G. S. Corrado, and J. Dean. Zero-shot learning by convex combination of semantic embeddings. In *2nd International Conference on Learning Representations, ICLR 2014*, 2014.

[160] C. K. Ogden and I. A. Richards. *The Meaning of Meaning: A Study of the Influence of Language upon Thought and of the Science of Symbolism*, volume 29. K. Paul, Trench, Trubner & Company, Limited, 1923.

[161] D. Oyen and T. Lane. Leveraging domain knowledge in multitask Bayesian network structure learning. In *Proceedings of the AAAI Conference on Artificial Intelligence*, 2012.

[162] M. Palatucci, D. Pomerleau, G. E. Hinton, and T. M. Mitchell. Zero-shot learning with semantic output codes. In *Advances in Neural Information Processing Systems*, pages 1410–1418, 2009.

[163] S. Pan and Q. Yang. A survey on transfer learning. *IEEE Transactions on Knowledge and Data Engineering*, 22(10):1345–1359, 2010.

[164] Y. Pan, T. Yao, Y. Li, Y. Wang, C.-W. Ngo, and T. Mei. Transferrable prototypical networks for unsupervised domain adaptation. In *Proceedings of the IEEE Conference on Computer Vision and Pattern Recognition*, pages 2239–2247, 2019.

[165] G. Papandreou, L.-C. Chen, K. P. Murphy, and A. L. Yuille. Weakly-and semi-supervised learning of a deep convolutional network for semantic image segmentation. In *Proceedings of the IEEE International Conference on Computer Vision*, pages 1742–1750, 2015.

[166] S. Parameswaran and K. Q. Weinberger. Large margin multi-task metric learning. In *Advances in Neural Information Processing Systems*, pages 1867–1875, 2010.

[167] N. Parikh, S. Boyd, et al. Proximal algorithms. *Foundations and Trends® in Optimization*, 1(3):127–239, 2014.

[168] G. I. Parisi, R. Kemker, J. L. Part, C. Kanan, and S. Wermter. Continual lifelong learning with neural networks: A review. *Neural Networks*, 2019.

[169] D. Pathak, P. Krahenbuhl, and T. Darrell. Constrained convolutional neural networks for weakly supervised segmentation. In *Proceedings of the IEEE International Conference on Computer Vision*, pages 1796–1804, 2015.

[170] G. Patterson and J. Hays. Sun attribute database: Discovering, annotating, and recognizing scene attributes. In *Proceedings of the IEEE Conference on Computer Vision and Pattern Recognition*, pages 2751–2758. IEEE, 2012.

[171] J. Pennington, R. Socher, and C. D. Manning. Glove: Global vectors for word representation. *Proceedings of the Empirical Methods in Natural Language Processing (EMNLP 2014)*, 12:1532–1543, 2014.

[172] J. Peters and S. Schaal. Natural actor-critic. *Neurocomputing*, 71(7):1180–1190, 2008.

[173] J. Rabin and G. Peyré. Wasserstein regularization of imaging problem. In *Proceedings of the 18th IEEE International Conference on Image Processing*, pages 1541–1544. IEEE, 2011.

[174] J. Rabin, G. Peyré, J. Delon, and M. Bernot. Wasserstein barycenter and its application to texture mixing. In *Proceedings of the International Conference on Scale Space and Variational Methods in Computer Vision*, pages 435–446. Springer, 2011.

[175] R. Raina, A. Battle, H. Lee, B. Packer, and A. Y. Ng. Self-taught learning: transfer learning from unlabeled data. In *Proceedings of the 24th international conference on Machine learning*, pages 759–766, 2007.

[176] A. Rannen, R. Aljundi, M. B. Blaschko, and T. Tuytelaars. Encoder based lifelong learning. In *Proceedings of the IEEE Conference on Computer Vision and Pattern Recognition (CVPR)*, pages 1320–1328, 2017.

[177] B. Rasch and J. Born. About sleep's role in memory. *Physiological Reviews*, 93:681–766, 2013.

[178] I. Redko, A. Habrard, and M. Sebban. Theoretical analysis of domain adaptation with optimal transport. In *Proceedings of the Joint European Conference on Machine Learning and Knowledge Discovery in Databases*, pages 737–753. Springer, 2017.

[179] A. Rehman, M. Rostami, Z. Wang, D. Brunet, and E. Vrscay. SSIM-inspired image restoration using sparse representation. *EURASIP Journal on Advances in Signal Processing*, 2012(1):16, 2012.

[180] S. R. Richter, V. Vineet, S. Roth, and V. Koltun. Playing for data: Ground truth from computer games. In *European Conference on Computer Vision*, pages 102–118. Springer, 2016.

[181] A. Robins. Catastrophic forgetting, rehearsal and pseudorehearsal. *Connection Science*, 7(2):123–146, 1995.

[182] B. Romera-Paredes and P. Torr. An embarrassingly simple approach to zero-shot learning. In *Proceedings of the International Conference on Machine Learning*, pages 2152–2161, 2015.

[183] K. Roose. His 2020 campaign message: The robots are coming. *New York Times*, 2018.

[184] G. Ros, L. Sellart, J. Materzynska, D. Vazquez, and A. M. Lopez. The SYNTHIA dataset: A large collection of synthetic images for semantic segmentation of urban scenes. In *Proceedings of the IEEE Conference on Computer Vision and Pattern Recognition*, pages 3234–3243, 2016.

[185] M. Rostami. Compressed sensing with side information on feasible region. In *Compressed Sensing with Side Information on the Feasible Region*, pages 23–31. Springer, 2013.

[186] M. Rostami. Transfer of knowledge through collective learning. In *Proceedings of the AAAI Conference on Artificial Intelligence*, pages 5050–5051, 2017.

[187] M. Rostami. *Learning Transferable Knowledge Through Embedding Spaces*. PhD thesis, University of Pennsylvania, 2019.

[188] M. Rostami, M. Babaie-Zadeh, S. Samadi, and C. Jutten. Blind source separation of discrete finite alphabet sources using a single mixture. In *2011 IEEE Statistical Signal Processing Workshop (SSP)*, pages 709–712. IEEE, 2011.

[189] M. Rostami, N.-M. Cheung, and T. Q. Quek. Compressed sensing of diffusion fields under heat equation constraint. In *2013 IEEE International Conference on Acoustics, Speech and Signal Processing*, pages 4271–4274. IEEE, 2013.

[190] M. Rostami and E. Eaton. Lifelong learning networks: Beyond single agent lifelong learning. In *Proceedings of the AAAI Conference on Artificial Intelligence*, pages 8145–8146, 2018.

[191] M. Rostami and A. Galstyan. Sequential unsupervised domain adaptation through prototypical distributions. *arXiv preprint arXiv:2007.00197*, 2020.

[192] M. Rostami, D. Huber, and T.-C. Lu. A crowdsourcing triage algorithm for geopolitical event forecasting. In *Proceedings of the 12th ACM Conference on Recommender Systems*, pages 377–381. ACM, 2018.

[193] M. Rostami, D. Isele, and E. Eaton. Using task descriptions in lifelong machine learning for improved performance and zero-shot transfer. *Journal of Artificial Intelligence Research*, 67:673–704, 2020.

[194] M. Rostami and S. Kolouri. System and method for transferring electro-optical (EO) knowledge for synthetic-aperture-radar (SAR)-based object detection, Aug. 20 2020. US Patent App. 16/752, 527.

[195] M. Rostami, S. Kolouri, E. Eaton, and K. Kim. Deep transfer learning for few-shot SAR image classification. *Remote Sensing*, 11(11):1374, 2019.

[196] M. Rostami, S. Kolouri, E. Eaton, and K. Kim. Deep transfer learning for few-shot SAR image classification. *Remote Sensing*, 2019.

[197] M. Rostami, S. Kolouri, E. Eaton, and K. Kim. SAR image classification using few-shot cross-domain transfer learning. In *Proceedings of the IEEE Conference on Computer Vision and Pattern Recognition Workshops (CVPRW)*, 2019.

[198] M. Rostami, S. Kolouri, and K. Kim. Decentralized collective lifelong learning agents. US Patent.

[199] M. Rostami, S. Kolouri, K. Kim, and E. Eaton. Multi-agent distributed lifelong learning for collective knowledge acquisition. In *Proceedings of the International Conference on Autonomous Agents and Multiagent*, pages 712–720, 2018.

[200] M. Rostami, S. Kolouri, Y. Owechko, R. Eaton, and K. Kim. Zero-shot image classification using coupled dictionary embedding. *https://arxiv.org/abs/1906.10509*, 2019.

[201] M. Rostami, S. Kolouri, and P. K. Pilly. Systems and methods for continual learning using experience replay. US Patent.

[202] M. Rostami, S. Kolouri, and P. K. Pilly. Systems and methods for unsupervised continual learning. US Patent.

[203] M. Rostami, S. Kolouri, and P. K. Pilly. Complementary learning for overcoming catastrophic forgetting using experience replay. In *Proceedings of the International Joint Conference on Artificial Intelligence*, 2019.

[204] M. Rostami, S. Kolouri, P. K. Pilly, and J. McClelland. Generative continual concept learning. In *AAAI*, pages 5545–5552, 2020.

[205] M. Rostami, O. Michailovich, and Z. Wang. Gradient-based surface reconstruction using compressed sensing. In *2012 19th IEEE International Conference on Image Processing*, pages 913–916. IEEE, 2012.

[206] M. Rostami, O. Michailovich, and Z. Wang. Image deblurring using derivative compressed sensing for optical imaging application. *IEEE Transactions on Image Processing*, 21(7):3139–3149, 2012.

[207] M. Rostami, O. V. Michailovich, and Z. Wang. Surface reconstruction in gradient-field domain using compressed sensing. *IEEE Transactions on Image Processing*, 24(5):1628–1638, 2015.

[208] M. Rostami and Z. Wang. Image super-resolution based on sparsity prior via smoothed l_0 norm. *arXiv preprint arXiv:1603.06680*, 2016.

[209] K. Roth, A. Lucchi, S. Nowozin, and T. Hofmann. Stabilizing training of generative adversarial networks through regularization. In *Advances in Neural Information Processing Systems*, pages 2018–2028, 2017.

[210] A. A. Rusu, D. Rao, J. Sygnowski, O. Vinyals, R. Pascanu, S. Osindero, and R. Hadsell. Meta-learning with latent embedding optimization. In *International Conference on Learning Representation (ICLR)*, 2019.

[211] P. Ruvolo and E. Eaton. ELLA: An efficient lifelong learning algorithm. In *Proceedings of the International Conference on Machine Learning*, pages 507–515, 2013.

[212] A. Saha, P. Rai, H. Daumã, S. Venkatasubramanian, et al. Online learning of multiple tasks and their relationships. In *Proceedings of the Fourteenth International Conference on Artificial Intelligence and Statistics*, pages 643–651. JMLR Workshop and Conference Proceedings, 2011.

[213] K. Saito, K. Watanabe, Y. Ushiku, and T. Harada. Maximum classifier discrepancy for unsupervised domain adaptation. In *Proceedings of the IEEE Conference on Computer Vision and Pattern Recognition*, pages 3723–3732, 2018.

[214] S. Sankaranarayanan, Y. Balaji, A. Jain, S. Nam Lim, and R. Chellappa. Learning from synthetic data: Addressing domain shift for semantic segmentation. In *Proceedings of the IEEE Conference on Computer Vision and Pattern Recognition*, pages 3752–3761, 2018.

[215] F. Santambrogio. Optimal transport for applied mathematicians. *Birkäuser, NY*, pages 99–102, 2015.

[216] A. M. Saxe, J. L. McClelland, and S. Ganguli. A mathematical theory of semantic development in deep neural networks. *Proceedings of the National Academy of Sciences*, page 201820226, 2019.

[217] T. Schaul, D. Horgan, K. Gregor, and D. Silver. Universal value function approximators. In *Proceedings of the International Conference on Machine Learning*, pages 1312–1320, 2015.

[218] T. Schaul, J. Quan, I. Antonoglou, and D. Silver. Prioritized experience replay. In *Proceedings of the International Conference on Learning Representations*, 2016.

[219] C. Schwegmann, W. Kleynhans, B. Salmon, L. Mdakane, and R. Meyer. Very deep learning for ship discrimination in synthetic aperture radar imagery. In *Proceedings of the IEEE International Geoscience and Remote Sensing Symposium*, pages 104–107, 2016.

[220] H. S. Seung and D. D. Lee. The manifold ways of perception. *Science*, 290(5500):2268–2269, 2000.

[221] S. Shalev-Shwartz and S. Ben-David. *Understanding Machine Learning: From Theory to Algorithms*. Cambridge university press, 2014.

[222] R. Shang, J. Wang, L. Jiao, R. Stolkin, B. Hou, and Y. Li. SAR targets classification based on deep memory convolution neural networks and transfer parameters. *IEEE Journal of Selected Topics in Applied Earth Observations and Remote Sensing*, 11(8):2834–2846, 2018.

[223] A. Sharif Razavian, H. Azizpour, J. Sullivan, and S. Carlsson. CNN features off-the-shelf: an astounding baseline for recognition. In *Proceedings of the IEEE Conference on Computer Vision and Pattern Recognition Workshops*, pages 806–813, 2014.

[224] Y. Shigeto, I. Suzuki, K. Hara, M. Shimbo, and Y. Matsumoto. Ridge regression, hubness, and zero-shot learning. In *Proceedings of the Joint European Conference on Machine Learning and Knowledge Discovery in Databases*, pages 135–151. Springer, 2015.

[225] H. Shin, J. K. Lee, J. Kim, and J. Kim. Continual learning with deep generative replay. In *Advances in Neural Information Processing Systems*, pages 2990–2999, 2017.

[226] J. Shotton, M. Johnson, and R. Cipolla. Semantic texton forests for image categorization and segmentation. In *2008 IEEE Conference on Computer Vision and Pattern Recognition*, pages 1–8. IEEE, 2008.

[227] K. Simonyan and A. Zisserman. Very deep convolutional networks for large-scale image recognition. *arXiv preprint arXiv:1409.1556*, 2014.

[228] J. Sinapov, S. Narvekar, M. Leonetti, and P. Stone. Learning inter-task transferability in the absence of target task samples. In *Proceedings of the 2015 International Conference on Autonomous Agents and Multiagent Systems*, pages 725–733, 2015.

[229] J. Snell, K. Swersky, and R. Zemel. Prototypical networks for few-shot learning. In *Advances in Neural Information Processing Systems*, pages 4077–4087, 2017.

[230] R. Socher, M. Ganjoo, C. D. Manning, and A. Ng. Zero-shot learning through cross-modal transfer. In *Advances in Neural Information Processing Systems*, pages 935–943, 2013.

[231] A. Srivastava, L. Valkov, C. Russell, M. U. Gutmann, and C. Sutton. VEEGAN: Reducing mode collapse in GANs using implicit variational learning. In *Advances in Neural Information Processing Systems*, pages 3308–3318, 2017.

[232] S. Stan and M. Rostami. Privacy preserving domain adaptation for semantic segmentation of medical images. 2020.

[233] S. Stan and M. Rostami. Unsupervised model adaptation for continual semantic segmentation. In *Thirty-Fourth AAAI Conference on Artificial Intelligence*, 2020.

[234] S. Stan and M. Rostami. Privacy preserving domain adaptation for semantic segmentation of medical images. *arXiv preprint arXiv:2101.00522*, 2021.

[235] B. Sun and K. Saenko. Deep coral: Correlation alignment for deep domain adaptation. In *European Conference on Computer Vision*, pages 443–450. Springer, 2016.

[236] R. S. Sutton and A. G. Barto. *Reinforcement Learning: An Introduction*. MIT press, 2018.

[237] R. S. Sutton, D. A. McAllester, S. P. Singh, and Y. Mansour. Policy gradient methods for reinforcement learning with function approximation. *Advances in Neural Information Processing Systems*, 99:1057–1063, 1999.

[238] M. Svetlik, M. Leonetti, J. Sinapov, R. Shah, N. Walker, and P. Stone. Automatic curriculum graph generation for reinforcement learning agents. In *Proceedings of the AAAI Conference on Artificial Intelligence*, pages 2590–2596, 2017.

[239] C. Szegedy, W. Liu, Y. Jia, P. Sermanet, S. Reed, D. Anguelov, D. Erhan, V. Vanhoucke, and A. Rabinovich. Going deeper with convolutions. In *Proceedings of the IEEE Conference on Computer Vision and Pattern Recognition*, pages 1–9, 2015.

[240] M. E. Taylor and P. Stone. Transfer learning for reinforcement learning domains: A survey. *The Journal of Machine Learning Research*, 10:1633–1685, 2009.

[241] M. E. Taylor, P. Stone, and Y. Liu. Transfer learning via inter-task mappings for temporal difference learning. *The Journal of Machine Learning Research*, 8(Sep):2125–2167, 2007.

[242] Y. Teh, V. Bapst, W. M. Czarnecki, J. Quan, J. Kirkpatrick, R. Hadsell, N. Heess, and R. Pascanu. Distral: Robust multitask reinforcement learning. In *Advances in Neural Information Processing Systems*, pages 4496–4506, 2017.

[243] S. Thrun. Is learning the n-th thing any easier than learning the first? In *Advances in Neural Information Processing Systems*, pages 640–646, 1996.

[244] R. Tibshirani. The lasso problem and uniqueness. *Electronic Journal of Statistics*, 7:1456–1490, 2013.

[245] J. Tighe and S. Lazebnik. Superparsing: scalable nonparametric image parsing with superpixels. In *European Conference on Computer Vision*, pages 352–365. Springer, 2010.

[246] T. Tommasi, N. Quadrianto, B. Caputo, and C. H. Lampert. Beyond dataset bias: Multi-task unaligned shared knowledge transfer. In *Proceedings of the Asian Conference on Computer Vision*, pages 1–15. Springer, 2012.

[247] Y.-H. Tsai, W.-C. Hung, S. Schulter, K. Sohn, M.-H. Yang, and M. Chandraker. Learning to adapt structured output space for semantic segmentation. In *Proceedings of the IEEE Conference on Computer Vision and Pattern Recognition*, pages 7472–7481, 2018.

[248] E. Tzeng, J. Hoffman, K. Saenko, and T. Darrell. Adversarial discriminative domain adaptation. In *Proceedings of the IEEE Conference on Computer Vision and Pattern Recognition (CVPR)*, volume 1, page 4, 2017.

[249] M. F. Valstar, B. Jiang, M. Mehu, M. Pantic, and K. Scherer. The first facial expression recognition and analysis challenge. In *Proceedings of the 2011 IEEE International Conference on Automatic Face & Gesture Recognition and Workshops (FG 2011)*, pages 921–926. IEEE, 2011.

[250] C. Villani. *Optimal Transport: Old and New*, volume 338. Springer Science & Business Media, 2008.

[251] T.-H. Vu, H. Jain, M. Bucher, M. Cord, and P. Pérez. Advent: Adversarial entropy minimization for domain adaptation in semantic segmentation, 2018.

[252] C. Wah, S. Branson, P. Welinder, P. Perona, and S. Belongie. The caltech-UCSD birds-200-2011 dataset. Technical report, California Institute of Technology, 2011.

[253] B. Wang and J. Pineau. Generalized dictionary for multitask learning with boosting. In *Proceedings of the International Joint Conferences on Artificial Intelligence*, pages 2097–2103, 2016.

[254] C. Wang and S. Mahadevan. A general framework for manifold alignment. In *Proceedings of the AAAI Conference on Artificial Intelligence*, 2009.

[255] J. Wang, M. Kolar, and N. Srerbo. Distributed multi-task learning. In *Proceedings of the Conference on Artificial Intelligence and Statistics*, pages 751–760, 2016.

[256] Q. Wang and K. Chen. Zero-shot visual recognition via bidirectional latent embedding. *International Journal of Computer Vision*, 124(3):356–383, 2017.

[257] Q. Wang, L. Zhang, L. Bertinetto, W. Hu, and P. H. Torr. Fast online object tracking and segmentation: A unifying approach. In *Proceedings of the IEEE Conference on Computer Vision and Pattern Recognition*, pages 1328–1338, 2019.

[258] Z. Wang, L. Du, J. Mao, B. Liu, and D. Yang. SAR target detection based on SSD with data augmentation and transfer learning. *IEEE Geoscience and Remote Sensing Letters*, 2018.

[259] R. J. Williams. Simple statistical gradient-following algorithms for connectionist reinforcement learning. *Machine Learning*, 8(3-4):229–256, 1992.

[260] A. Wilson, A. Fern, S. Ray, and P. Tadepalli. Multi-task reinforcement learning: a hierarchical Bayesian approach. In *Proceedings of the International Conference on Machine Learning*, pages 1015–1022. ACM, 2007.

[261] D. Wu. Online and offline domain adaptation for reducing BCI calibration effort. *IEEE Transactions on Human-Machine Systems*, 47(4):550–563, 2016.

[262] Z. Wu, X. Han, Y.-L. Lin, M. Gokhan Uzunbas, T. Goldstein, S. Nam Lim, and L. S. Davis. DCAN: Dual channel-wise alignment networks for unsupervised scene adaptation. In *Proceedings of the European Conference on Computer Vision (ECCV)*, pages 518–534, 2018.

[263] Y. Xian, Z. Akata, G. Sharma, Q. Nguyen, M. Hein, and B. Schiele. Latent embeddings for zero-shot classification. *Proceedings of the IEEE Conference on Computer Vision and Pattern Recognition*, 2016.

[264] Y. Xian, C. Lampert, B. Schiele, and Z. Akata. Zero-shot learning-a comprehensive evaluation of the good, the bad and the ugly. In *Proceedings of the IEEE International Conference on Computer Vision*, pages 17140–17148, 2017.

[265] Y. Xian, C. H. Lampert, B. Schiele, and Z. Akata. Zero-shot learning-a comprehensive evaluation of the good, the bad and the ugly. *IEEE Transactions on Pattern Analysis and Machine Intelligence*, 2018.

[266] S. Xiang, G. Meng, Y. Wang, C. Pan, and C. Zhang. Image deblurring with coupled dictionary learning. *International Journal of Computer Vision*, 114(2-3):248, 2015.

[267] L. Xie, I. M. Baytas, K. Lin, and J. Zhou. Privacy-preserving distributed multi-task learning with asynchronous updates. In *Proceedings of the 23rd ACM SIGKDD International Conference on Knowledge Discovery and Data Mining*, pages 1195–1204. ACM, 2017.

[268] E. P. Xing, Q. Ho, W. Dai, J. K. Kim, J. Wei, S. Lee, X. Zheng, P. Xie, A. Kumar, and Y. Yu. Petuum: A new platform for distributed machine learning on big data. *IEEE Transactions on Big Data*, 1(2):49–67, 2015.

[269] R. Xu, P. Liu, L. Wang, C. Chen, and J. Wang. Reliable weighted optimal transport for unsupervised domain adaptation. In *Proceedings of the IEEE/CVF Conference on Computer Vision and Pattern Recognition*, pages 4394–4403, 2020.

[270] X. Xu, T. M. Hospedales, and S. Gong. Multi-task zero-shot action recognition with prioritised data augmentation. In *Proceedings of the European Conference on Computer Vision*, pages 343–359. Springer, 2016.

[271] X. Xu, F. Shen, Y. Yang, D. Zhang, H. T. Shen, and J. Song. Matrix tri-factorization with manifold regularizations for zero-shot learning. In *Proceedings of the IEEE International Conference on Computer Vision*, pages 3798–3807, 2017.

[272] B. Xue, Ya and Liao, Xuejun and Carin, Lawrence and Krishnapuram. Multi-Task Learning for Classification with Dirichlet Process Priors. *Journal of Machine Learning Research*, 8:35–63, 2007.

[273] F. Yan, S. Sundaram, S. Vishwanathan, and Y. Qi. Distributed autonomous online learning: Regrets and intrinsic privacy-preserving properties. *IEEE Transactions on Knowledge and Data Engineering*, 25(11):2483–2493, 2013.

[274] J. Yang, Z. Wang, Z. Lin, S. Cohen, and T. Huang. Coupled dictionary training for image super-resolution. *IEEE Transactions on Image Processing*, 21(8):3467–3478, 2012.

[275] J. Yang, J. Wright, T. S. Huang, and Y. Ma. Image super-resolution via sparse representation. *IEEE Transactions on Image Processing*, 19(11):2861–2873, 2010.

[276] Y. Yang, D. Lao, G. Sundaramoorthi, and S. Soatto. Phase consistent ecological domain adaptation, 2020.

[277] Y. Yang and S. Soatto. FDA: Fourier domain adaptation for semantic segmentation. In *Proceedings of the IEEE/CVF Conference on Computer Vision and Pattern Recognition*, pages 4085–4095, 2020.

[278] M. Ye and Y. Guo. Zero-shot classification with discriminative semantic representation learning. In *Proceedings of the IEEE International Conference on Computer Vision*, pages 17140–17148, 2017.

[279] H. Yeganeh, M. Rostami, and Z. Wang. Objective quality assessment for image super-resolution: A natural scene statistics approach. In *2012 19th IEEE International Conference on Image Processing*, pages 1481–1484. IEEE, 2012.

[280] H. Yeganeh, M. Rostami, and Z. Wang. Objective quality assessment of interpolated natural images. *IEEE Transactions on Image Processing*, 24(11):4651–4663, 2015.

[281] Z. Yu, F. Wu, Y. Yang, Q. Tian, J. Luo, and Y. Zhuang. Discriminative coupled dictionary hashing for fast cross-media retrieval. In *Proceedings of the 37th international ACM SIGIR conference on Research & development in information retrieval*, pages 395–404, 2014.

[282] T. Zeng, B. Wu, and S. Ji. DeepEM3D: approaching human-level performance on 3D anisotropic EM image segmentation. *Bioinformatics*, 33(16):2555–2562, 2017.

[283] F. Zenke, B. Poole, and S. Ganguli. Continual learning through synaptic intelligence. In *Proceedings of the International Conference on Machine Learning (ICML)*, pages 3987–3995. JMLR. org, 2017.

[284] D. Zhang, D. Shen, A. D. N. Initiative, et al. Multi-modal multi-task learning for joint prediction of multiple regression and classification variables in Alzheimer's disease. *NeuroImage*, 59(2):895–907, 2012.

[285] F. Zhang, J. Cao, W. Tan, S. U. Khan, K. Li, and A. Y. Zomaya. Evolutionary scheduling of dynamic multitasking workloads for big-data analytics in elastic cloud. *IEEE Transactions on Emerging Topics in Computing*, 2(3):338–351, 2014.

[286] J. Zhang, D., W. Heng, K. Ren, and J. Song. Transfer learning with convolutional neural networks for SAR ship recognition. In *Proceedings of the IOP Conference Series: Materials Science and Engineering*, volume 322, page 072001. IOP Publishing, 2018.

[287] L. Zhang, T. Xiang, and S. Gong. Learning a deep embedding model for zero-shot learning. In *Proceedings of the IEEE Conference on Computer Vision and Pattern Recognition*, pages 2021–2030, 2017.

[288] Q. Zhang, J. Zhang, W. Liu, and D. Tao. Category anchor-guided unsupervised domain adaptation for semantic segmentation. In *Advances in Neural Information Processing Systems*, pages 435–445, 2019.

[289] R. Zhang and J. Kwok. Asynchronous distributed ADMM for consensus optimization. In *Proceedings of the International Conference on Machine Learning*, pages 1701–1709, 2014.

[290] Y. Zhang, P. David, and B. Gong. Curriculum domain adaptation for semantic segmentation of urban scenes. In *Proceedings of the IEEE International Conference on Computer Vision*, pages 2020–2030, 2017.

[291] Z. Zhang, S. Fidler, and R. Urtasun. Instance-level segmentation for autonomous driving with deep densely connected MRFs. In *Proceedings of the IEEE Conference on Computer Vision and Pattern Recognition*, pages 669–677, 2016.

[292] Z. Zhang and V. Saligrama. Zero-shot learning via semantic similarity embedding. In *Proceedings of International Conference on Computer Vision and Pattern Recognition (CVPR)*, pages 4166–4174, 2015.

[293] Z. Zhang and V. Saligrama. Zero-shot learning via joint latent similarity embedding. In *Proceedings of the IEEE Conference on Computer Vision and Pattern Recognition (CVPR)*, pages 6034–6042, 2016.

[294] L. W. Zhong and J. T. Kwok. Convex multitask learning with flexible task clusters. *Proceedings of the International Conference on Machine Learning*, 1:49–56, 2012.

[295] B. Zhou, A. Lapedriza, J. Xiao, A. Torralba, and A. Oliva. Learning deep features for scene recognition using places database. In *Advances in Neural Information Processing Systems*, pages 487–495, 2014.

[296] D. Zhou, O. Bousquet, T. N. Lal, J. Weston, and B. Schölkopf. Learning with local and global consistency. In *Advances in Neural Information Processing Systems*, volume 16, pages 321–328, 2003.

[297] J. Zhu, T. Park, P. Isola, and A. A. Efros. Unpaired image-to-image translation using cycle-consistent adversarial networks. In *Proceedings of the International Conference on Computer Vision (ICCV)*, pages 2223–2232, 2017.

[298] Y. Zhuang, Y. Wang, F. Wu, Y. Zhang, and W. Lu. Supervised coupled dictionary learning with group structures for multi-modal retrieval. In *Proceedings of the AAAI Conference on Artificial Intelligence*, volume 27, 2013.

Index